MONTY

MARK KEOHANE

ALSO BY MARK KEOHANE

Chester
Springbok Rugby Uncovered
Champions of the World
Monty (Illustrated)

Monty: His Life Story
First published 2008

2004 03/1056/03, Highbury Safika Media, 8th floor, Metlife Centre,
7 Coen Steytler Avenue, Foreshore, 8001, Cape Town, South Africa

Editor: Simon Borchardt
Designers: Rory Ross, Kirsty Reid
Copy Editors: Ross Edwards, Nick van Rensburg
Proofreaders: Patrick Farrell, Gary Lemke
Statistician: Kobus Smit
Index: Linda Retief
Repro Artists: Karin Livni, Donnevan van der Watt, Janette Wright,
Adri van der Watt
Cover Photo: Julian Finney/Getty Images/Gallo Images
Other Photos: Montgomery Collection, Gallo Images, Getty Images, AFP
Marketing Manager: Kara Ross
Printer: Paarl Print

ISBN 978-0-620-42103-4.

CONTENTS

AUTHOR'S NOTE

When Percy Montgomery called to ask if I would be interested in doing his authorised biography, his first question was not if I would write his life story, but if it was *windgat* (big headed) of him to believe he was worthy of a book.

I said if he had played for England he would be on his fifth book because their players tend to write one after every 20 Tests. I felt that as Springbok rugby's most capped player, record point-scorer and a World Cup winner, he was worth a book and I was flattered to be the one to write it. He said he wanted to tell his story and did not want to use the book to insult people or to settle any scores. And tell his story is exactly what he has done.

Monty and those close to him have been incredible in how they have opened up and that is what sets apart this biography from other rugby ones I have worked on or read. For someone who refused to say much during his professional career, he avoids nothing in reflecting on it and his journey from South West Africa (now Namibia) to Cape Town, overseas and finally back to Cape Town. His greatest attribute is his humility, and his story is as much about internal hardship as it is about winning the World Cup. He is anything but *windgat*. I want to thank him for his honesty during the writing of the book and I also want to thank his mom, Lillian, and wife, Tasmin, for keeping scrapbooks of his career because they proved invaluable in recording accurately the time and place of events.

A special thanks also to editor Simon Borchardt, designers Rory Ross and Kirsty Reid, copy editors Nick van Rensburg and Ross Edwards, as well as Kobus Smit, who provided the most comprehensive statistics of Monty's first-class career.

Mark Keohane
Cape Town, October 2008

FOREWORD BY JAKE WHITE

Monty's worth will only be fully appreciated when the next South African comes along and attempts to play Test rugby for an 11-year period, control matches from the back and accumulate points with such regularity.

Let's see how the next Springbok fullback reacts to having four or five different coaches, is asked to play in four different positions, is told he can't kick the ball in his first Test as a flyhalf and is asked not to miss a kick at goal in a World Cup semi-final and final.

Let's see how the next Springbok fullback deals with being booed by South Africans when playing at home on the same days he scores 20-odd points.

As Bok coach, I would always make a fuss about Monty's Test experience. Young guys would think they'd arrived on the Test scene after five or six matches and I'd hear them talking of the emotional and physical demands of playing for their country. I'd then emphasise Monty's sacrifice, professionalism and dedication to the Springboks when handing over the jerseys before every Test. The day before the 2007 World Cup final, it went something like: 'No 15, Percy Montgomery, 94th Test. Think about it, guys … 94 times Monty has been called up to get a jersey … 94'. I wanted it to sink in and I needed the young players around him to know the enormity of the achievement. It used to embarrass him and he'd always ask me not to make a big deal about his Test matches or his Test records, of which he held something like 90 when we won the 2007 World Cup.

His nature is such that he didn't want to be singled out by his team-mates or me, but he deserved the recognition because not enough South Africans have ever been willing to acknowledge what he meant to Bok rugby.

There is the disgraceful story of him walking to the Bok team bus after a Test at Ellis Park and seeing blokes dressed in Bok jerseys urinating against his picture on the bus. Those guys should be ashamed of themselves.

Monty's team-mates have always known how good he is and he will always have their respect.

In my association with Bok rugby, dating back to when I was the technical adviser to Nick Mallett's Springboks in 1997, I'd never experienced a player as passionate about Bok rugby or as dedicated to the team ethos.

The players in the squad called him 'Bok *befok* [crazy]' because of how much Springbok rugby means to him. His ritual on the night before every Test was to dress up a chair in his room with a springbok skin, on which he would neatly place his jersey and kit. That skin went everywhere on tour with him.

The success of the 2007 World Cup Springboks had more to do with Monty's play and belief in the traditions and values than anyone outside of the squad could ever know or appreciate.

His value as a player speaks for itself through his records, but equally impressive is his humility as a person. He has never forgotten those who helped him in his development as a person and rugby player.

He should never have been dropped from the Springboks in 2001 and his international comeback to influence the 2004 Tri-Nations and 2007 World Cup triumphs defines his legacy. His influence was so big that I would go as far as to say the Boks would not have won the World Cup without Percy Montgomery.

* *White coached the Springboks in 54 Tests, with 36 victories (66.6% win rate). He was in charge when the Boks won the Tri-Nations in 2004 and the World Cup in 2007.*

1

'JUST STRAP IT ... I'LL BE FINE'

'It's my fucking knee,' screamed Percy Montgomery. 'I think it's gone.'

Montgomery was cursing the situation and his misfortune. He was angry that his right knee had to give way 39 minutes into a World Cup final. For the last seven minutes of the first half he had hobbled around the Stade de France in Paris with his mind in control, even if he knew his right knee wasn't. Now he accepted it was serious and that's why he was swearing when Springbok physiotherapist Clint Readhead got to him.

Montgomery had played in the 1999 World Cup and been part of a Springbok team dramatically beaten in an extra time semi-final to Australia at Twickenham. He had kicked two drop goals to beat the All Blacks in the 1999 play-off for third place in Cardiff, but a bronze medal was not why he played this game. He wanted gold and he wanted to be a contributor to a Springbok World Cup win.

Montgomery never got to play in the 2003 World Cup because of a six-month suspension for an attack on a touch judge, but ever since 2004, he had transformed his game and rewritten the record books of Springbok rugby. No Springbok had played more Tests. No Springbok had kicked as many conversions. No Springbok had kicked as many penalties. No Springbok had scored as many points. But as he lay on his back at the Stade de France on 20 October 2007, he knew that all those records meant nothing if his international career was to end on a stretcher. Montgomery was 33 years old and he knew there would never be another World Cup for him. The opportunity to win gold was the night of 20 October. But his right knee was gone.

He was even angrier because his knees had never been a problem. He had never missed a Test in 10 years because of crocked knees, but he did not need medical experts to tell him there was a problem. The knee was hurting, but the greater pain was the prospect that it could all be over and he didn't want to contemplate it.

In two previous matches at the Stade de France at the 2007 World Cup, Montgomery had succeeded with every kick at posts. In the final, he had already kicked two penalties from two attempts to go with 14 from 14 against England and Argentina in the pool game and semi-final wins. He was the most prolific point-scorer at the tournament and teams feared the effectiveness of his left boot. His legacy would be defined in the final, but only if he kicked the points and the Springboks won gold.

Montgomery knew people remembered the misses more than the successes, but he also knew no one forgot the World Cup final. He had missed crucial kicks, as a schoolboy and as a Test player, and he had won many matches for the Springboks. But only one match mattered in a player's career – and lying on his back in the World Cup final, he refused to accept it was going to end in injury. He had been picked to kick the points and he was determined to do that.

Montgomery admits the first book he bought and read from start to finish was the iconic Springbok flyhalf Naas

Botha's guide to kicking. His high school 1st XV coach, Simon Perkin, tells of Montgomery missing a kick to win the match for SACS (South African College Schools) against DF Malan. The kick would have ended the opposition's unbeaten run. Montgomery missed and SACS lost.

The next morning, Montgomery, a school boarder, was on the field at the same position, kicking for goal. That it was Sunday probably made it more poignant because kicking was his religion and a rugby field was his place of worship. Only this Sunday's kicking session was more like confession because each time he succeeded it only reinforced the failure of the previous day.

'I watched him take kick after kick that Sunday morning, and each time it went over he just shook his head,' says Perkin. 'It was as if he couldn't believe he had missed the penalty the previous day.'

Goal kicking was Montgomery's inspiration at school, but in his early professional career he was never given the responsibility and in his first 50 Tests he was asked to kick on just 17 occasions. He had a reputation for inconsistency, although it is a perception based more on three failed matches than statistical reality. Montgomery, in those 17 Tests, had an average strike rate of 70%, but no one in South Africa seemed prepared to forgive him for a penalty and two conversion misses against the Lions in the second Test in 1997, which the Lions won 18-15. South Africa, beaten in the first Test at Newlands, lost the Test series that night and Montgomery was the scapegoat. That first-choice Bok kicker, Henry Honiball, also missed two penalties and André Joubert failed with a conversion, was a statistical afterthought.

Then, in 1998, with the Boks one match away from a world-record 18th successive Test win, Montgomery missed a sitter against England at Twickenham with the scores level at 7-all. England would win the game 13-7 and Montgomery would again take a beating in the media, despite there being 30 minutes to play after his penalty miss.

In 2001, his third Test failure to convert kicks into a Bok win against the All Blacks at Newlands saw him dropped, and when Braam van Straaten kicked the Springboks to victory against Australia a week later in Pretoria, there would be no place back for Montgomery in the Bok starting XV until June 2004. Singling out Montgomery for the All Blacks defeat was unfair because his goal kicking had won the Boks Tests and in the majority of matches when he was tasked with goal kicking, he delivered. It was Montgomery's seven from eight that crushed the Wallabies in the 1998 Tri-Nations decider in Johannesburg. Earlier in the tournament he had also out-kicked Australia's Matthew Burke in Perth and out-performed New Zealand's Carlos Spencer in the Springboks' 13-3 victory against the All Blacks at the notoriously windy Athletic Park in Wellington, New Zealand.

Montgomery, from when he first kicked a ball, wanted the responsibility of goal kicking, but in the first half of his international career he was never forceful enough to demand it become part of his job responsibility. It was only when Springbok coach Jake White brought him back to South Africa in 2004 after two years in Newport, Wales, that a Bok coach told Montgomery his primary responsibility in the team was to kick points.

'You miss more than you get and you are out,' White told him. 'Your first job is to kick points. Then we look at the rest of your game.'

And that is exactly what he did in the 44 Tests he played under White, when he averaged closer to 80%. He was no longer the 'hit and miss' 70% player who had left South Africa in 2002.

In June 2007, he had twice played against Jonny Wilkinson – England's 2003 World Cup hero and goal-kicking genius – and twice he had won the battle. In Bloemfontein, Montgomery kicked 10 from 10 to Wilkinson's two from three and in Pretoria, he again outdid the man considered the best goal kicker in the world. At the 2007 World Cup, he again upstaged Wilkinson, who was averaging 60% to Montgomery's 80%.

But now he was on his back and contemplating the moment. He had done everything asked of him at the World Cup. He had missed just one penalty kick and that was one that hit the post against Fiji in the quarter-final. He had already succeeded with two penalties in the final to Wilkinson's one. The Boks were leading 6-3 and Montgomery's boot was dominant, but in the 32nd minute, England lock Ben Kay thudded into Montgomery at a tackle, clipping the fullback's right knee with his head. Montgomery got up, in pain, but was sure he could run off the bump. Initially, he thought it was a bit of a dead leg, but each time he tried to cover ground, the pain seemed to get worse. The medical team saw him struggling but as they got no word from him, they assumed it was not serious.

The Springboks were attacking the English line in a frantic end to the first half and the forwards surged and came close to scoring. The Boks attacked the English pack and only the cynicism of a professional foul prevented the quick release of the ball. This time, Irish referee Alain Roland was unforgiving of the English foul and he awarded a penalty to South Africa, but even more appealing to Montgomery at that very moment was the break in play. He dropped to the ground, in pain and unsure whether he would get up again. Montgomery had every reason to swear. And he did.

Readhead felt the knee and knew it was serious.

'Monty doesn't swear easily on the field when it comes to dealing with pain, but he did that night,' recalls the physiotherapist. 'I knew he was in trouble when he went down and didn't get up and my first reaction when running towards him was that his World Cup could be over. I knew the half-time break was a minute away so I did not rush the treatment. I also knew there would be time to treat him in the change room, but I also knew Jake wanted him kept on as long as possible.

'I was aware of the possible disruption to the backline if Monty had to be replaced. Ruan Pienaar could play at fullback but it was also possible Frans Steyn [playing at inside centre] would have to go to fullback and Wynand Olivier would come on at 12. Butch James would then have to take over the goal kicking. It had the potential to change the entire dynamic of the game because we'd be losing our most experienced player and the tournament's best goal kicker. Monty's influence on a youngster like [right wing] JP Pietersen was also immense and England had been kicking a lot onto JP in the first half. Monty's positional play was superb and he was constantly directing JP and [left wing] Bryan Habana when to drop back and when to push up.

'I ran the touchline all the time so I heard a lot of what was said by the players. What the crowd and cameras never picked up was the influence Monty had on our defensive pattern from the back. He was like a conductor in how he was orchestrating them – that is why Jake was so anxious for him to stay on. It wasn't that he didn't have faith in the guys on the bench. It was more a case of who he would be losing.

'When I got to Monty, I told him to relax while I felt the knee for an assessment. I knew immediately there was ligament trouble, just by the way he refused to move it. I felt the knee and it was spongy and there was no stability, which is the first indicator he had done his ligaments. I didn't know the extent of the injury but if it had not been a World Cup final, I'd have taken him off immediately. As a medical team, we had always erred on the side of caution and when in doubt, our first instinct was to pull a player. But this was a World Cup final and the players had met with us beforehand to emphasise how bad any injury had to be for them to come off. No player was prepared to leave that field unless it was physically impossible for him to continue and Monty reminded me of this agreement while I was treating the knee. Jake had told me to keep Monty positive, but it wasn't something I had to do as he was adamant he wasn't going off. I told Monty the knee was damaged but that it was treatable and that we would also have the 10-minute half-time break to work on it.'

The Boks, leading 6-3, had been awarded a penalty and Montgomery was determined to kick at goal. White told Readhead to do everything to keep Montgomery on the field and to ensure he took the kick.

'I was shitting myself he would come off,' recalls the former Bok coach. 'I had to have him on the field and I told Clint to talk him through whatever pain it was he was feeling in the knee. Monty had been brilliant for us throughout the World Cup and he had consistently been one of our most influential players for the last four years. To lose him in the World Cup final, one minute before half-time, was something I had never thought of simply because I didn't want to think it was even possible.

'His goal kicking and line kicking were unmatched in the tournament and I knew that if it came down to a penalty shoot-out with Wilkinson, he would come through for us. He also needed to kick the penalty because in the context of the game, it was worth so much more than three points. We had come close to scoring a try and we deserved more than a three-point lead at half-time.

'Monty hadn't missed a kick at the Stade de France during the World Cup and those three extra points would mean we went into the change room on a high. I felt if England went in only three points down, they'd start believing a win was possible and our guys might start doubting themselves – that for all their control they were only up by three points. I told Clint we could reassess Monty at half-time, but for now, he needed to take that kick.'

No encouragement was needed.

'Just strap it ... I'll be fine,' Montgomery told Readhead. 'Make it fucking tight.'

Readhead strapped the knee as hard as he could.

'I don't even know how he moved because I strapped it

so tight, but he did. He got up and hobbled over to take the kick. He said he would make a call after the kick once he had felt how the knee had responded to the pressure. But I was not sure he would make it.

'As a left-footed kicker, all the pressure would be on his right knee during the follow-through and he would have to rely on the strength of the right knee for balance and stability. In four years of working with him, he'd shown his mental toughness, but I felt he would need as much luck as bravery to finish the match. Even if he coped with a one-off kick at posts I didn't think he could last another half because of how much kicking there was in the match and how much pressure he would be putting on the knee every time he made a line kick or kicked for posts. And what if the game went into extra time? There was no strength in the right knee and any sharp turn on the knee or change in direction would aggravate the injury.

'We briefly discussed the risk of him taking the kick as medically I was obliged to caution him, but he was in another zone and I don't even think he was listening to what I was saying. He seemed to be swearing at himself as much as the situation. I just made sure the strapping was tight.'

Montgomery lined up the kick. Readhead closed his eyes and only opened them for the left-footed Montgomery's landing on the right knee.

'The crowd roar seemed secondary at the time because I was more focused on what happened between the kick and it going over. I had expected him to fall over once he had kicked, but he stood firm in his follow-through, turned and started jogging back to the tunnel for half-time. I ran next to him and asked him how it felt. He said he would be fine.'

In the change room, White hesitantly enquired as to his player's well-being, admitting he did not want to make too much of a fuss about it.

'I didn't want to complicate anything by showing I was also worried. I could see he was in pain, but I could also see he was on a high after kicking the penalty. He told me the knee was sore, but that he would play on. He didn't want an injection. All he wanted was for the strapping to be made tighter.'

Readhead briefly treated the strapping but there would be no reassessment of the knee at half-time or again in the match.

'There was no need to assess it. I knew that ordinarily he should be off, but I wasn't going to tell him that. He insisted his role was to kick the points and that he would only come off if he couldn't do that anymore. We did not talk about it again at half-time.'

What White and Readhead did not know was Montgomery had already briefed Bok utility back Ruan Pienaar that it was probable he would be replacing him.

'I knew how bad my knee was and I didn't think I'd be able to last another 40 minutes,' says Montgomery. 'I wanted to make sure Ruan was calm and prepared for the match situation. If he came on, there wouldn't be time to settle in. I told him to concentrate on the basics and on playing the percentages, as per the game plan. Ruan is a brilliant runner and an instinctive ball player, but this final demanded discipline in not playing risk rugby because we knew England could not beat us with their limited attack, but we could beat ourselves through a poor counter-attacking option, an intercept or one bad call.

'Wilkinson was not getting his usual distance with his punting so I gave Ruan an indication of how far back to stand and to ensure he aimed for accuracy and not length in returning his kicks. I was calm and so was Ruan. We spoke naturally and without panic, because I knew we could win this Test, whether or not I was on the field. We had a team of good players and between Butch, Frans and Ruan, we had three capable goal kickers.

'I also knew the value of experience in finals, and I still believe that if Smitty [John Smit] and myself had not been substituted in the Super 14 final, the result could have been different. One disappointment was bad enough and I didn't want to remember 2007 as the year of two shattering experiences in finals. I was worried about my knee but I wasn't going to go off. If I never played again after the final because I aggravated the knee then that was the risk I was willing to take. Playing in a World Cup final and winning it was everything we as a team had worked for and this was why I played the game – to be part of a World Cup final and to be making a contribution. I wasn't going to let it end like this after four years of sacrifice and I wasn't going to walk away from the challenge because my knee hurt. If I was a liability to the team, and was letting them down because I couldn't perform my primary role of kicking points, then I would walk off, otherwise no one was getting me off.'

Within two minutes of the restart, England centre Matthew Tait stepped inside of Steyn, broke the line and beat Montgomery in the tackle. Montgomery was down again, but now he was operating on adrenalin and once back up, he took off to try and stop England winger Mark Cueto from scoring. Montgomery got there too late, but Bok No 8 Danie Rossouw's lunge at Cueto saved the try.

It was a dramatic opening to the second half and the worst possible situation for Montgomery because he was stood up in defence by a very good stepper in Tait. The defensive action meant he twisted and turned the knee without thinking. When that happened, the medical team thought he would not be able to play on, but within a few seconds he was on his feet and part of the scrambling defence to try and stop Cueto from scoring.

There was more drama to follow. Roland referred the try-scoring act to the TMO (Television Match Official), Australian Stuart Dickinson, who after nearly a minute ruled Cueto had put a foot in touch just before scoring. Readhead says the intensity of that opening two minutes overshadowed any thoughts of sympathy for Montgomery.

'Monty was right in there, talking and calming the backs down and using every bit of experience to help resist the English burst. The last thing on his mind seemed to be his knee.'

Montgomery – who would be involved in 17 actions from catching, to kicking, to hitting a ruck, to tackling and to passing in the final 35 minutes – says the occasion numbed the pain but he knew that with every minute he was on the field, he was doing himself damage.

'I had to see out the job. Jake brought me back from Wales and reinvented my international career and he believed in me. How could I hobble off with the score at 6-3 or 9-3 or 12-6? It was only when Frans kicked the long-distance penalty to take us to 15-6 that I felt comfortable England did not have the capability of scoring twice against us, but I hadn't come this far to watch the last few minutes from the sidelines. I wanted to be there at the end and I wanted to be adding something to the win. I wanted to be on the field when that final whistle went and we won the World Cup.'

Montgomery could have been carried off the field in the 39th minute of the World Cup final with his reputation intact, safe in the knowledge he had done his bit for Springbok rugby. He had not missed a kick in the play-off matches and medical opinion would always defend any decision for him to leave the field. Montgomery will argue that he was not schooled to walk away when things got tough.

As a boarder at SACS for a decade, he had been taught you were judged on how you got up and not how many times you stumbled. He was also taught that any action had to benefit his team-mates and it's why he insisted he would only leave the Stade de France if continuing to play would disadvantage the Springboks. He had satisfied himself that Pienaar had been sufficiently briefed and that was his plan B. Plan A was to continue playing.

Pienaar never got to play fullback in the World Cup final. Montgomery kicked another penalty in the second half, took his World Cup strike rate at the Stade de France to 18 from 18, and scored 12 of the Boks' 15 points in the final.

Later that night, the Bok medical team confirmed he had a grade-two medial co-lateral ligament sprain and that it would be 10 weeks before he could play rugby again. There could be no guarantee how strong the knee would be in the future.

2

HEARTACHE AND HOPE

Percival Montgomery Senior, Monty's dad, spent his early years in Hermanus, 115km southeast of Cape Town, born to an Afrikaans fisherman father and raised Afrikaans. They were not particularly close and his recollection of his father is that he was often at sea.

'It was different in those days when it came to relationships between parents and kids,' he says. 'Your father worked and provided for you. I knew he cared about us as a family but back in those days, as a kid you did your thing and were seen and not heard. I don't have these memories of us doing things together and of him being there because, most of the time, he was out at sea and working. Then one day he went out fishing and had a heart attack. When the boat came back, he was dead.'

Life would change forever for the seven-year-old Percival Montgomery and the free-spirited days spent along the Hermanus coastline would make way for the unforgiving world of an orphanage when his mother had an accident and was physically incapable of caring for her children. Percival Montgomery and his brothers were sent to school at Jan van Riebeeck in Cape Town's City Bowl and housed at the orphanage in Hoff Street.

'My mom would come and visit on weekends, but she was struggling with her health and she also did not have money, so my brothers and I accepted the situation and just got on with it. We had a roof, food and were getting an education and there were others who weren't as lucky, but hell, I missed Hermanus and I missed walking on the rocks and most of all, I missed being able to explore. I missed smelling the sea every morning and I always said I would come back here one day and now I am here, back in Hermanus. It has taken more than 50 years, but I made it and I am walking those rocks again and smelling that sea.'

For a moment, Percival Montgomery Senior is back on the rocks, seven years old and exploring.

'Did Percival tell you we want to buy the house in Church Street, the one in which I lived before my father died?'

Monty hadn't told me yet, but would when we next spoke and he detailed the difficulties his father had to overcome as a youngster, testing times his father had spoken of as a matter of fact and without a hint of bitterness or self pity.

'Ja, those were hard times, Markie, but we were not alone. Hey, a lot of people had it hard and you do what you have to and in our case me and my brothers got our *boere* [Afrikaans] matric [standard eight or grade 10], as everyone called it in those days, and then got working. Once you were 16, you could find work and that's when I started my journey back to Hermanus and, bloody hell, it took me some time to get here. But I am here.'

Montgomery Senior laughs at just how long it took him to be in a position to walk those rocks again as he lights up a cigarette and offers me coffee and toast.

'Percival hates me smoking. He has always hated being near anyone smoking. One night, early on in his and Tazzie's

[Tasmin Tobitt's] relationship we were bonding and chatting and she had a few puffs of my cigarette. Jesus, he lost it.'

More laughter follows.

'I tell you, he is still pissed off with me for breaking one promise … I told him I would quit smoking if he made the Western Province U21 team.' Montgomery Senior inhales and with the smoked release comes a naughty grin: 'Hell, he needed the motivation at the time, and he hasn't forgiven me. You know I've tried to stop, but it is bloody hard, and at least I keep in shape by riding the bike and walking the rocks. They say each man has his vice and mine must be smoking. I want to give it up, but it is bloody enjoyable. Come let me show you the jersey Percival gave me before he left for the World Cup. It means everything to me and there he has written a message to me on the front, thanking me for all the support and for being there for him. You know, I wish I was there for him more and that as a family, we were all in the same city, but it was not possible at that stage. Lillian and I were both working hard to try and make a success of our fish and chips shop in Swakopmund [west of Windhoek].'

Work opportunities had taken Montgomery Senior from Cape Town to Namibia, when it was still South West Africa and a province of South Africa. It was there he met Lillian, also originally from Cape Town. The marriage would be her second, with her three daughters (Sharon, Lesley and Tracey) from the first marriage raised under the roof of her first husband's home.

Montgomery Senior shows off the framed, signed jersey and it is the backdrop to his corner dining-room bar at the rented house, with the lease giving him an option to purchase in a year's time. Next to it is a painting of Monty, presented to the Bok fullback in recognition of his 50th Test.

'I've got lots of other stuff from Percival but it is all in boxes and I've only been in this Hermanus house for a month and Lillian only finishes off with her work in Cape Town in a month. But when you come again, she will be in Hermanus, the boxes will have been unpacked, everything will be up and we'll have the photo albums and all his scrapbooks for you to go through. You know, I have every one of his 1st XV matches at SACS on video. I occasionally got down to see him play, but I used to follow his progress through the videos I was sent and then I'd call him and we'd chat about the game. Never cheat on fitness and never cut corners with the basics were two rules no player can break. I used to tell him that those things I took for granted he was doing and I also knew he was getting good coaching from HO de Villiers, who was one of the greats of Springbok rugby. You know people think Percival had it easy at SACS, but that boy worked hard for what he got and he's a tough and determined bugger. Hell, I'm proud of him.'

When I spend time with Monty in Perpignan he tells me about the house in Church Street and how much he would like to buy it for his dad and mom. He also tells me how hard his dad had it as a youngster.

'I'd love to buy him that house and give him something he wants, but the owners aren't keen to sell. I want him to be happy and I want my mom to be happy. They deserve happiness and quality in their life. Hey, bugger, they had it tough when they were younger.'

Monty tells me about his early days at SACS and how he battled with being away from his parents and his sister, Haley, but he adds that he lived like royalty when compared to how his dad had it as a kid.

'In the beginning, I found it tough at boarding school. I wasn't used to the structure and the discipline and the traditions and I just wanted to be back in Namibia. In that first year, I cried a lot on the phone and whenever I went home for the holidays I felt empty when I had to go back to school, which had nothing to do with the school. I liked it but I just wanted to go home and be with my family and be carefree. My parents had a fish and chips shop in Swakopmund and after school I'd race in, finish my homework and get out of there as fast as I could to play with my friends. And I remember there was always an endless supply of Wilson's toffees at the shop. They were my favourite and I'd always sneak a few on the way through to the kitchen and on the way out to play.'

If Montgomery's memories of the fish and chips shop are nostalgic, then Montgomery Senior's recollections are of toil and not triumph.

'Lillian and I wanted to give him more time, but it wasn't possible as we were trying to make the takeaway work as a business. I had left the fisheries in Walvis Bay to try and get the shop working and we spent five years there before we went back to Walvis Bay. But we'd look at Percival sitting at the back of the shop doing his homework and we knew it wasn't right for the young boy. He needed an environment that would be more caring and he needed to have the attention on schooling that we were just not in a position to give him.'

Montgomery says he understands why his parents sent him to boarding school in Cape Town, but as a kid he said knowing it was for his own good did not make it easier because he missed home.

'I know they wanted to give me opportunities they never had and I know how hard they worked. You know they never denied me anything. When I was at SACS, many of the boys were wealthy and they always had the latest bikes, games and skateboards. I remember phoning home one day and asking my dad if I could have a skateboard and predictably he told me it was too expensive and that we just didn't have money to spend on such luxuries. I was distraught and cried out of disappointment, telling him all the other boys had the latest skateboards. He was firm with me and told me it wasn't possible. Then he asked me how things were going in my sport and with my art as he knew those were the two things I liked to do and didn't mind talking about. He would always remind me to work hard and appreciate the luxury of being at such a good school and not to waste the opportunities. Before he hung up he said he would think about the skateboard again, but he couldn't promise me it was possible because he never made me a promise he knew he couldn't keep. Then the skateboard, as an example, would arrive at the school a few weeks later. I knew that they had sacrificed something, worked harder or taken from the savings account to get me what I wanted. You don't forget those kinds of things. You just don't.'

When I meet Montgomery Senior for the first time, I tell him Monty should have made sure someone put him on TV 10 years ago and then the Afrikaans rugby public would have loved Monty because they'd have known he is half a *boertjie* [little Afrikaner].

'That's what pissed me off so much about people who judge him and don't know him. Percival's always been a very private person and so have we as a family. The two of us used to joke at how people would assume he was a rich and spoilt boy from the southern suburbs in Cape Town and make assumptions about his character. You know how many times I have gone to a pub to watch the Springboks and I hear the shit they talk about him. These okes in the bar don't know I am his father and they have a full go, whether he is scoring tries, kicking points or making a tackle, it doesn't matter, and it always comes back to him being this spoilt *soutie* [Englishman] and show pony from Cape Town. The Boks win, he kicks the points and plays well and still they talk *kak* [shit]. There have been times when I have come close to *klapping* [hitting] an oke because of the *kak* they talk about him. I've learned to walk away from it now, but it isn't easy. People make assumptions and have opinions but they don't actually know anything. It was like when the Springbok team left for the 2007 World Cup and I walked past these Afrikaans-speaking Bok supporters who were from Pretoria and were getting autographs from the Bulls players and typically weren't very flattering about Percival.

They must have heard me speaking Afrikaans and when I went over to speak to Percival, who I speak English to, they must have made the assumption I was his father and they started cheering on Percival and telling me how proud I must be as a father to have a son who has done so much for the Springboks. I told them to get lost. All these years, guys like that have booed him at Loftus out of ignorance because of who they think he is, but now they hear his old man can speak Afrikaans and they suddenly accept him. Come on, it doesn't work like that. Judge him on how he has played and his commitment to the Springboks.

'I am a South African who speaks Afrikaans and English. My son's a South African who plays for the Springboks and gives 100% every time he puts on that jersey, but those people who bad mouth him have an opinion of him because in their eyes he comes from Western Province and has a surname like Montgomery, so they just assume certain things and boo him. They don't know him at all … they don't know how hard he has worked to be a Springbok and stayed there. They don't know what shit he has had to put up with and they don't know what that jersey means to him every time he plays. I do …

'You know, Markie, these people think they know him because they see an image on TV. How many of them would even think his dad could be Afrikaans? How many of them would even think Percival enjoys Leon Schuster's music, loves to braai and fish and go hunting? Schuster was the one guy Percival always wanted to meet.'

There is laughter with the mention of Schuster's name.

'Jeez we had one big night in Newport when he first played there. I think it was 2002 and Taz was supposed to go with him and she didn't because they were at that stage of their relationship when it was on one week and off the next. Lillian and I had moved back to Cape Town by then and we were living in Table View and I got this call from Percival saying we were going to Newport. He said he needed my support and he wanted company in his first few months while settling into his new club, so I went with him to Wales. But he was pissing me off with the amount of money he was spending on phone calls to Tazzie in Cape Town and it was starting to annoy me.

'One night he was missing South Africa so badly and Tazzie in particular, so he said, "Bugger this, I'm going to braai and listen to Leon Schuster's music". It was pissing with rain and cold, but he got the braai going and on came the music and out came the beers. He and Tazzie had been having this war of words on the phone for a few weeks and I probably went where I wasn't supposed to go and I told him to sort out his relationship and stop wasting money on phone calls to South Africa. I said it was bullshit how much money he was spending on calls – thousands of rands – and he was solving nothing. We had both had a few drinks and he told me to mind my own business.

'The one thing about Percival is that he has always shown me respect as his father and never backchatted me, but this night he did talk back and I told him that he may be a Springbok rugby player but to me he was a son first and that he was never too old to get a hiding. We had a stand-off – he turned around, walked away and went to bed and fortunately nothing came of it. I felt awful and I think he also felt bad about it and to tell you the truth, when I had sobered up the next day and thought about what I had said about giving him a hiding I wasn't so sure about it any more. Hey, he's not a *laaitie* [youngster] anymore.'

He laughs again. 'It was the first and last heated argument between the two of us, but somehow it also bonded us that much more, even if it took a couple of days for him to get over it.'

Again there is some laughter.

'It took a few days because the next day I got a call from the travel agent to say he had changed my flight and I was leaving Wales that week. I told her to change it back to the original date as I was going nowhere and when he got home from training I told him I was staying. We had to deal with the situation and sort it out like men. I had come to support him and I was leaving when my original ticket said I had to leave. When you don't grow up in the same house, you aren't used to these kinds of arguments and differences that would be normal between father and son. We had to work it out and we did and I left for South Africa on the day I was meant to return.'

I mention the incident to Monty.

'My dad told you that … hey, that's embarrassing.'

It's life, I say. It happens. Fathers and sons argue and sort it out.

'My old man calls it straight,' says Monty. 'There's no bullshit from him. What you see is what you get. I can't believe he actually told you about that night. Hey, we were both angry.'

Montgomery admits there are still occasions he gets angry with his father and he makes no secret that his father's love for a drink and a cigarette will always be an issue for him.

'My dad will describe himself as a social guy or a pub person, but I can't stand the fact that he smokes and his drinking has embarrassed me in the past and caused a lot of heartache in our family. The drinking caused destruction and contributed to my parents getting divorced. That they are back together again is like a fairytale for me, but I am constantly at my dad to drink less and to live healthier. I want him to have a longer "career" with his son and his wife.

'Tasmin's parents were also divorced and are now back together again, so she also knows the heartache of a broken family. I want all-round happiness for my family and it scares me that my parents could separate again because my dad is not looking after himself or taking my mom into consideration. He will tell you I am being dramatic when I say these things, but it troubles and upsets me because I have seen how destructive it can be. I love the guy, but he has his faults and I don't want to spend the next 20 years resenting him for being a pub person as I did many of the last 20 years.'

The two concede that their relationship is different to the norm because it has always been long distance. From the decade of boarding school to Monty's professional rugby career, he has never stayed with his parents for a period in excess of six weeks. But geographic distance, say both, should not be interpreted as emotional distance.

'We are close, but in a different way because our interaction was not of a father and son growing up in the same house. At school, I spoke telephonically to my parents nearly every day and my dad followed my rugby career closely. I knew he was interested in what I was doing and how well I was doing it. That was good enough for me because he used to watch my games on tape, phone me and discuss the game and give me some advice. He always said that if a person was not fit he couldn't play the game. That was the first rule, and he always told me never to play with an injury because I would only be letting my team-mates down as I wouldn't be able to do my job on the field.'

Montgomery Senior played for South West Africa (now Namibia) in the 1970s in the era of Springbok flank Jan Ellis, and coached club rugby in Walvis Bay and Swakopmund. It is here where Monty was introduced to days spent next to the field and the freedom of running with a rugby ball.

'The match days were the best,' says Monty. 'I always knew I would get to play all afternoon, get to run with the ball and kick it as much as I wanted it. And I'd always get my *blikkie* [can] coke and packet of chips.'

Monty, in his first year at junior school in Namibia, wanted to play rugby but the English school his mother insisted on him attending only had soccer. He was then given permission to play rugby for a neighbouring Afrikaans school, but the situation was never ideal.

'His love for rugby contributed to us sending him to a good school that invested in sport, but the main reason was we had to give him a better life. Lillian and I used to hate watching him come home from school and have to do his homework on his own in the kitchen while we were working at the shop. He needed stimulation and interaction we couldn't give him because of our work situation. And then there was the rugby. If he wanted to play rugby and do well, he needed to be in a good school. Friends of ours in Walvis Bay suggested SACS and we sent him there on their recommendation. It's one of the best decisions we ever made.'

3

BLUE AND WHITE DELIGHT

There are two stories that quintessentially define Percy Montgomery's schooling career at SACS. The first is less than charitable and it is of a young standard four (grade six) Montgomery being hung out of a second-storey window by a teacher who, to quote the man, was going to 'shake your brains from your arse into your head'. The second and more significant one is of a teenager who lived for first and second break and couldn't wait to get onto the practice field to kick and pass a rugby ball, and if he wasn't on a rugby field, he was in the pool, swimming or playing water polo.

Montgomery, then and now, understood the distance from the pass to the tackle more than he appreciated nouns and adjectives and whatever they taught in mathematics back then. He loved drawing and painting and excelled at art, but he was not a scholar by definition, never wanted to be and has never pretended to be one. But he was a good rugby player in his U9 year and by the time he left SACS 10 years later, he was the best schoolboy fullback in South Africa.

Springbok fullback of the 1960s, HO de Villiers, guided Montgomery's schoolboy talent from the age of 16. I would have said he 'coached' him but HO prefers to use the term 'guide' because he says there was very little coaching of a player who would get better with experience but would not be any better than he already was at 16 because someone taught him how to kick, catch and pass a ball.

'I didn't walk in and teach him how to play,' recalls De Villiers. 'There wasn't a great deal to teach Percy and all I could offer him were insights gained from having played Test rugby and from having been around a bit longer.'

Simon Perkin, deputy headmaster of SACS and 1st XV coach during the Montgomery era, asked HO to have a look at the 'boy wonder' because Perkin was convinced Montgomery was the best rugby player he had seen at SACS. De Villiers started with a simple exercise in contact practice sessions in which he would position himself behind Montgomery and play the practice as if he was the fullback. De Villiers says Montgomery ran and he hobbled, but the purpose of it all was to understand Montgomery's feel for the game and to study his natural appreciation of how to use the width of the pitch and how he read the play of the opposing flyhalf.

'Monty was instinctive in a lot of what he did and that is a gift some have and others never get. I told him that he was playing fullback and I was playing fullback, and decision-making was what defined a fullback, so every time at training, in defence or on attack, both of us would have to play the moment as we saw it. I wanted to get a sense of his appreciation of depth, space and field position and I had to put myself in the same position to read the play and react at the same time. I told him that if one of us went right and the other went left then one of us was getting it wrong and it didn't mean it was him. On most occasions, we took a similar option and there were times when he went right and I went left and I thought I'd taken the wrong decision.

'What I spoke to him about in the beginning was decision-making – of understanding the qualities or limitations of his team-mates and of backing himself to have a go. If he stuffed it up, but in his heart he felt it was on, then it was not necessarily the wrong decision, but the wrong execution. I knew I could impart knowledge that I had gained through experience and because of his age, that was one thing he didn't have. He didn't play in particularly strong SACS teams yet he always excelled and his influence won many games.

'We worked on him dominating the opposition flyhalf because of superior positioning on defence and how he could turn the flyhalf's clearances into an advantage for his own team. Most flyhalves were right footed and because of this they would kick onto Percy's strongest foot, which is his left. It was important for him to watch the ball onto the boot of the flyhalf, and not the flyhalf himself, because that half a second was worth the critical metre a fullback gets when anticipating where the ball would go.

'Percy was also one of the quickest players and I thought that he could be as much a success on the left wing as he was at fullback. I'd have loved to see him on the wing playing alongside André Joubert at fullback, with Percy then having moved to fullback when André retired. It never happened that way but I always thought Percy would have gained enormous benefit from André and that André would have enjoyed having a specialist fullback among his wingers.

'Some believed flyhalf was Percy's best position, but my view was he would be too restricted at flyhalf and he was a greater danger at fullback or wing where he could roam. The fact that he has played flyhalf, centre, wing and fullback for the Springboks shows his versatility but 15 always was the number he coveted and history will judge him as one of South Africa's finest 15s, who got there because of natural talent and an incredible determination to succeed.

'Percy's longevity is because of his discipline in training and his willingness to listen and learn. During those 1st XV school days, he was like a sponge, taking in whatever information I shared and I made sure it was a two-way thing because an old dog can always learn a few things from a young one. I challenged him to show me a few things and I think that encouraged him to think about the game even more. Some would say I coached him, but I never saw it like that. He was a boy in need of an older pal, with a bit more life experience and I think that's the role I played for him.

'He adored his parents and he talked a lot about his father's rugby days in Namibia and about his dad's advice about rugby, but naturally as a boarder who only saw his parents during holidays, he missed the interaction any boy would have with his dad on a day-to-day basis. The last thing I ever wanted to be was a surrogate parent or a substitute for a father and fortunately Percy never saw our relationship like that. If anything, I was more like an older mate and he treated me like that from the age of 16 and has never stopped treating me in this way.

'When he first became professional, I managed his affairs, but quickly realised he needed a specialist in that field but we've never lost touch. I'd leave a message on his voicemail before every Test, which would be in keeping with what I used to say to the 16-year-old SACS *laaitie*, and he would always get back to me after the game with a thank you and, if needed, a short discussion about what worked or perhaps didn't. As two guys who live for rugby, we instantly had a connection and that has never changed.'

Montgomery's recollection of working with De Villiers is of the respect he and the other players got from him on the training field, and that he was always a buddy more than a master in a school where tradition dictates that older blokes and coaches aren't mates, but educators.

'He was amazing to work with because he never preached or spoke about when he was a Springbok. I can't ever remember him speaking about himself and he really didn't have to because everyone I knew who had seen HO play spoke about how good he was. I just liked him and felt I could speak to him and that he would never judge what I had to say.

'When we trained I could ask him questions without feeling stupid and he would give me a rugby explanation if he felt I could have done something better or why my execution of a kick, pass, tackle or move was poor. I knew I was lucky to have a mentor like that but I was as lucky to have a school master in Simon Perkin who allowed the relationship to develop and was never threatened by HO's influence at training.'

Perkin still teaches at SACS and his classroom has all the standard high-school trappings of chairs, desks and that wonderful smell of wood, but it could also be a rugby museum to Montgomery with his exploits in the SACS No 15 jersey equally prominent in the wall-to-wall classroom display alongside Montgomery, the Springbok. The walls boast newspaper clippings of the brilliant schoolboy Percival Montgomery and one particular match report is of the influence of Montgomery in trouncing Jan van Riebeeck, coincidentally the school attended by Montgomery Senior. There are provincial reports of Montgomery and there are the more obvious ones of Montgomery the World Cup-winning hero, and there are pictures, many of them. There are also gifts of Springbok memorabilia – from Montgomery to Perkin and from Montgomery to SACS.

'He does anything and everything for the school and he does it without us asking,' says Perkin. 'He donates signed Bok kit to help the school raise funds and when in Cape Town, he has always phoned to say hello and see if the school needs him to do a fundraiser or donate anything that can help us. When he was playing for Western Province and had already made the Springbok side, I once asked him to come down and work with the U14C team because they were in need of a boost and I thought that having the Springbok fullback, who just happened to be a SACS old boy, helping out at training would motivate them and show we cared about them as much as we did the U14A team. Monty only asked what time he had to be there and on what afternoon. Whenever he has been in town with the Springboks, he has made an effort to connect with the school and in 1998 when he was on tour with the Springboks in England, he even took the train from London to watch SACS' 1st XV play a tour game two hours outside London. He sat in the stands, popped into the change room and said hello to everyone afterwards, got back on the train and returned to London to be with the Boks. You can only imagine what that did for the schoolboys because he had come on his own accord when he heard SACS were on tour.'

Other SACS old boys make the wall, with Western Province trio Paul Delport, Ross Skeate (now with Toulon) and Isma-eel Dollie's achievements honoured, but the walls in this classroom belong to Montgomery.

'This is it,' says Perkin. 'This is Monty's old class, although he will tell you his class was outside on the Memorial Field and he won't be wrong because all he ever wanted to do was to be on the field kicking and training. He liked art and design and in 1992, when SACS hosted an arts festival, it was Monty's painting that was chosen as the programme cover. He enjoyed being creative but academics was not his strength, as I am sure he has told you.'

Montgomery has never pretended to be anything he is not. A giant among academics? He laughs when asked about schoolbooks and exams.

'I was definitely Perkie's A student and whenever I e-mail him, I remind him of that in the way I say goodbye. It usually goes: "Your number-one A student, Monty". I know he gets the humour in it because he used to get it at school when I used to tell him the same thing whenever he had to speak to me about my grades. I always found sport easier than academics and I had greater interest in a ball than a book. I wasn't a lazy student, but being in a classroom was not something I found easy. I just wanted to play rugby, run, swim and play water polo. We had a crazy water polo coach in Alan Footman and some of my fondest school memories are water polo tours and sessions in which Footie killed us in the pool.

'However, rugby was always the priority for me. In matric, I made the WP Schools waterpolo team and I asked Footie if he thought I had a chance of making SA Schools. He said yes, but I had to choose between the water polo national trials and going on tour to England with the SACS 1st XV. I had never been overseas and Footie told me I'd probably never get to go on another overseas rugby tour. He suggested I take the rugby tour at the expense of the water polo national trials.'

Footman, at the 2008 SACS Old Boys reunion, reminded Montgomery of the advice, given that for the last 14 years he spent nearly as much time touring overseas with rugby teams as he did at home, before finally settling in Cape Town in 2008 to play out his final year with WP and the Stormers.

'I dreamed of playing for Western Province at Newlands and of the SACS blue and white being the WP blue and white. My ambition was to play for the Springboks but to get there, I first had to play for Province and I used to love going to Newlands as a schoolboy, watching the rugby and getting lost in my own world where I was playing for Western Province and not a schoolboy on the side of the field. Those were great days, taking the walk down from SACS to Newlands to watch Province play. Perkie always used to say my favourite subjects were first and second break because I could go on the field and practise my kicking and be in my own world and he was right. I loved the Memorial Field and I used to run Newlands Forest most mornings before the other guys in the boarding house were even awake, get back to the boarding house, sneak a carton of milk, down it, have a shower and be ready for first break's kicking. If they had given grades for sport, for getting up early and for dreaming big about being a Springbok, then I would have been top of the class.'

Montgomery, the most capped Springbok of all time, the most capped Test fullback in the history of the game, Tri-Nations and World Cup winner, is SACS' most famous modern rugby son, but Perkin will tell you Montgomery is also the school's most humble celebrity. Humility is the word everyone uses to describe Montgomery, and schoolmasters, housemasters, coaches and old school class-mates all just say he was a popular kid but he was a normal kid, who loved sport and wasn't that keen on being in a classroom. They all remember him as a boy with strong values and simple tastes.

'If you gave him a ball to play with, he was at his happiest and that is how we remember him at SACS,' says Perkin, who also talks of Montgomery's loyalty to a school whose members were family. 'This is where he spent his entire youth and the connection between Monty and the school must be how most kids would relate to life at home because when most kids went home in the afternoon, Monty went to Memorial Field to train and then to have fun. He only went home for holidays and as he got older and toured with schools and provincial sporting teams, those holidays at home either got shorter or on occasions didn't happen. I know he loved going home to Namibia because of his close bond with his parents, but SACS was his home for more than 10 years and I think that is why he is so comfortable coming back here and why he always wants to give so much back to the school. He certainly is not your average past pupil.'

Perkin adores Montgomery, as a dad to a son and an older brother to a younger sibling. He never speaks of them being mates and the relationship will always have the respect of schoolmaster and pupil. Montgomery's work ethic is singled out, as is his loyalty to people. Perkin gives one example of Montgomery's loyalty and appreciation to those who have helped him throughout his career, describing the evening Montgomery was selected for the SA Schools team in 1992.

'The WP Schools team arrived back from Craven Week and Monty was to spend the evening at the home of team-mate and friend Johan van Schalkwyk in Oranjezicht in the City Bowl. I got a message from Johan's dad asking me to be at the house as Monty needed to see me urgently. He didn't know what was so important but he asked if I could be there by the time he got back from the airport, at midnight. When I got there, Monty and the Van Schalkwyk family were already there, waiting for me to celebrate his selection for the SA Schools team. He wouldn't open the bottle of champagne unless I, as his school coach, was there to share the moment. He thanked me for supporting him and for always believing in him. I was overwhelmed that he would involve me in what was his celebration and he has never lost that quality of always being prepared to honour anyone he feels has played a part in his development or success.'

Montgomery played more than 60 games for SACS' lst XV in three successive seasons, which Perkin believes is a school record, although the inconsistent keeping of documents for records, appearances and points scored means it can't be verified. Perkin also can't guarantee Montgomery is the school's most prolific point-scorer as Anton Chait, who would play flyhalf for WP in the 1990s, was an outstanding schoolboy goal kicker and a SACS points machine.

'SACS have had some wonderful players over the years. Peter Kirsten [who played cricket for South Africa and rugby for the Junior Springboks] is the most prominent of our flyhalves and Anton Chait was a big star for SACS,' says Perkin. 'But Monty has been the most successful rugby player in the school's history because he played SA Schools for two successive years and only Warren Kruger, in 1975, had made the SA Schools side.'

In 1992 and 1993, Montgomery scored half of the 1st XV's points, played for WP Schools and SA Schools, with the SA Schools match against a Nampak Academy XV at Newlands in 1992 the apex of his schools rugby career.

'We were the main curtain-raiser to the Bok match against the Wallabies, who had won the World Cup the year before, and the atmosphere at Newlands was incredible. I scored my first-ever try at Newlands and the only disappointment was that we played in white jerseys and black shorts and the Academy team, which was like an SA Schools B team, played in green and gold. We were told it had to do with politics and we weren't allowed to play in green and gold as the national schools team. We won and the occasion is still one of the most memorable of my career.'

It was also the only time Montgomery's mother and father saw him play a live schools game and it so nearly didn't happen. The SACS Old Boys had raised the funds to sponsor return flights from Namibia and accommodation for the Montgomerys, but they couldn't get match tickets because the Wallabies were in town. Newspaper reports changed that and Hugh Wiley, head of sponsorship at Norwich Union (WP team sponsor), ensured the Montgomerys would be their guests at the curtain-raiser and Test match. Montgomery scored one of three tries in a 15-13 win that also featured the mercurial talents of Herschelle Gibbs, who's now an international cricketer, at flyhalf. Montgomery is still of the opinion that he hasn't seen a schoolboy flyhalf as good since playing against and alongside Gibbs.

'He could kick the ball for miles and because of the distance of his kicks, it made it very difficult to play against him and I don't remember us winning much against Bishops when he was there,' says Montgomery. 'As a fullback, I had it easier when he was at flyhalf for the SA Schools team. He was also bloody naughty and when the pranks were played or a few rules were broken, you always knew Herschelle would be in there somewhere. He never took himself seriously and back then, among schoolboys, that was just perfect.'

If Gibbs was the superstar at Bishops, then Montgomery held a similar status at SACS, although he says no individual was ever allowed to get ahead of himself, even though it was not in his nature to behave like he was better than any other player.

'If any guy thought they had made it, the other guys would quickly cut him down to size. Boarding school teaches you to always clean up, it gives you discipline and it also creates an environment that doesn't tolerate individuals. It didn't matter if I had scored the winning points or made the SA Schools team, my responsibilities and duties remained the same. The team ethos always came before the desires of any individual.'

Montgomery talks up the virtues of boarding school, suggests his 12-year-old son, Nicholas, could do with the experience and then admits it is unlikely to ever happen.

'I would never get his mother [Tasmin Tobitt] to agree to it and in any case, I am too close to him and wouldn't want him away from us.'

Montgomery was a boarder at SACS in Newlands from standard two (grade four), but it was a situation forced on his parents through circumstance and ideally they would have wanted him at home.

'I know why my parents sent me to boarding school and the experience shaped my character, so if the circumstances were similar and I felt Nicholas would benefit more in that environment then I would have no fear sending him to boarding school, based on my own experience.'

Montgomery, on his return to Cape Town in 2008, enrolled Nicholas at SACS, but not as a boarder, as their Camps Bay home is a 20-minute drive from the school.

'To be able to send Nicholas to SACS is special for me,' says Montgomery. 'And what will make it even more enjoyable is being able to watch him develop and to be able to share some of my memories with him because he will be in a position to relate to the place and the traditions. Who knows, maybe Perkie will even teach him.'

Despite the plaudits for SACS' boarding school environment and the school itself, Montgomery admits his first year, as an eight-year-old, was painful and that it is difficult to articulate the loneliness and the confusion in understanding how the absence of a traditional home life was actually a good thing. In that first year, he often felt nauseous and home sick and he craved those afternoons at the rugby field watching his dad play or coach, and most of all, he longed for the freedom of doing as he pleased as a six- and seven-year-old in Namibia. Rugby days there were days of being treated and of treats.

Montgomery Senior and Monty speak of the bond there has always been between the two, but a long-distance relationship comes with restrictions and neither father nor son can talk of intimacy during the decade Monty was in Cape Town as a schoolboy and Montgomery Senior was in Namibia. It is why Monty is so determined to make up that time post-rugby.

'I want to get closer to my family and I also want to make more of an effort with old school friends. I seem to have been on the road since I was eight years old, but being back in Cape Town with Taz, Nicholas and [daughter] Taneal, and having my folks an hour's drive away in Hermanus, makes me feel settled and content. I am desperate to make up for lost time, especially with my mom and dad, and I will always want to give back to a school that gave me so much.'

It is at SACS that Montgomery was taught discipline and to work hard, and while you can sense the hurt and humiliation when he tells of being hung out of a window by a school teacher and embarrassed in front of his class-mates, the tears of a young boy lessened as the teenager thrived and triumphed. Montgomery, despite times of loneliness in his first few years, never talks of feeling neglected.

'My parents were a phone call away and in the boarding house people cared about us and there were always invites from class-mates to spend the weekends at their homes. I missed my home, but I never felt unloved and the more I got involved with sport, the less time I had to feel lonely.'

SACS junior-school headmaster, Stuart Anderson, who retired at the end of 2008, described Montgomery as an honest and well-liked boy. Anderson, like those who taught Montgomery at junior school, can't recall anything out of the ordinary, other than the obvious sporting talent that saw Montgomery play for the U13A cricket side and captain the U13A rugby team. Montgomery doesn't tell any remarkable junior-school stories either. He missed the normality of home life and of doing things without constant supervision. But in time, he would learn to miss SACS more than Namibia, especially as he prospered in his rugby and water polo, and most holidays were spent on tour with the rugby team. Montgomery calls himself 'a boy in blue and white for life'. He has played professional rugby in Wales and France and spent two years playing for the Sharks, in KwaZulu-Natal, on his return to South Africa in 2005. But in his heart, the only rugby home he knows is in the suburb of Newlands.

'Wearing blue and white hoops was all I knew at SACS. When I played for WP Schools, the only difference was that the blue hoops were wider than the ones we wore at school, but the colours remained the same. From there the blue and white hoops were of the WP U21 side in 1994 and 1995, before I finally got to wear the most famous blue and white hoops of them all, that of the senior WP team late in 1995.'

Montgomery recalls that U21 team as among the most naturally gifted and potent he has ever played in.

'No one could beat us. We were phenomenal and we had some of the best players I had seen at that level. A lot of those guys went on to play provincial and Test rugby and nearly half of them were in the WP team that won the Currie Cup in 2000 and 2001, but in 1995 not only were they brilliant rugby players, they were quality okes who enjoyed having fun as much as they enjoyed playing rugby.'

Montgomery had played against many of them at school, with the trio of Robbie Fleck, Dave von Hoesslin and Selborne Boome at Bishops – the traditional school rivals of SACS –

while the Paarl Boys' High duo of Wium Basson and Corné Krige were the enforcers of pain on any opposition. Hottie Louw and Bob Skinstad were from out of town, but their personality type was such that they slotted in immediately and Montgomery spent a year rooming with Louw while both tried to attend classes at Cape Technikon.

'Hottie and I became good mates in that U21 year and the friendship stayed strong as we progressed to the seniors. Grant Hinckley, who would become my best friend, also moved down from Johannesburg and we all shared a digs in the City Bowl. We lived as any students would – lots of fun, late nights and between Hottie and Grant, a fair amount of drinking, while I focused on the ladies. Our common bond was we all played rugby, but as mates we just got along and when Robbie Kempson moved to Cape Town from Durban, he also became a very good friend.'

Kempson, who would play many Tests in the same Bok team as Montgomery, remembers first meeting him when they played for SA Schools, but the cultured Kempson, who lists piano playing, show jumping (and, in particular, dressage) and tequila drinking as his hobbies, would only connect with Montgomery a few years later when both were permanently based in Cape Town. Of that WP U21 side – who never lost a match in 1995 and humiliated Free State 50-10 in the final played in Bloemfontein – Montgomery, Fleck, Louis Koen, Basson, Louw and Von Hoesslin would all play for the Boks and Skinstad and Krige would captain them. Rhys Botha (Fleck's centre partner), Cassie Carstens (scrumhalf) and Marius Goosen (flyhalf) would all play provincial rugby.

'It was a hell of a team and if Kempo had been there it would have been even better. Outside of Os du Randt, Kempo has to be one of the best props to have played for South Africa in my time, and like Os, he gives any backline player that extra comfort that in a time of crisis they are never far away,' says Montgomery, who ideally wanted to return to Western Province from Wales in 2005. He had left in 2002 on good terms, with WP coach Gert Smal on record as saying that despite the player's disillusionment with South African rugby, he was always willing to sacrifice for Province and that he gave it his all until the final minute of the 2002 Currie Cup season.

WP managing director, Rob Wagner, also says that in an ideal world, the union would have wanted Montgomery back in 2005, but economics determined otherwise.

'We have always known him as one of ours and even when he played for the Sharks for two seasons, it was like he was on loan because of enforced circumstance,' says Wagner. 'He has always done us proud and he has always had an appreciation for everyone here. When he left for Wales, he came into the office and thanked everyone personally for helping him at WP and all the ladies at the office received flowers. Contrary to the media speculation at the time, he left us with a name as good as the young teenager who first walked into the WP change room.'

Montgomery admits the ideal would have been to play for Province when he got back to South Africa in 2005, but he understood the combination of his contract cost and the limited availability for Currie Cup games meant he had to look elsewhere.

'First prize when I got back to South Africa in 2005 would have been playing for Western Province, but they were rebuilding a team and it was explained to me that they didn't think they would see much of me because of Springbok commitments and they were not comfortable with spending money on a high-profile contract when they were unsure what playing value they would get in return. I accepted they had budgetary restrictions and I got an approach from Sharks coach Dick Muir to play in Durban. Dick and I had played together at WP and for the Springboks at the end of 1997 and I enjoyed him as a person and rated his insights on rugby. He is always positive about life, and outside of the obvious rugby benefits from playing in a strong Sharks squad, there was the added lure of Taz's folks having moved to Durban from Johannesburg. Taz, after our three years in Newport, wanted to be close to her folks and with them in Durban, it was not a difficult decision to make.

'I would never have considered playing for the Lions, Cheetahs or Bulls. I like the players from those regions and the guys I tended to hang with in the Boks were the Bulls players, but I am a Province man who played most of his rugby close to Newlands or at Newlands and it would just be wrong for me to be wearing a Bulls, Lions or Cheetahs jersey. It would have been like seeing Naas Botha in a Western Province jersey. Percy Montgomery in a Bulls jersey? No, and I know the locals in Pretoria would have felt the same way as I did. But thanks to Dick's interest, I could settle back in South Africa in 2005 and not have to play for the Boks as an overseas-based player, which also delighted Jake White, who always wanted me to return to South Africa once he had picked me for the Boks in 2004.'

Montgomery played for the Sharks between 2005 and 2007 and in his first year, he played in a losing Sharks team in a Currie Cup match at Newlands.

'It was among the strangest days to go back to Newlands and play in another jersey and be given the "treatment" by the people I have always considered my home fans. But it emphasised to me that the fans are loyal to a jersey and not any player and on that day they saw me as part of the opposition and a threat to Western Province.'

Montgomery, in 2008, played again for WP, a situation he says he never thought possible, but it also reinforced his love for the blue and white jersey.

'To start and finish my career in the Province jersey is just unbelievable. When I left Province for Newport in 2002, I never thought I'd get to wear the blue and white again. As a schoolboy, I used to train on Memorial Field and stare at Newlands, which was just down the road. The thought of playing at that stadium always inspired me and when I'd feel tired in training or when doing my own training I'd always seek out the view of Newlands to give me a second wind. It also helped that SACS had such a strong Western Province and Springbok tradition, even though there haven't been many Boks produced by the school in the last 50 years.'

Montgomery's modesty is highlighted here because he has been the only SACS Bok Test player since Cecil Moss played in 1948. The tradition Montgomery refers to was born when SACS, then the South African College (SAC), played the first-ever match at Newlands against Bishops. The 2nd XVs had the honour and the second match, between the 1st XVs, followed. SACS also gave Western Province their blue and white hoops, a playing strip they had gained by default and not design.

Sir Henry Juta, in the history of SACS, is quoted as saying that SACS' players initially turned out in whatever each man fancied or possessed, but when they played Bishops, who always dress in dark blue, this prompted a change and SACS' players decided they too wanted a uniformed strip. Rugby historian Paul Dobson writes that SACS' players had to take what was available from an Adderley Street supplier, Porter Hodgson's. The only jerseys he had in stock, in two sizes, were those with blue and white hoops and they became SACS' official colours. Western Province, winners of the Currie Cup in 1892, wore SACS jerseys because their captain Ben Duff was a SACS man and they have worn the blue and white hoops ever since.

When Montgomery was at school, he was taught about those who helped shape the tradition of SACS and of the exploits of those who would play for South Africa in various sports. Among the famous stories is that of Billy Millar, who survived typhoid fever as a baby, went to SAC and ran away at 16 to join the Cycling Corps in the Anglo-Boer War. He nearly lost an arm and to strengthen himself, took up boxing and walking and became the Cape Colony amateur heavyweight champion. Millar played for South Africa in 1906. Tom Hepburn is another famous name because he kicked the conversion in South Africa's first-ever Test win in 1891.

But the most remarkable story of SACS rugby is that after producing the first Springbok selection in 1891, when Ben Duff was alphabetically listed as the first South African national team player against the British Isles, the school would 117 years later produce the first Springbok to win 100 Test caps in Percival Montgomery.

4

MOSQUITOES, MENDOZA AND MUSCLES

When Western Province coach Harry Viljoen returned from his side's pre-season tour of Argentina in 1997, he said he had found the most explosive centre in South Africa and he raved about Percy Montgomery's strength in the tackle, his aggression and his pace.

Percy Montgomery? The same guy Viljoen's predecessor, Alan Zondagh, considered too frail to start consistently at fullback in the 1996 Currie Cup? Percy Montgomery? The same guy the Bloemfontein crowd called 'Mosquito' on his Western Province debut in the Test Unions Day? Now, 18 months after being mocked for having the physical presence of an insect, Montgomery was this menace in the Province midfield and physically capable of troubling defences?

Viljoen, before his arrival at Western Province in 1997, had not coached for three years and he was not familiar with the Cape players, especially the younger ones who had come through the Cape schooling system. But when he saw Montgomery at training during the pre-season and playing on the tour to Argentina, he was adamant Montgomery was the most special backline player in South Africa and that he had the X-factor to be a game breaker and a match winner.

Viljoen told the Cape press they had missed a good thing in Mendoza and Buenos Aires and that the career of a very special professional rugby player was born there during Western Province's tour. As no rugby writer had travelled with the team, they told Viljoen they'd wait until the domestic Nite Series (the forerunner to the Vodacom Cup) to see whether Montgomery had indeed turned into a midfield mongrel. Viljoen, throughout his coaching career, believed a good big player was always a better investment than a good little one and his first experience of Montgomery was in pre-season training in 1997 when he weighed 85kg and not the 78kg Zondagh considered a liability in the last line of defence.

'He will play for the Springboks this year,' Viljoen told me at the time. 'You should have seen how good he was in Argentina, playing at outside centre and at flyhalf. He has power and pace and he has got bigger since he first started playing for WP. He also gives any backline another attacking option because of the distance he gets on his kicks and he is eager to learn.'

It took one match back in South Africa for the local media to join the cheerleading of Montgomery's virtues. In the domestic Nite Series, Montgomery destroyed defences with his explosiveness. He was confrontational in contact situations, playing with the confidence of a muscle man and showing no frailty of the 'Mosquito' who visited Bloemfontein at the end of 1995. But with the praise and media awareness, came the rumblings that Montgomery had been on anabolic steroids – accusations he dismissed then and now as malicious.

'I am all eggs, creatine and protein,' Montgomery told me in an interview for the *Cape Times* in 1997. 'I have heard all the rumours that I have taken performance-enhancing substances and I think it's a joke what is being said. My increase in weight has been blown out of proportion as well. I got injured in June last year and did not play for Western Province again, so I had six months to work in the gym.'

Montgomery, as WP Schools, SA Schools and primarily WP U21 left wing in 1994 and 1995, toured with the WP Super 12 squad to Australia and New Zealand in 1996 where he played occasionally at fullback, but mostly from the bench. When he wasn't playing Super 12 rugby in 1996, he was playing fullback and wing for Cape club side Villager, with his pace and left boot on one occasion contributing 20 points in Villager's memorable 25-13 win against a powerful Stellenbosch University side in the premier Cape league. Any win against Maties, as Stellenbosch University's 1st XV are called, is worth noting and it also confirmed Montgomery had the game to excel in company older, wiser and more physical than his 21-year-old frame.

Montgomery could play alright and his mentor, HO de Villiers, and former Northern Transvaal and Bok fullback, Pierre Edwards, were convinced he would play Test rugby. De Villiers made the statement after working with Montgomery at SACS for three years and Edwards, headmaster of Affies in Pretoria, told the media he had seen a future Springbok at Craven Week in Pretoria in 1992, when Montgomery was selected as SA Schools fullback. But between 1992, when he was the premier schools No 15 in South Africa, and 1996, when he started at fullback for WP against the Otago-based Highlanders at Newlands in the Super 12, Montgomery was never seen as an imposing physical presence. Now, in the week of a Nite Series derby between Boland and Western Province, officials and players from Boland were insistent that the player called 'Mosquito' had been sucking on more than blood to bulk up. With both teams in contention for the final, which ironically both would make and Province would win a month later, Boland officials argued they wanted a fair contest and the accusation was Province were selecting a player who had an unfair advantage over the opposition. The player supposedly was Montgomery and Boland team officials and players wanted him tested, even though the norm was that players got tested randomly on match day once the match had been played.

Montgomery, in a week of high drama, was tested and the results were negative, but it silenced none of the doubters and the accusations went from him being on the juice to somehow beating the system.

'I was satisfied when his test was negative and when I became Bok coach, I had no problem in selecting him,' says Nick Mallett, who at the time was coaching Boland.

Montgomery insisted he had done nothing illegal and that the additional weight was because of an intense pre-season gym programme designed to build muscle and add weight. He said his training had been aggressive and that it had been specific to adding bulk and that he knew he had to add between 8 and 10kg to his frame if he was to be a professional player. He attributed the weight gain to being on a specific conditioning programme for the first time in his life.

'Throughout my high-school career, I had never done gym-specific training and even in my two years of playing for WP U21, there wasn't a great focus on gym work or diets because rugby was still an amateur sport,' says Montgomery. 'I weighed around 85kg at the start of the 1997 season and I have weighed between 85 and 88kg for the last 11 years. My body-fat percentage has been the same since 1997 and it is because I am disciplined about my body and my training.'

Montgomery's protests of innocence in 1997 did not stop the mutterings or the mocking and when he and his best friend, Grant Hinckley, returned from Johannesburg, where they had been training for four months at the end of 1996 and beginning of 1997, the mocking turned to malice.

'In the beginning, it was a joke among some of the Province boys. I remember walking into La Med in Camps Bay with

Monty early on in 1997, and Robby Brink and Simon Berridge, two of the Province guys Monty got on really well with, came over and asked us if we had been vacationing at an animal farm. They were amazed at how much Monty had bulked up, but then they had not seen him for four months and the programme we were on was high protein and intense. Monty told them it was all egg whites.

'"Fuck off," they said, pissing themselves,' says Hinckley, whose own provincial career would be ended as a 22-year-old in 1998 because of injury. 'Monty laughed it off but it didn't mean it went away and there was a lot of talk about Monty's weight in the media and a lot of speculation that he had been on the juice.'

For the team-mates who made light of it, there were others who wanted him tested and privately claimed the transformation was too quick and the results too dramatic. Protein shakes were one thing. Creatine – the popular muscle builder used by rugby players in the late 1990s – was another but the change in Montgomery, they were sure, was because of substance use. Montgomery never wavered in his stance, took the random test, in-season, and in the past 11 years has never failed a doping test in South Africa or abroad.

Did he take juice?

He says no, and every doping test performed on him says no, yet others still say he did. However, you won't find anyone prepared to go on record with that assertion.

In 1997, influential Cape-based rugby writer Gavin Rich was incensed at the manner in which Montgomery had been treated. He condemned the South African Rugby Football Union's (Sarfu) doping procedures and their singling out of Montgomery.

Rich, in his *Sunday Argus* column, called for a blanket drugs test on all the country's contracted players to avoid a repeat of what happened to Montgomery.

'It will also prevent the dope issue from turning into a divisive witch-hunt, which, on the evidence of the way the Montgomery case was handled, could end up landing someone in court. For those who did not read the report, the Cape public was informed on the morning of the Boland game that Montgomery was the subject of a special probe by Sarfu. Although Montgomery was given space to protest his innocence and was cleared when Sarfu announced that the test was negative on Friday, there remained a clear inference that the player was suspected of having used steroids to bulk up during the off-season.

'WP coach Harry Viljoen claims the first he heard of the matter was when he read about it in the newspapers, while Montgomery was informed by journalists of the pending drug test, which was carried out at his home. By singling Montgomery out so publicly, Sarfu placed unnecessary pressure on a player whose only crime was that he had put on 7 or 8kg during a four-month off-season. It has undeniably slighted his character as an individual. Although he was subsequently exonerated, Montgomery had to live through a week where he had to carry the stigma of being a potential cheat. All of this on the flimsy evidence provided by potentially jealous players and officials from another province, which in this case just happened to be the same one WP were playing the day Montgomery's name was dragged through the mud.'

Rich also described Viljoen as being incensed at the timing of the drug testing and quoted Western Province and later Springbok team-mate Fritz van Heerden defending Montgomery.

'What irritated me about the whole way Percy was singled out was that I knew how hard he worked to improve his physical presence,' said Van Heerden. 'A few years ago, in an effort to bulk up, I went on a similar training routine to the one followed by Percy. By spending time in the gym and eating six eggs a day, I went from 85 to 100kg. At the time everyone was joking that I had used steroids, which I just took as a compliment to the hard work I had put in.'

Montgomery's weight gain, concluded Rich, was nowhere near that of Van Heerden and he asked whether the national governing body was going to test up-and-coming Western Province utility back Breyton Paulse once he had also picked up 5kg through a gym programme. Viljoen considered Paulse, who weighed 72kg, too light for the WP senior team, and the player was told to add at least 5kg. Rich's point was that in the professional era, with specialised diets and weight-gaining programmes, players would get heavier, especially those who had never been exposed to gym work as schoolboys. South African rugby at the time was considered the doping capital of world rugby, and within the fraternity, everyone had a story to tell about players on steroids, from schoolboy level through to the national squad. Everyone seemed to know a player who was getting a little help from doctors, but for all the talk, South African rugby's medical director and member of the International Rugby Board's (IRB) anti-doping committee, Dr Ismail Jakoet, believes those who were playing with the fire of using anabolic steroids got burned.

'No one can say with certainty that every player who was using performance-enhancing substances was caught but I am confident that in those early days of professional rugby, when the support structures were not that good in terms of advising players against substance abuse and there was also confusion regarding what was legal, we in South Africa policed it effectively,' says Jakoet. 'We were the most vigilant of all the countries when it came to testing in the early years of professional rugby and that is why our numbers of guilty players were higher than other countries. Now, I believe, everyone around the world is on the same page and there is consistency everywhere when it comes to testing. Every rugby nation has aggressive educational programmes because the common view on the best way to fight it is to educate players about the long-term harm to their bodies and risk to their careers.'

On Montgomery, Jakoet says: 'I instructed the South African Institute of Drug-Free Sport to do a random test on Montgomery in 1997. There was too much talk going on, in the media and in the corridors. We had requests to test him and I even had a call from his mentor, HO de Villiers, asking how to deal with the rumours because he was adamant they were rubbish. I said there was only one way to deal with it and that was to single Montgomery out for what is called a "target" test. That would end all the speculation. In those days, the normal testing always came straight after a match, but if there was suspicion a player was using performance-enhancing substances then he could be tested in any environment. We sent testers unannounced to a training session and he was tested. The result was negative and since then Monty has been one of the most tested Springboks because he has played at the highest level for so long. He has never returned a positive test and no player whose weight has stayed consistent in the mid-80kgs could be using performance-enhancing substances and beat the system for more than 10 years.'

Jakoet makes no apologies for the random test done on Montgomery because on the same day, Blue Bulls prop Frikkie Bosman was also subjected to a random test at his house.

'We had information that Bosman was possibly using illegal substances and there were suspicions that Montgomery was on something, so we tested both of them. Bosman was positive [and banned for two years] and Montgomery was negative, which was a vindication of the testing. For me, it was vindication of our actions because we could not afford to take any chances and dismiss any allegations being made, and the positive for Montgomery was that his name was cleared of all the rumours in a year in which he made his Test debut.'

5

A HISS, A ROAR AND A MISS

It was each man for himself when Percy Montgomery walked into a Springbok team room for the first time in 1997. There were no grand welcomes, high fives or tutoring. Those who had survived from the first Test defeat against the British & Irish Lions in Cape Town were intent on making it past Durban and onto Johannesburg for the third Test. Those who were new to the environment just wanted to make it through the 80 minutes at Kings Park. Montgomery, a controversial inclusion, did not have the luxury of an abundance of provincial team-mates in the starting XV, with left wing Pieter Rossouw the only other Western Province player getting a start. Provincialism in those days was more powerful than national unity and you only had to walk into a team room to know which province a player represented. This was a tribal environment and after the defeat in Cape Town against the Lions, it was also a troubled one.

'I have never experienced such anxiety in more than 10 years of being with the Springboks,' says Montgomery.

'I have known tough times and there have been difficult years but that week was something else. The team unexpectedly lost 25-16 in Cape Town and the players were fighting for their Test careers and the pressure on Carel du Plessis as coach was massive. There was a lot of emotion in the squad and I sensed there was not a lot of confidence in Carel and [Bok assistant coach] Gert Smal, with the media writing them off and the senior players not convinced they were good enough to be there. I thought Carel and Gert were brilliant because they were the guys who had just made me a Springbok.

'I admired Carel when he played wing for the Springboks and he was one of the game's best. I liked him immediately as a person when we first met and I respected his knowledge of the game, but I was only a kid in that environment and the older and more experienced players did not share that opinion. They were sceptical about his ability to be as good an international coach as he was a player and losing to the Lions only added to the view that he would not cut it.

'There were complaints that he did not communicate effectively and there seemed to be confusion about what he wanted the players to do. I tried to distance myself from that and I only wanted to reward him for picking me. I was desperate to do well and I wanted Carel to succeed. I knew he rated me and that was good enough for me. He was also the Springbok coach and I felt he deserved more respect because of that but no losing Springbok team gets done any favours and this was a team under siege with a coach who had no track record.

'When I got to Durban, I was excited, confident I could do anything against anyone and not fearful in the least. There was nothing to be scared of because by being selected, I already felt I had won and my form in 1997 had been good. I was young, ignorant about the history and tradition of the Lions and, as far as I was concerned, I was bullet proof. I saw it as my first Test and not as a Test to save the series against the Lions. It would take 10 years of playing Test rugby for me to understand that some Tests are bigger than others and that a series against the Lions is the biggest thing outside of the World Cup.'

Montgomery, who had been part of the initial Bok training squad of 27, had never shared a change room with the likes of André Joubert, Henry Honiball, Os du Randt, André Venter, Ruben Kruger, Mark Andrews, Joost van der Westhuizen and Gary Teichmann. They were Durban, Bloemfontein and Pretoria-based players, but more importantly, some of them were World Cup winners in 1995 and all of them were Springbok icons to Montgomery, who says there was a pecking order within the team he was always willing to respect and one he agreed with.

SACS, his junior and senior school, had taught him about pecking orders and he had learnt as an eight-year-old in his first year at boarding school that you earned respect. It was not something given to you on arrival in a new environment. He could only prove to his team-mates he belonged in the Springbok change room through on-field performance and through an attitude that showed a willingness to listen and learn.

'I was shy by nature and in that kind of environment, I kept to myself. It was not the era in which young okes would hang out with the Bok captain, invite him for a cup of coffee or join his table. It just didn't happen in the Bok set-up that old mixed with young when I got to Durban before my first Test. As a youngster, you also didn't have an opinion and if you did you didn't share it with guys who had won the World Cup. I shut up and spoke when spoken to, which wasn't very often that week.

'What made it a bit easier was that Danie van Schalkwyk, who made his Bok debut in 1996, had also been recalled to play inside centre. Danie played for the Bulls and was in his early 20s and we got on well. I enjoyed his vibe. He was a funny guy, outgoing and did not take himself too seriously.

We found ourselves in the same position, with so many people doubting our ability and questioning how we could stand up to the Lions midfield of Scott Gibbs and Jeremy Guscott. They were world-class performers who had played everyone and we were two kids who had only recently met, but would be playing together for the first time.

'Danie had made his Test debut in Durban against the All Blacks a year earlier and you don't get much tougher than that. He seemed relaxed and I was very calm because I backed myself to do well. I think it surprised the older guys that we seemed so comfortable with the occasion, even though they never said anything to us. I can't recall much being said to us by the senior players and with so many of them being under pressure after losing the first Test in Cape Town, each guy seemed to be looking after himself. It wasn't a "them and and us" situation but because of all the uncertainty about individual places in the team and pressure on winning the Test, each guy, whether it was his first or 50th Test, had to fend for himself.

'I found Danie easy to get on with and we seemed to enjoy the same things. He didn't think there were many combinations better in the game than Gibbs and Guscott. He respected what they had achieved but, like me, he was not overawed by their reputations. Carel believed we were good enough to handle them and that was good enough for me.

'There were no big one-on-ones with Carel that week and he confined his talking to me at training. It was also at training where he told me to do a bit of goal kicking because I might get used in the Test. I didn't seriously think I would be kicking because Henry Honiball and André Joubert were starting and they were the top two in the pecking order when it came to goal kicking. Gary Teichmann, who was captaining the side, never mentioned to me in the week that I would be used as a kicker during the match and my preparation was about playing centre and doing it as well as I had for WP in the 1997 Nite Series, which we had won.'

Goal kicking would become the hottest topic after the Test but in the build-up, all Montgomery would hear were the names of Gibbs and Guscott, with Gibbs the dominant of the two. The advice, in the rugby media and among the public, was consistent. Gibbs, they felt, was too strong for Montgomery, even though it was Guscott who was playing at outside centre.

'Don't take a step backwards or you will never play again for South Africa.' 'Don't be intimidated by his reputation, his size or his aggression.' 'Know that he is going to target you.' 'Know that they see you as a kid out of your depth and not capable of playing Test rugby.' All week, Montgomery heard how powerful Scott Gibbs was, how brutal he was and how big he was. 'Scott Gibbs is a monster.' 'Scott Gibbs is a brick shithouse' and the 'toughest player in their backline'. 'Scott Gibbs …', 'Scott Gibbs …' Wherever Montgomery went in Durban in the week of his Test debut against the Lions in 1997, he heard of this Welshman, who weighed more than 100kg and, because of his rugby league background, liked to tackle as much as he liked life itself.

Montgomery had heard the same thing the week Western Province played the tourists in Cape Town and it never bothered him because the talk was of how another league player, Scotland's Alan Tait, would physically be too strong for the youthful likes of Montgomery. It also did not faze him because in that game he had introduced himself early to Tait in a tackle, swung a few punches, taken a couple and then settled into what he describes as a good experience as Province led 21-7 before losing 38-21.

'The sideshow when WP played the Lions was between James Small and their winger John Bentley. They were at each other all game and I'd never heard two guys going at one another like that before. They were calling each other every name in the book and neither was prepared to back down and if they were too far apart for verbals, they were gesturing insulting signs at each other, from wanker to up-yours. James accused Bentley of eye-gouging him and each guy was trying to outdo the other in showmanship.

'I am sure the crowd loved it, but I found it a bit over the top. I have never been one for swearing at opponents or for getting psyched up that way. James, as I would find out in my career, was very vocal and would see his verbal sparring with the opposition as part of a battle within a battle and I can't remember an opponent who revelled in that approach as much as Bentley did. It was an education watching the two of them and while some of the comments between them were crude, others were bloody funny.

'We scored three tries in the match but they were too experienced and strong in the second half and they ended up winning quite easily, but I enjoyed the occasion. I would also play centre against them for the Emerging Springboks, but I did not think I was in contention for a Test place as I was one of the five guys to drop out of the training squad for the one-off Test against Tonga and the first Test against the Lions, both of which were at Newlands. A lot was made of [WP coach] Harry Viljoen moving me from outside centre to flyhalf for the Lions match and the media also questioned my ability to cope with the physicality of the Lions backs and their loose forwards, but I thought I handled them OK.'

Now Montgomery was hearing the monster stories again and being told Gibbs, in a Test, was a different beast to Tait and that Guscott would be better than he was against Western Province. Montgomery did not think too much about Gibbs because he rated his midfield partner, Guscott, as the more dangerous runner and better distributor. Gibbs had physicality, but Guscott was all class, according to Montgomery.

The Lions had stunned the Springboks in the first Test in Cape Town and the coaching obituary of Du Plessis was already being written. The Boks had been favourites to win the series 3-0, but that was before the shock Cape Town result. Montgomery's selection was as big a shock as that loss, but Du Plessis touted Montgomery as the future of Springbok rugby and said it was time to move on from those players who had won South Africa the World Cup in 1995. Du Plessis, his selections bold and his rugby philosophy even bolder, believed in expansive rugby and was dismissive of restrictive game plans.

The Newlands defeat had shocked him, but he was adamant he had picked a team capable of scoring tries and smashing the Lions. As it was, Du Plessis was not far wrong in his view of the Lions, but the one thing he would have taken for granted at Kings Park, the Boks' goal kicking, flopped.

'There was no emphasis on the goal kicking going into the Test,' says Montgomery. 'Henry and André were the recognised kickers and I'd kicked for WP in the pre-season tour to Argentina, in the Nite Series final against Boland and against the Lions, but that was the total of my kicking in 1997 and I never thought I would be taking the kicks in my Test debut. There was not much intensity about how I practised my goal kicking that week. I'd have a few kicks with Henry and André after training and that was it. They did not say much to me and they kept to themselves. I just observed as much as possible. The mood among all the players was selfish because if the Boks were going to win, each guy had to ensure he did his primary job well and mine was not going to be the goal kicking. I had to make sure I beat my man if put into space and I had to make my tackles. There was no fear for the Lions. The fear I felt in the squad was about the Springboks failing again. The players could not believe they had lost in Cape Town and were convinced they were too good to lose again in Durban, even though they knew they would have to play well to win.'

The Springboks played well enough to win, outscoring the Lions three tries to nil, but between Honiball, Joubert and Montgomery, they missed three conversions and three penalties. The Lions won 18-15 thanks to five Neil Jenkins penalties and a late drop goal from Guscott. The media and public slammed Montgomery for the defeat after he missed a penalty and two conversions, but Honiball's two first-half penalty misses and Joubert's second-half conversion miss did not get the same press.

Montgomery says he has never blamed himself for the defeat because he had not been picked to kick the goals.

'Obviously I wanted to get them over, but I was not the first-choice kicker and did not think I would be kicking – that makes a difference to any player's approach during the week. Henry started the game as the goal kicker and after he missed twice, Gary handed me the ball and told me to give it my best. On the day, my best wasn't good enough and when we scored our third try to take the lead, André was given the responsibility of adding the two points and I was only too pleased he would be kicking. I had scored a try in the match and thought I'd done well, but I knew the defeat could influence whether I got selected for the third Test in Johannesburg.

'I don't remember much detail from the game, but I won't forget the minutes before the start when we sang the anthems or the scenes at the final whistle when they had won. I couldn't believe we had lost and that the series had been lost. In the game, I felt we were so much better than them and had dominated them in every aspect of the game. But they had kicked their penalties and we had missed ours and I was a part of those misses and, while I don't blame myself for losing the Test, I know a lot of people have never forgiven me for those misses and don't seem to remember I wasn't the only one who missed that day.

'There is nothing specific I recall from playing Gibbs and Guscott, although Gibbs bouncing Os du Randt was a big moment for the Lions in the Test and it seemed to lift their intensity and belief. It was a strange game and it felt like we had them on the ropes all the time but couldn't finish them off and then, out of nowhere, they landed a sucker punch through the Guscott drop goal.

'Afterwards, I wanted to feel down because of the result, but I also felt happy at having played my first Test. I was a Springbok and it felt good, even though it felt terrible to lose to a team when you know your team is better. The dressing room mood was down because of the series defeat and that fear of being dropped for the third Test at Ellis Park became even greater among the players. Uncertainty over selection is an awful thing to feel when you are a player.

'Carel was dejected and so was Gary, but both of them were dignified in the change room. Neither blamed anyone for the defeat and both gave me the reassurance I'd done well, even if the conversation was limited to a few words. There was also no blame among the players in the change room. There were long periods of silence and reflection. Every player knew the media were going to be harsh and Carel seemed to prepare for the worst. I felt sorry for him and I felt I had let him down because if just two of our six kicks had gone over, we'd have won, but none of them had and we had lost. If you asked me before the game if I thought it was possible that between Henry, André and myself, we would miss six out of six, I would have said never, but it happened.'

Teichmann would also never have bet on the probability of six misses from six attempts. In his autobiography, *For the Record*, he writes that Honiball, Joubert and Montgomery were all recognised goal kickers, who had previously won games with their boots and would do so for the Boks. He felt it was an aberration that came at the worst possible time – a series-deciding match – but he also accepted blame for unintentionally creating uncertainty about who would be doing the goal kicking and he underestimated the need for one of them to have been told they would be doing it.

Du Plessis, talking to Dale Granger in the *Cape Times*, took the blame for the goal-kicking stuff-up after the convener of selectors, Mickey Gerber, had blasted Teichmann in the media. Gerber told Granger: 'Percival Montgomery was selected as the kicker, but was not used as intended. The captain did not start with him, and whose fault is that? It has nothing to do with the selection. You can't go into Test matches and give away so many penalties against a kicker like Neil Jenkins, who can kill you stone dead.'

Du Plessis defended Teichmann in the same article.

'I gave Teichmann the green light to use Honiball at first, if he was feeling confident. If Honiball battled, then Teichmann was to bring in Montgomery. In the week before the Test, both Montgomery and Honiball were successful with 70% of their kicks in training. Honiball was used initially because he has kicked for South Africa before and was playing on his home ground.'

Everyone had an opinion on the goal-kicking woes and former Bok flyhalf Naas Botha felt neither Honiball, Joubert nor Montgomery were recognised goal kickers, and he called for an established goal kicker to be selected, with Free State's Jannie de Beer the most prominent of the contenders.

'When I think of New Zealand's Andrew Mehrtens and of Wales and Lions flyhalf Neil Jenkins, then I immediately think of them as goal kickers, but when I think of Joubert and Honiball, I think of them as rugby players before I think goal kicker,' said Botha in an interview with Afrikaans newspaper *Rapport*. Botha then defined what it took to be a world-class goal kicker and questioned the techniques of the Springbok goal kickers in Durban, asking whether they had what it took.

Joel Stransky, the 1995 World Cup-winning drop-goal hero, who was playing for Leicester in 1997, told the *Cape Times* that Montgomery should never have been given the responsibility as he was not a first-choice goal kicker and did not have the necessary composure in his debut Test to cope with the pressure. Stransky said it was unfair on Montgomery, as was the post-mortem crucifying Montgomery's misses.

Montgomery says it had nothing to do with pressure or the occasion and that he struck the ball badly.

'Two of the three misses were angled conversions and they came with a lot of time still to play so I didn't feel the pressure of having to make the kick to win the Test. We were in the lead when I missed the kicks, so that pressure wasn't there. It was just one of those days and in 13 years of playing provincial and Test rugby, I've had a couple of them sandwiched in between some very good days.'

Honiball and Joubert, like Montgomery, accepted it had just not been a good day with the boot. Neither were beating themselves up about it because they had also won matches for teams with good goal kicking.

England and Lions loose forward Lawrence Dallaglio, in his autobiography, *It's in the Blood: My Life*, mocked Sarfu's decision to play the first two Tests of a three-Test series at sea level in Cape Town and Durban because it suited the tourists and meant they did not have to worry about playing at altitude until the series had been decided. But Montgomery believes that at sea level or altitude, the Boks played well enough to win in scoring three tries to nil at Kings Park.

'You can look for any excuse but it will never change the result. This game is about getting lucky as well. In 1998, we beat Australia in Perth when Matthew Burke missed a sitter from right in front of the posts and we celebrated a famous win, but if he had got that kick, we would have been beaten.

'Who knows whether Carel would have kept his job as Bok coach if the goal kicks had gone over in Durban and the Boks had won the series? When you look back at Carel's time as Bok coach, not much went for the team until that last game against the Wallabies in Pretoria, but by then it was too late and there was always this feeling among the players that he was going to be axed no matter how well we played in Pretoria.'

Montgomery, zero from three in 1997 against the Lions, would not miss a kick in the 2007 World Cup semi-final and final. But that night in Durban he would not know there would ever be a World Cup final in which the accuracy of his left boot would be celebrated. That night in Durban was one of reflection and angst because he did not even know if there would be another Test match for him.

'I had felt lonely when I first walked into a Bok change room, but the feeling of being in a *losing* Bok change room is far worse than loneliness. I looked at those icons around me and wondered if I would get to know the feeling of victory in a Springbok jersey. We'd lost the Test and the series and not only had Guscott finished us off with a drop goal, he'd also humiliated me by refusing to swap jerseys after the Test. I was stunned when he said no as I assumed it was the done thing. I'd never heard of a player saying no to his opponent and when I asked him, it never occurred to me that he would refuse. I thought he was a prick for saying no, but who knows, he may argue I didn't deserve his jersey.'

Dallaglio roomed with Guscott in the week of the final Test. In his autobiography, he writes how Guscott gave his Lions kit to the cleaning ladies after the series because he couldn't be bothered taking it back to England. Dallaglio writes that he did the dutiful thing and packed Guscott's bags for him because the midfielder's leg was in a plaster cast after being injured in the third Test and he thought he would struggle with his packing. But when Guscott got back to the room, he just tipped everything on the floor and told Dallaglio he wasn't going to cart all the Lions kit back to England and he gave it to the hotel staff who were cleaning their room.

Montgomery, though, got in a bit earlier than the cleaning ladies as Guscott relented to another request after the third Test and gave his young opponent his jersey.

'It wasn't the same as getting it after my debut but it made the experience of playing Test rugby complete. I had scored tries in my first two Tests, measured myself against two of the best midfielders of the time and got initiated by one of the legends of South African rugby in Joubert.'

Of the initiation, Montgomery remembers the burning sensation of being caned, but didn't think it out of order or out of the ordinary. 'I went to school in an era when caning was accepted and part of the school package, but I can tell you André didn't hold back and anyone who has seen him tee off on the golf course will know he has an impressive swing. I think he gave me three on the arse and each one of them hurt, but I wore the bruising like a badge of honour for the next couple of weeks. The humiliating part of the initiation was when I had to strip down to my jocks [underwear] and act out my favourite sex positions to the squad.

'The way it works in initiation sessions is that the new guy is always embarrassed and belittled. Don't ask me why, but that is just the way it has always been like in every sporting team I have been part of. The senior guys, who run the initiation ceremony, always look to make you feel like a fool and then later on build you up to feel special. I had a feeling that it could get pretty messy with me, and the senior players honed in on this playboy lifestyle they said they'd heard I had, but that was utter nonsense. I knew not to talk back and come across as a young smart arse, so I just listened. They said they'd been impressed by what they'd heard, but they needed a demonstration of my skills in the sack and instructed me to act out what I considered my best sexual positions. It was a huge piss-take, and having been part of initiations at different levels of my sporting career I took it in that spirit, although I don't know if I actually managed to impress them, and I wasn't about to ask them either. Shut up and move on – I knew that was the best way to deal with these kinds of things. While it may sound simplistic, that was the approach I took to my career, and I think it contributed to me surviving for so many years in so many teams under so many coaches. I never saw the point of upsetting the opposition or my team-mates with over-the-top quotes in the media and I also never reacted in the media to stir up controversy. The less of a public opinion I had with regards to rugby's issues meant the less there was to be judged on. This doesn't mean I didn't have opinions or think about things, but I believed it wiser to keep them to myself and in that way, give people less ammunition to use against me. And in any event, at that time of my career, I did not feel I had the right to make bold statements or to speak my mind in the team environment.

'I was a youngster who was doing his international apprenticeship and I was prepared to be the duty boy, carry tackle bags and do whatever else the new guys did. I knew that if I stayed in the set-up long enough, there would be newer guys who would take over that role and I'd be the guy sleeping till 6am while the new caps were up at 4am as duty boys assigned to load everyone's bags onto the bus.

'The only thing that mattered to me after the Lions series was that I was a Test Springbok. I had been inducted into a special rugby brotherhood. I finally had an opposition Test jersey after playing at Ellis Park and I had experienced the feeling of playing in a winning Test.

'I did not know if I would be picked for the third Test after we lost in Durban. But after playing that game against the Lions at Ellis Park [which the Boks won 35-16], I was confident of doing well against the All Blacks at the same venue. Carel had told me he was pleased with my performance in the third Test, even though I had been substituted after 55 minutes because I had been battling with flu in the build-up. He told me to get my mind right for the All Blacks as Frank Bunce would be even tougher than Guscott. I also knew Bunce would be less of an arsehole, having chatted to the boys who had played Super 12 rugby against him. You play this game to measure yourself against the best and he at the time was the best. I couldn't wait to play the All Blacks for the first time in my career.'

6

TRIALS, TRIBULATIONS AND TRIUMPH

The moment Percy Montgomery took Frank Bunce on the outside from a standing start and beat him for pace was the moment Springbok coach Carel du Plessis knew he had made the right call in Montgomery. And when Bunce brushed off Montgomery's defensive effort later in the 1997 Tri-Nations match at Ellis Park, Du Plessis remained convinced that Montgomery was good enough to be an international player.

'We could always teach him to be a better defender,' says Du Plessis. 'And in any case, I never agreed with the criticism that he was afraid to tackle or was physically not big enough to defend in the midfield. A lot of the early defensive lapses were down to inexperience and lack of communication between Percy and Danie van Schalkwyk, who had only started in two Tests when we played the All Blacks. When I picked Percy, I backed his attacking qualities ahead of any possible defensive vulnerability and I was always willing to invest in an outside centre whose strength was that he could attack from first phase and create try-scoring opportunities because of his out-and-out pace. There was no other outside centre in the country who could match him for explosiveness in 1997 and I made a call to go for a player who gave me more on attack than defence. That was a risk I was willing to take and I was prepared to live with the criticism of him missing some tackles because of the attacking dimension he gave our backline.

'Percy was a player I had identified as having the potential to break the mould of South African outside centres because he was not physically imposing and didn't weigh 110kg, but he had an understanding of space and movement, and a natural feel of when to run and when to pass. I also rated the quality of his field kicking and, to me, we had something rare in an explosive left-footed outside centre who was as quick as anything I had seen over the first 20m. I had to play him against the best in the world to confirm my gut feeling that he was good enough and I never doubted he would make an impact in Test rugby.

'What people forget is he played against Jeremy Guscott, Frank Bunce and [Australia's] Jason Little in his first six Tests and those guys were consistently rated the top three outside centres in the game, and Percy never stood back for any of them. I was impressed with his tenacity against the Lions and his willingness to get stuck in.

'But the biggest moment was when he showed the skill and pace to beat Bunce at Ellis Park, although Bunce did use every bit of his experience to turn, scramble in defence and just manage an ankle tap to break the momentum of Percy's run. Bunce won the contest on points but Percy showed me enough to confirm that South Africa had something very special in this guy.'

The South African rugby media did not share Du Plessis's enthusiasm for Montgomery and sections of the press in the north and south crucified Montgomery for lacking the defensive presence to be a Test midfielder.

'It was unfair on him but even at such an early stage of his Test career, he showed good mental strength to cope with the criticism,' says Du Plessis. 'I never made an issue of it and each week I just gave him a few reassuring words. The biggest compliment I could give him was to continue to select him. Once the Lions series was finished, I committed to playing him in all four Tri-Nations Tests as I did not want him playing with the burden of each Test being his last and this was communicated to him. Gary Teichmann also had a quiet chat to him to make sure he was OK and Percy's response was that he couldn't wait for the next Test.

'He worked hard in training and was prepared to learn and that impressed the other players because he matched his training work ethic with better performances in every Tri-Nations Test and his attacking performance against the Wallabies at Loftus in 1997 was brilliant. I don't believe he ever got fair press in the six Tests he played under me and there was not an acknowledgement from the critics of how much he had improved from his Test debut against the Lions to that stunning win against the Wallabies in Pretoria.'

Montgomery says he didn't give much thought to the reputation of who he was playing against in that first season of Test rugby and focused on his own game.

'Guscott, Bunce and Little had all been very successful and I knew they were world-class players but they only had two legs and two arms and I was confident that I could match them in a one-on-one situation. I was learning about defensive patterns with every match and Danie and I were improving as a combination the more we played together. Carel seemed happy with the way we had gone against the Lions and told us to ignore what was being written and said in the media. He said we had to work hard on minimising defensive errors and never stop believing in ourselves when we got the ball. Before every Test, he told me to back my pace and to attack my opposite number on his outside shoulder because none of those guys would be adequately prepared for my pace. Guys like Bunce and Little had never played against me in the 1997 Super 12 because I was playing for WP in the domestic Nite Series.'

In 1996, the All Blacks had won a series in South Africa for the first time and despite New Zealand's four wins in five Tests that year, Du Plessis was convinced he had picked a team with the attacking qualities to surprise the All Blacks, who had lost the 1995 World Cup final and the final Test of the 1996 series at Ellis Park.

All Blacks prop Craig Dowd added to the intensity of the build-up when he said he hated South Africans in an interview with the Auckland-based *Sunday Star-Times*.

'I had never taken much notice of South African rugby until I started playing for the All Blacks and people spoke of the tradition in playing them. When we toured South Africa [in 1996], it confirmed why I hate them.'

All Blacks captain Sean Fitzpatrick responded that it would need more than hate to beat the Springboks and that it would require a certain level of skill to beat them in South Africa.

'Hatred of the Springboks and South Africans certainly isn't something the team talks about or uses as motivation. The challenge is to beat the Boks. They are the ultimate challenge for any All Black. It is as simple as that.'

All Blacks coach John Hart also dismissed the media view that the All Blacks were jinxed when playing at Ellis Park after being reminded that the All Blacks lost the World Cup final in 1995 and the last Test against the Boks in 1996.

'There is no hoodoo. You'd have to be into witchcraft for that kind of thing. The All Blacks won there in 1992, so it is not a case of us not being able to win at Ellis Park,' said Hart. 'And I do subscribe to the view that the All Blacks are probably a better side when playing at Ellis Park.'

Hart promised the All Blacks would play expansively and Montgomery and Van Schalkwyk's selection in the midfield was seen as a weakness the All Blacks could exploit. Bunce confirmed the visitors felt it was an area the All Blacks could use to their advantage, but he also spoke of Montgomery's pace and the threat he presented on attack.

'We know they [the Bok midfield] are inexperienced but they are Springboks and I will give both of them the necessary respect,' said Bunce, who would put in some crunching tackles and score two tries in a thrilling 35-32 All Blacks victory.

Montgomery's recollection of the game is the intensity and pace at which it was played and the physicality of both teams.

'They had picked Carlos Spencer ahead of Andrew Mehrtens at flyhalf and we knew they felt they could beat us with a running game, but we were sure we had the pace to match them in the midfield and out wide. André Snyman proved this when he chased down Tana Umaga in the first few minutes of the game and put in a great tackle. The All Blacks had attacked from inside their own 22, but we were up to it and that early contest won by André over Umaga seemed to unsettle them. We took control of the first 30 minutes and raced into a healthy lead. They showed their quality by scoring two tries in as many minutes just before half-time and that first 40 minutes seemed more tiring than if you had put the two Lions Tests together and played them on the same night. I felt like it was going from one end to the other and it was a lot quicker and more intense than against the Lions.

'Bunce was very good against us and I remember him beating me in the tackle a few times and me going around him once when I did exactly what Carel encouraged me to do, which was to attack him on the outside shoulder, swerve and accelerate. Bunce was a fierce competitor and a true professional. We got into an early skirmish after he put in a late tackle on me and I ended up on top of him and with my hands around his neck. We tugged at each other and then got up to follow the play. I said nothing to him and he said nothing to me and we just got on with the game. The more I played rugby against him at Super 12 and Test level, the more I appreciated what a quality player and top guy he was. He wasn't into sledging and, like Scott Gibbs, he just played the game bloody hard. People hadn't given us much of a chance of beating the All Blacks, but with three minutes remaining, Jannie de Beer hit the upright with a penalty that would have levelled the game at 35-all.

'The first time Bunce spoke to me was after the final whistle when he walked over, shook my hand and said well played. I asked him if we could swap jerseys and he said fine. He had a humility I didn't see in Jeremy Guscott and I left Ellis Park that evening inspired that rugby was a great game and that the rivalry between the All Blacks and Springboks was everything it had been made out to be.

'I found facing the haka enjoyable but it was not something that scared me or something I thought about before the Test although in the next 10 years, as the haka became more hyped commercially, it seemed to become more significant to Springbok players experiencing it for the first time.

'The way Bunce played the game at Ellis Park in 1997, and his humility afterwards, was an example to me as a young bloke and that was the most significant lesson I took from the match. I was only playing my third Test but he showed me respect as a Test player and that was something I promised myself I would do in my Test career because any opponent considered good enough to play for his country deserves to be respected.

'I have come across the odd bloke in Test rugby who doesn't understand that you earn the right to mouth off and then it still doesn't make it right. The great players did not rely on verbal intimidation and they did not play the match insulting your mother, your sister or your culture. They insulted you with skill and if you happened to do it back to them during the match, they were the first to acknowledge it afterwards. Bunce always impressed me with his attitude on the field and that is why I was surprised a month later when he was quoted in the New Zealand media saying what he enjoyed about Test rugby was running over 80kg guys in the midfield. My response was that the thing I enjoyed most about Test rugby was running around 50-Test veteran centres, who weren't the quickest. I know it was a childish response but I thought his remark was childish and inappropriate and more so when I considered how professional and competitive he was on the field.

'When you first get into provincial rugby, you hear all the talk about Test rugby being a different occasion, and what adds to the intensity is the media scrutiny and the unrelenting national and international focus on one individual, which in those first few months of my Springbok career was me. I thought I had experienced that against the Lions, but in my first Test against the All Blacks, I felt I finally knew what Test rugby was all about. In the next few weeks, in Australia and in New Zealand, I'd get an even greater idea that Test rugby is defined when you play the best teams away from home. That is the true test of any player's ability.'

Du Plessis, in speaking to the media afterwards, applauded the courage and skill of the Springboks, and captain Gary Teichmann defended his decision to kick for posts with three minutes remaining, saying it was not a willingness to settle for a draw but showed intent to win the game. Teichmann told the media he was confident De Beer would kick the penalty, level the scores at 35-all, and that the Boks could still win the match from the kickoff in the last few minutes as the altitude seemed to have sapped everything from the All Blacks.

Du Plessis also refused to blame Montgomery and Van Schalkwyk for Bunce's tries and the defeat.

'I don't regret my decision to play the youngsters. They did well and our midfield defensive lapses can be attributed to a breakdown in communication. It will improve. I thought they did exceptionally well on attack.'

The significance of the win was that the All Blacks edged ahead 23 wins to 22 in 48 Tests played between the teams. In the next decade, that one-win advantage would grow as high as 12 after the Boks led the rivalry 21-16 in 1992.

'It was an important win for us and it showed victory is possible for the All Blacks at Ellis Park,' said New Zealand coach John Hart. 'We appreciate how big the victory is because it is a very good Springbok team and when they play at Ellis Park, they are always harder to beat than anywhere else.'

Montgomery's first experience of Ellis Park had been the 35-16 third-Test win against the Lions but he remembers that night being very different to playing the All Blacks.

'We had already lost the series to the Lions and while the crowd was noisy, there wasn't intensity about the fixture. This time, when our bus pulled into Ellis Park, it was like we were playing in a final. The crowd was really loud, aggressive and buoyant and all I heard when I got off the bus was the chant of 'Bokke, Bokke, Bokke'. I can imagine how intimidating a packed Ellis Park must be for any visiting team, especially when the South African anthem is sung and the crowd gets as excited for a match against the All Blacks as the players do. I always got the feeling the South African public took the result personally when we played the All Blacks, more so than against any other team.'

The South African media, myself included as rugby correspondent for the *Cape Times*, took it very personally at Ellis Park and the criticism was that Du Plessis, Teichmann and his team were celebrating a defeat while the All Blacks generally had come across as sombre in their post-match analysis. I wrote at the time that if you didn't know better, you'd have thought the Boks won.

Du Plessis's response was that they had won on many fronts except the scoreboard and this enraged the media.

'Percy's performance was one positive from the game and Jannie de Beer's goal kicking was very good. The pack had played well and the players were becoming more comfortable in trusting their attacking skills,' says Du Plessis. 'I was criticised for playing Jannie at No 10, but two years later in Paris, he produced the most amazing performance against England in a World Cup quarter-final, and 10 years later, Percy would be one of the stars in a World Cup final.'

But in 1997, there was no Nostradamus to back up Du Plessis's belief in players like De Beer and Montgomery and he spent the next month on the defensive as the Springboks lost by 12 points against the Wallabies in Brisbane and conceded 55 points at Eden Park against the All Blacks a week later.

Ironically, Montgomery's defensive game was applauded against the Wallabies in Brisbane in a match when the Bok pack struggled and the backs played mostly behind the gain line.

Du Plessis, on departure for Australia, was under pressure for single-mindedly trusting youth ahead of experience and World Cup-winning backs James Small and André Joubert were told they would be going to Australia and New Zealand to carry tackle bags and provide cover for those in the starting XV.

Joubert, internationally acclaimed as the 'Rolls Royce of fullbacks' and brilliant for the Springboks in the 1996 win against the All Blacks at Ellis Park, refused to waste his time as a tourist and the media wouldn't accept that Border's Russell Bennett was a better option at fullback.

Joubert, in withdrawing from the tour, said at the time: 'What would be the point of me sitting on the bench for three weeks? I haven't played for two weeks and I need to get going. Instead of going to Australia and New Zealand and doing nothing, I want to play for Natal in the Currie Cup. I want to get stuck in for Natal so that I can prove my fitness and form. This is not the end of me. I will be back.'

Du Plessis would be forced to send an SOS to Joubert a day before the Boks' final Tri-Nations Test against Australia in Pretoria, but when he left South Africa it was with the view that Joubert was a spent force, as were Henry Honiball and Small.

Du Plessis insisted that with Van Schalkwyk at No 12 and De Beer at No 10, there would be no place for Honiball in his starting XV and, at best, he would be an option among the backline reserves.

Montgomery, on arrival in Australia, defended the selection of youngsters by asking how else they were to get experience. 'Surely experience comes with playing,' Montgomery told the Australian media. 'The youngsters have confidence in one another and the experienced guys have been tremendous. They have focused on the positive and we are developing a squad-system culture that goes beyond the starting XV.'

Montgomery now says where Du Plessis's squad system failed was in his inability to effectively communicate it to the older players.

'James Small was very down about not being in the starting XV and he struggled to accept the situation because he was such a competitor and he refused to believe any right wing in the country was better than him. James, who had joined Western Province in 1997, had been very good to me when I first came into the WP team that year. I liked his energy and how he was prepared to be himself, no matter how much he got criticised. One of the first bits of advice he gave me was to always be myself, to believe in who I was and how good I was and to never accept being second best. He also told me never to try and change to please other people. This guy, a World Cup winner in 1995, treated me as an equal on the rugby field with Province in 1997 when I had hardly played a first-class game. And now, a few months later, I was starting for the Springboks and he was down in the dumps, on tour with the Boks but among the reserves. Yet, despite his predicament, he was there for me on the tour and protected me from any negativity. He made sure I did not doubt myself, which at the time I didn't because I was just happy to be a Springbok and whether Carel had started with me or used me off the bench, it wouldn't have mattered. But it was strange to be in the starting XV when icons like James and Henry were on tour but not in the team and a guy like André was not making the team.'

The Australian media found it more than strange and Queensland coach John Connolly, who would coach the Wallabies at the 2007 World Cup, identified the Bok backs as the weakness.

'The Bok pack is the most fearsome in world rugby but the backs are the Achilles heel. They will miss [centre] Japie Mulder and it is puzzling that a player of Small's experience is warming the bench. Youth prospers in the company of old hands and there are not many of the latter in the Bok team. Individually the Bok backs are all talented and Montgomery looks a fine player, but as a unit they lack experience. I know they did very well against the All Blacks on attack, but they were vulnerable defensively and when put under pressure. My advice to Australia would be to keep going at the midfielders.'

The Wallabies did just that in winning 32-20, with Os du Randt and replacement Small the best of the Springboks.

All Blacks coach John Hart said he couldn't believe how poor the Springboks were, but that he anticipated the real Boks would turn up in Auckland.

'I haven't seen them play worse. I believed they would win comfortably. Sadly for us, the All Blacks are their main targets and we bring the best out of them. I am not sure they actually rise to the Wallabies.'

Du Plessis, as in South Africa, was unrepentant about his selections, but his comments continued to cause confusion among the players and the media.

'I don't regret playing the young combinations but we will have to look at bringing in experience against New Zealand. The youngsters were under pressure because of the quality possession Australia had and it is not ideal to have a backline where the youngsters are the majority. Although they are keen, motivated and committed, there were a few bad decisions under pressure. We can get this balance with the experienced guys back from injury and in form.'

Du Plessis, after emphasising the need to reinvest in experience, then ignored Pieter Müller as a replacement for the injured Van Schalkwyk and put the uncapped Golden Lions centre Joe Gillingham on standby as midfield cover before settling on Honiball as the inside centre against the All Blacks. Honiball, who was left on the bench for 77 minutes in Brisbane while the youngsters battled, and Small had big match experience Du Plessis simply could not ignore against the All Blacks, especially if he was to get the balance of the starting team right. Joubert, back in South Africa, was also getting mixed messages after Du Plessis had contacted him to establish his availability to fly to New Zealand. Joubert said he was ready to go, but a few hours later Du Plessis told the travelling South African media that Joubert lacked the versatility he required. Du Plessis had also enquired about the availability of Müller and another Sharks midfielder, Joos Joubert, but then drafted in Gillingham, who was not even a regular in the Golden Lions team.

The theory at the time was that Du Plessis needed youngsters around him to establish his authority because the senior players did not believe in him as he had never coached prior to his appointment as the Bok coach. And when the Boks lost in Brisbane, the distance between Du Plessis and the senior players only increased after the Bok coach blamed them for the crushing defeat against the Wallabies and suggested captain Teichmann had not been decisive in his decision-making.

Mark Andrews, in particular, got a caning from Du Plessis, who said the player had neglected his basics against the Wallabies.

'Mark knows what we expect from the forwards, especially the tight five, and that is to do the basics. There is no way you can get away from that. The way we decide to play the game is to play to the ball in threes and fours and that means you've got to do the dirty work. The only time we allow a forward to stay out is when we split the pack so that when the ball moves from wide onto the left and right half of the field, we are looking for quick ruck ball to bring it back again. Then we allow for someone to stay out. But there is no way they are allowed to stay out and be part of the backline. It is going to take an effort from people, especially senior players like Mark, to get that sorted out.'

Singling out Andrews to the media angered the senior players, especially because Du Plessis defended the team's inexperienced players.

'The problem is that important players, who have been there for a few years, are not up to standard. And that makes a huge difference. This experienced core of players is needed to lift the youngsters. These older players have to face up to the reality. They have to make a difference and it is no use trying to find an excuse.'

The All Blacks, with Sean Fitzpatrick captaining the side for the 50th time and Frank Bunce playing his 50th Test, were overwhelming favourites. The Boks took a beating from the New Zealand media for staying on in Brisbane after the Wallabies defeat and only flying to Auckland on the Thursday. This would give the players one day in New Zealand to acclimatise to the Test-match atmosphere, which Montgomery concedes was a shock to the system.

'You hear about playing the All Blacks in New Zealand and how intense the week can be but you can only know it once you have been through it. I don't know, maybe the management felt they were protecting the players from new scrutiny by staying in Australia, but it proved a disaster. We only got in late on the Thursday and the management's organisation of those few days in Auckland seemed non-existent. We couldn't have a proper captain's run at Eden Park on the Friday and went through the drills on the

B field because their officials said we had got the field time wrong. On match day, the bus was late in picking us up from the hotel and we got to the stadium 25 minutes before the kickoff. There wasn't time for a proper warm-up and the next thing I knew, I was playing the All Blacks in New Zealand.'

For all the disarray, the Springboks scored in the first few minutes of the match through Ruben Kruger. Teichmann got a try after Joost van der Westhuizen made a great tackle on Christian Cullen and in the 29th minute Montgomery scored a freakish try when he misdirected his up-and-under, but the ball bounced back into his hands. The Boks, incredibly, were leading 21-11, but that is as good as it got and after an hour the All Blacks had scored 39 unanswered points to lead 50-21.

'Everything was frantic when we got to the ground. It was one rush from the bus to the change room and onto the field, and it seemed to stay that way in the first half. I scored one of the more bizarre tries of my Test career when I miscued an up-and-under that was supposed to go centre-field in their 22m line. As I mis-hit the kick and it flew towards the corner flag on the grandstand side of the field, I could almost hear the laughter of the New Zealand crowd but I just kept on chasing the kick and the ball bounced back into my hands and I scored. I couldn't believe what had happened and when I later saw the replay of the try on TV, I found it even more disbelieving that I could have scored against the All Blacks like that.'

There would be little else for Montgomery or the Boks to celebrate as the All Blacks slaughtered the Boks in the first 20 minutes of the second half and two late Bok tries would not soften the reaction to the biggest-ever Springbok defeat against the All Blacks and the first time 50 points had been scored against the Boks.

The New Zealand bookies had given the All Blacks an 18-point start, a margin bigger than any differential in 48 Tests between the two teams, and the 20-point winning margin was consistent with most pre-match predictions, which only angered Sarfu president Dr Louis Luyt, who had a full go at the players in the change room afterwards.

'The guys were crushed afterwards and as a youngster who said very little in the only winning Test I had experienced, I wasn't going to say anything to anyone in this environment,' says Montgomery. 'Dr Luyt blasted us and called us a disgrace to the Springboks and to the country. James Small got up and took him on about his reaction and had a full go at the management, saying they were a disgrace and the organisation of the tour was a joke. He asked how anyone could take us seriously with the logistics around the Test when no one could even get the time right for the captain's run or the bus pick-up to the Test. Luyt just glared at him and then told him to shut up and remember who paid his salary. No one else spoke up after that.'

The mood at the press conference did not get any better with the New Zealand media accusing the Boks of being thugs after flank André Venter had been sent off for stomping and Small had been yellow-carded for an attempted trip on All Blacks fullback Christian Cullen.

In one question at the post-match press conference, Du Plessis was asked how he would cope with Springbok rugby's blackest day, given the sending offs, a 20-point defeat and the All Blacks scoring 55 points.

Du Plessis responded: 'When was the last time a team scored five tries and 35 points against the All Blacks?'

The Kiwi journalist hit back: 'Mate, the All Blacks scored seven tries and got 55 points and stopped playing for the last 20 minutes.'

On the accusation of the Boks being thugs, Du Plessis said: 'I don't think it was our blackest day. Certainly there was aggression from our players. Tempers can get fired up, but I am not concerned about that. The discipline of the team was fine.'

Hart, when told of Du Plessis's response, was emphatic in his assessment.

'I would then hate to see an ill-disciplined performance from a South African team,' said the All Blacks coach. 'If I was South African, I would be asking serious questions. It was not a good day for their rugby, but it was a good one for New Zealand. To comprehensively take South Africa apart has to be a psychological blow. The All Blacks now know the Boks can be comprehensively beaten.'

David Kirk, captain of the 1987 World Cup-winning All Blacks and a columnist for the *Sunday Star-Times,* condemned the Boks.

'I had the All Blacks to win by 31 and the score should have been nearer 55-10 than 55-35. That flattered the Boks. On ability there is a 40-point difference between the two sides. Call me fussy, but the 55-35 victory left me feeling slightly dissatisfied and most of the people sitting around me in the stand felt the same way. I have a suspicion we let them off the hook. The Boks are a team of rather ordinary players. They lack the creativity to make the whole more than the sum of the parts. There is no guile about their performance.'

Du Plessis, one of the great Bok players of his era, was fighting for his international coaching career, but still he refused to make any radical changes and for all the talk of experience being important to the balance of the side, he did not recall Joubert.

Experienced players expected the worst after the Eden Park beating and Small was one who did not know if he had a future should Du Plessis be retained as coach.

'I can't really say whether Carel will go or not. As players, we are just trying to go out and do the best we can, but we got a hiding against the All Blacks and it would be understandable if they did hit the panic button. We have got to get uniformity and consistency going. It is a freakish environment for us at the moment. It is very volatile and very up and down.'

Du Plessis, Sarfu and the players had two weeks to think about things as Australia would have to travel to Dunedin to play the All Blacks and then fly directly to Johannesburg. The feeling within South Africa was the Boks would win against the Wallabies in Pretoria but it would have more to do with facing a fatigued Australian team, who had been labelled confused and directionless by rugby analyst and former Wallabies loose forward Simon Poidevin in a scathing attack on coach Greg Smith.

'It is frustrating to watch the Wallabies play like a club side, and ultimately, the responsibility for the style and tactics must lie with Smith,' said Poidevin before the Dunedin Test. And when the Wallabies trailed 36-0 at half-time, Poidevin was even more animated in his condemnation of Smith, who unbeknown to anyone was suffering with a brain tumour that would kill him two years later.

The Wallabies fought back to score 24 unanswered points in the second half, but the strains of that Test and the long-haul flight to Johannesburg meant the battered Australians only arrived in South Africa three days before the Loftus match.

Du Plessis, despite the apprehension of senior players, only made injury and suspension-enforced changes for the Test, but the coach suffered even more embarrassment when, as a spectator at Western Province's 53-16 Currie Cup win against the Golden Lions, he was booed by a section of the Newlands crowd when leaving the grandstand. Du Plessis, once the Prince of Wings and darling of Western Province as a player, was finding the landscape had changed and that for coaches to be applauded, they had to be winning.

Sarfu CEO Rian Oberholzer defended Du Plessis and predictably insisted the coach would at least complete one year in the job.

'There are 13 Tests and let's assess him after those have been played. There are still six Tests left in the year,' said Oberholzer, who maintained the decision to appoint Du Plessis was the right one. 'We believe that if he gets the necessary assistance he needs, and the support of the provincial coaches, he will do well.'

The senior Bok players were not convinced and neither was the media with the majority demanding Du Plessis be axed irrespective of the result against Australia.

'It was tough on Carel and as a young player, I felt sympathy for the guy because everyone you seemed to talk to wanted him out,' says Montgomery. 'I expected the atmosphere in the Bok squad to be tense when we reassembled, but it was good considering the kind of season we had. The senior players seemed relieved and surprised they were still in the side and as a youngster you didn't have an opinion. Ruben Kruger was injured and André Venter was suspended but the rest of the side was the same as the one that played in Auckland and that seemed to give the guys some confidence. Carel was also upbeat about us winning and I think just being at home for a week had been very good for the players because it had allowed us to get away from the negativity and pressure we had dealt with for more than two months.'

Montgomery would also get to experience André Joubert at his best in a Springbok Test for the first and only time. Border No 15 Russell Bennett failed a fitness test and Du Plessis turned to the experience of Joubert at fullback a day before the Test.

'The only other time we had been in the same Bok team was on my debut in the second Test against the Lions and while I thought André was good then, he was unbelievable at Loftus against the Wallabies,' says Montgomery. 'He ran the show from the back, kept us on the attack with long kicks and wasn't afraid to run the ball out from anywhere. He controlled everything in the second half and I was fortunate to experience how good he could be. He showed he could do anything on a rugby field.'

Montgomery scored two tries, the most memorable one being when Joubert threw out an American Football overhead pass to him on the Boks' 22m line and Montgomery used his speed to outpace the Australian defence and run the length of the field to score.

'Of all the tries I have scored, at any level, that one stands out for me because of the way in which André set it up and the way I finished it off. [Wallabies centre] Jason Little had been unflattering about me in interviews during the week and it was one of the few times in my career that I wanted to chirp a player after I scored because I beat him so easily for pace. Little had told the South African media I wasn't up to it as a Test player and that I was not ready to play Test rugby, so when I went around him I certainly considered asking him what he was doing on the field if I wasn't up to it. But I didn't and I am glad I said nothing when running back past him. Afterwards I thought of how guys like Bunce and Gibbs played the game, with dignity, commitment in everything they did and with decisiveness, and in that movement I felt I had done the same.'

It was a good thing Montgomery did not chirp Little because what the South African journalist had told him was not the full story and it was another example of mischief-making to elicit a response from a young Springbok.

Little, in an interview with Brenden Nel in the *Pretoria News* on 20 August, said: 'Montgomery has the qualities to develop into a good centre. I haven't seen a lot of him because Western Province did not play in the Super 12, but from what I have seen he makes a lot of mistakes, but then also does good things. He has got to learn to cut out the mistakes at international level. On attack he's had a couple of good breaks, but I definitely would not call him the weak link in the side, not with Henry Honiball next to him. Honiball is tough. He brings strength to the midfield and makes it tougher. I won't be underestimating either of them on Saturday, though.'

At the press conference that followed the Boks' record 61-22 win against the Wallabies, Du Plessis announced the team had finally delivered on their promise, but it was a flawed statement because the player who had been the catalyst to the performance was Joubert and Du Plessis had refused to select him in the three previous matches.

Teichmann made special mention of Montgomery, who was seated next to him at the press conference, and urged the media to be big enough to give credit to Montgomery's performance. The Springbok captain praised the character of Montgomery and his mental toughness to survive the unrelenting criticism of the previous months and to produce a performance of such quality, which he said was made even better because of his international inexperience. Montgomery said very little at the time.

'It was my first Test at Loftus and it was a taste of things to come in my Springbok career when playing there. The crowd booed me, groaned when I got the ball and went up a few levels when they thought I had made a mistake or was responsible for something not going well. The only way I could answer them was to put my head down, try not to make mistakes and play well. It was the same with the media and I didn't see the point of arguing with them or antagonising them because I could gain nothing from it. I did make the point that I didn't feel I had proved anything to the critics because I played for my team-mates, for the coaches and for myself, and if I played well enough, it would make the South African public happy.

'I was not comfortable having to talk to people who had been so scathing of me and in some instances got very personal about me, and while it didn't upset me, I knew how angry it had made my family and friends. I didn't want to be sitting at a press conference and at that moment I'd much rather have been in the Springbok change room celebrating an incredible victory along with players who would go on to be legends of Bok rugby.

'I also didn't think that night that I'd never again play alongside André Joubert in a Springbok team. I don't have regrets in my rugby career but I certainly would have liked to have played more Tests in a backline that featured André as he was that night in Pretoria.'

Before the Brisbane Test, Connolly had said youth prospers around old hands. The performance of Montgomery and Joubert at Loftus added credibility to that statement and provided further evidence that experience wins you more Tests than it loses you.

The Bok coach, to his credit, refused to be arrogant in addressing the media.

'It was a fine achievement to beat the Wallabies in such a manner, but we cannot be lulled into thinking the last two months did not happen and it does not make up for the disappointment of a season that yielded three wins from eight Tests. One has to be disappointed with that. But I still believe I am the right guy to coach the Boks and am capable of being successful on the end-of-year tour.'

Sarfu's President's Council, despite Oberholzer's public support of Du Plessis, did not agree and the same provincial presidents who appointed the Bok coach in February 1997, fired him six months later.

Boland coach and former Western Province and Springbok No 8 Nick Mallett would succeed Du Plessis and he impressed on the media that size, power and experience were attributes he was looking for in a Test player.

Montgomery, he said, was not a Test centre and he would never play him in the midfield. But there was hope for Montgomery as Mallett added the player was good enough to be a Test fullback, even though he would initially not select him in the Test team.

7

MUSTANGS AND MAD MEN

Just for a moment in 1997, Percy Montgomery got to relax in a Springbok tracksuit and he got to smile. The rugby media were not on his case because new Bok coach Nick Mallett had not picked him to start at fullback on the end-of-year tour opener against Italy. Montgomery, after the turmoil of his international introduction under the sacked Carel du Plessis, was not a talking point when the squad left South Africa. Mallett had been emphatic the Western Province utility back's best position was fullback and not centre, and if he did not play fullback on the tour, he would help out on the wing.

Justin Swart, the form fullback of the Currie Cup, got Mallett's vote of confidence and Montgomery, who played outside centre throughout WP's victorious campaign (they beat Free State 14-12 in the final), would be his understudy at fullback. The rest period was brief and Montgomery's midweek jaunt stretched to one match before Swart injured a hamstring and Montgomery was given the No 15 jersey against France in the second of five Tests on tour.

A month later and the media tributes to Montgomery were being written, with this little pearler from me in the *Cape Times* among them: 'Montgomery's triumph in 1997 was not of the tries in Europe, the 70m effort in Pretoria or the eight tries in 10 Tests. It was not of the bravery evident when he scrapped with Scott Gibbs and Frank Bunce or when he took on All Blacks prop Olo Brown in the tackle, got dumped and got up to run him in from behind. His greatest achievement in 1997 was to stand tall when the clock froze momentarily and the demons of failure called.'

Having been outspoken in my criticism of Montgomery's defensive display during the Tri-Nations, it was necessary to be as vocal in applauding his transformation from Test centre to Test fullback. You call what you see and if I thought he struggled as a centre in the early months of his Test career, there was no doubt he flourished on that tour as a fullback.

As far as rugby writers go, I was not alone in dedicating column inches to Montgomery at the end of 1997, most of it in praise and part of it in apology for a player crucified at stages of the season, only to be voted one of the country's five players of the year by the South African rugby media. *Rapport*'s Louis de Villiers was complimentary of a player he described as the 'Mustang of fullbacks' and the *Cape Argus*'s Gavin Rich credited Montgomery's change of fortunes to Mallett's decision to play him at fullback and not in the midfield, where he had made his Test debut against the Lions and played his next five Tests.

Mallett has big opinions on players, but he also asks for opinions on players and in the case of Montgomery, a very relevant opinion was provided by HO de Villiers. Montgomery's mentor said if Mallett wanted to realise the player's potential then he would be doing himself a favour in selecting him at fullback, which was the view Mallett shared and obviously the one he didn't mind hearing.

'Percy, in my view, is first and foremost a fullback, and it is a view which has been endorsed by De Villiers, who has played a huge role in bringing Montgomery through at Villager,' Mallett told Rich prior to the squad's departure for Europe in 1997.

'HO feels Percy is primarily a fullback, then a wing and then a flyhalf. His view is that centre, where Percy has played most of his provincial and international rugby, is only his fourth-best position and the one he is least suited to.' Mallett added that the fact Montgomery had made his Test debut out of position was testimony to his outstanding natural talent and the influence of WP captain Dick Muir. 'Montgomery showed his potential when he played in the WP midfield in their last two Currie Cup games, but we have chosen Percy for this tour as a fullback, and if he does not play there he will be at wing. Of course, we also know he can play flyhalf and centre, and it makes it useful to have him among our backup players.'

Montgomery has always been happier at fullback, even though Bok coaches through the years have played him at flyhalf, inside centre, outside centre and on the wing. When Mallett gave him a first start against France in Lyon, there was no indicator he would keep the jersey for a Springbok record 24 successive starts or that, 11 years later, he would be the most capped fullback in the history of Test rugby. Only France's Serge Blanco has come close to Montgomery's Test appearances as a fullback, and for South Africa, André Joubert is the next best with 34. No other fullback in 100-plus years of Bok rugby has made it to 30 Test appearances. But on the day Mallett picked Montgomery against France, he did so confident the player would cope but also with a script defending why he selected Montgomery, who hadn't been particularly impressive for the midweek Boks in their 40-22 defeat against the French Barbarians in Biarritz.

Having WP assistant coach Alan Solomons in the national set-up helped Montgomery's cause, but the most significant contributors to his selection were his WP team-mates and Bok left and right wings – Pieter Rossouw and James Small.

'We were helped in our deliberations by the knowledge that James and Pieter will be on hand to help Percy. Pieter started his career as a fullback and moved to wing and James played the early part of his career as a fullback and we feel that the trio as a back-three unit will complement each other,' Solomons told the South African media in defending Montgomery's selection.

Montgomery's early troubles in Test rugby and his mental toughness had impressed Springbok captain Gary Teichmann. He insisted Montgomery would cope with the demands of playing France, saying the player had been through all the questions in the Tri-Nations and came out of the ordeal with flying colours.

'I am confident he will do well,' said Teichmann, and that was as big as endorsement as a player got from the Bok captain in those days.

'The atmosphere and team environment was the best I had experienced in the Springboks and I'd only know that same level of comfort, confidence and class among players 10 years later at the World Cup in France,' says Montgomery. 'You couldn't compare my first experience of Test rugby to this because when I walked into the set-up in Durban, players were fighting to save their Test careers and the Boks were in a must-win situation to save the series against the Lions. Back then, it was each man for himself, but on this tour, it was about being dynamic, enjoying the game and just having a go.

'I felt no pressure when the tour started because I was just happy to have made the squad. There had been criticism of my Currie Cup form after the Tri-Nations, but Harry persisted with me at outside centre and Dick, at inside centre, was very instrumental in encouraging me to keep on going and play my natural game. For me, 1997 had already been a brilliant year. I had played for the Boks against the Lions, All Blacks and Wallabies, and Province had won the Currie Cup. In my view, it couldn't get more memorable than that.

'Nick had picked me for the tour but I knew I was not in the starting XV because he had been straight with me about my role and I respected that. Nick is very different to Carel and he has presence when he walks into a room or talks. Whereas the Bok senior players seemed to doubt Carel's coaching ability, no one questioned Nick's and on that tour he formed a close alliance with the senior players and quickly identified who his senior guys were. It is something Jake [White] would also do in 2004 when he first coached the Boks and as a player, I think it is the winning formula. Identify who your leaders are and make it clear to them and the team and the youngsters tend to follow. It was something Carel didn't do, for whatever reason, and it certainly complicated his job at a time when it would have helped if everyone was a believer in his philosophy.'

Montgomery's introduction at fullback, as Solomons said, was made easier because of Rossouw and Small, and Montgomery still rates them as among the best he has played with.

'They were a fullback's dream because they had both played fullback and understood the value of a winger playing back, so their focus in the game wasn't just on getting the ball, going forward and leaving the fullback isolated. I had also played wing, so immediately we were all on the same page when it came to how we thought about the game,' says Montgomery, whose introduction to both would again defy convention. 'Most think I would have struggled with James because of his standing in the game and the type of character he was and that it would have been easy to slot in with Pieter, but it was the other way around. When I first got into the Province senior set-up, Justin Swart, Pieter and Vlokkie Cilliers were a close-knit unit. I was very much seen as this *soutie* from SACS and an outsider with the potential to break up combinations, which were established, but also contained players who were mates away from rugby. Justin and Pieter were good mates and Vlokkie was the Province goal kicker. I've never clashed with any player in my career but I must say I found it extremely difficult to connect with Vlokkie and initially hard to get along with Pieter and Justin, who in time would warm to me and become good team-mates and guys whose company I enjoyed.

'Pieter and I also got to know each other a lot better the more we played in the fullback-wing axis and I also got to understand his mindset of being a very private person who doesn't give too much away. I never took it personally as a youngster trying to make inroads in the team environment, but it doesn't mean it was any easier.

'With James, it was the opposite. He kind of just got on with me, took me under his wing and treated me as an equal on the rugby field, which is something I have never forgotten and will always respect. I rated him as a player before I met him and always enjoyed the fact that he didn't seem to care what people thought of him or how much they criticised him. He had a very good vibe with Harry Viljoen and came into the Province team from the Sharks as one of the main guys and played that role very well.

'There was friction between James and Christian Stewart, who was also one of my early influences in rugby, but neither ever put me in the middle of their differences and both helped me a lot with my game at centre and at fullback. Both are bloody mad and very competitive and both are dominant personalities, so it was probably inevitable there would be issues between the two of them. But Christian wasn't on the Bok tour in 1997 and James, as he did with Province, gave me a lot of guidance and made me feel that as a player, I could do anything and be anything. So when I played my first Test at fullback, I was very comfortable that I had two very good players looking after me in James and Pieter.'

The Boks would survive a late French comeback to win 36-32, but Montgomery's afternoon would start with a knock-on from the first ball kicked to him, and as *Rapport*'s

Clockwise from top: Filling up the pool; my sister Haley and I; my dad playing provincial rugby in South West Africa (now Namibia); my 'pretty-boy image' was formed when I was a baby.

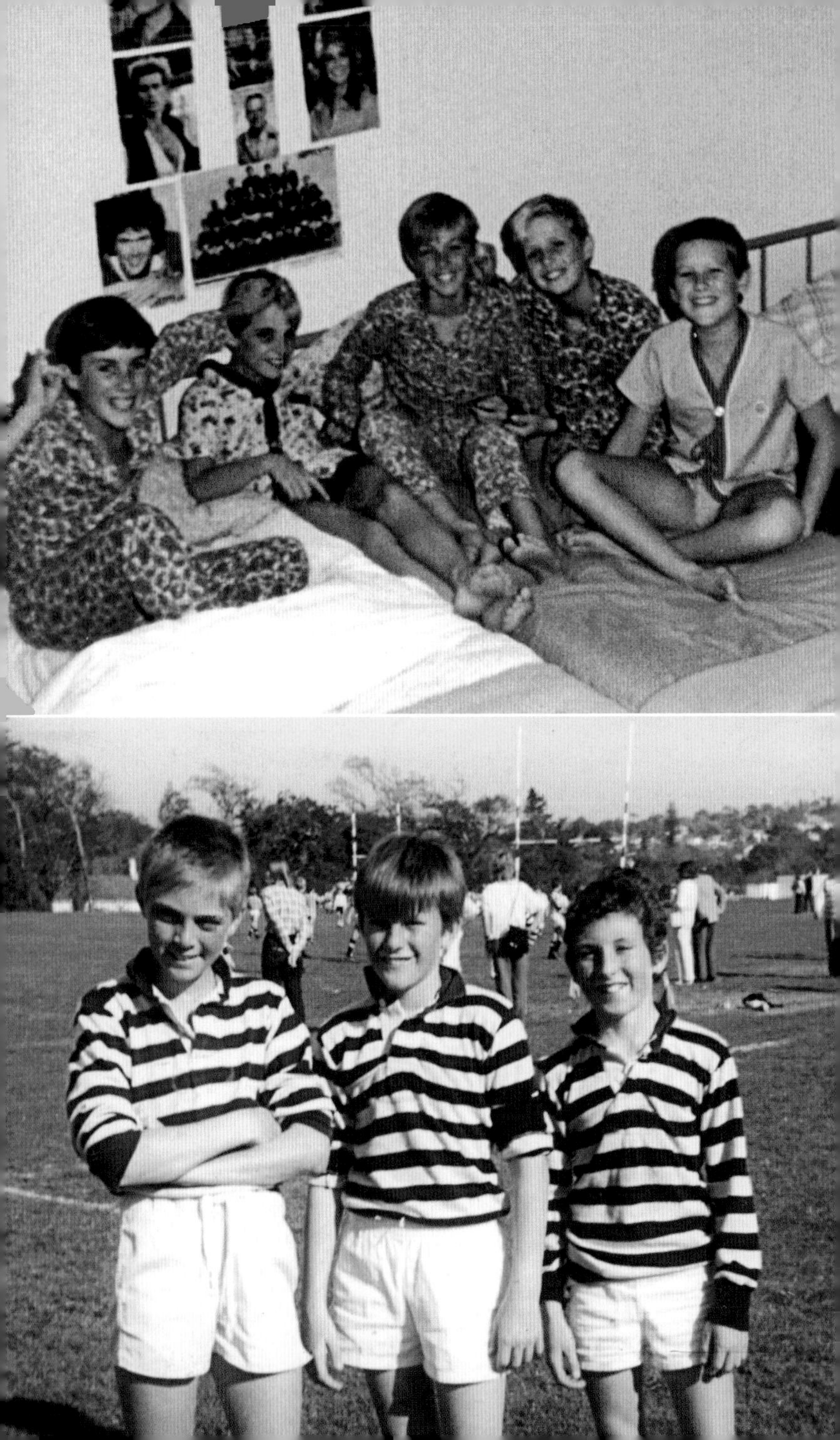

Opposite page: My friends and I at boarding school at SACS; my team-mates and I pose for the camera before a rugby match.
This page: Herschelle Gibbs was an outstanding schoolboy flyhalf and played with me for WP Schools; scoring a try for SACS; running the relay at an athletics meeting.

1883 – 1983

Opposite page: In a familiar pose and hopefully adding three points to SACS' total; scoring my first try at Newlands for SA Schools against SA Academy; with my dad and former 1st XV coach Simon Perkin after I made the WP Schools rugby team. Both played a huge role in my career.

This page: In action for SA Schools – I was disappointed we had to play in white, and not green and gold; in London with Wayne Fyvie, who would play flank for the Boks, during an SA Technikon tour; Robbie Fleck, Grant Hinckley and Hottie Louw were team-mates of mine in the WP U21 side.

FEDSURE
adidas

Western Province won back-to-back Currie Cup titles in 2000 and 2001 by beating the Sharks in both finals. In 1998, the Western Stormers played in these terrible jerseys – the combined colours of WP, South Western Districts and Boland.

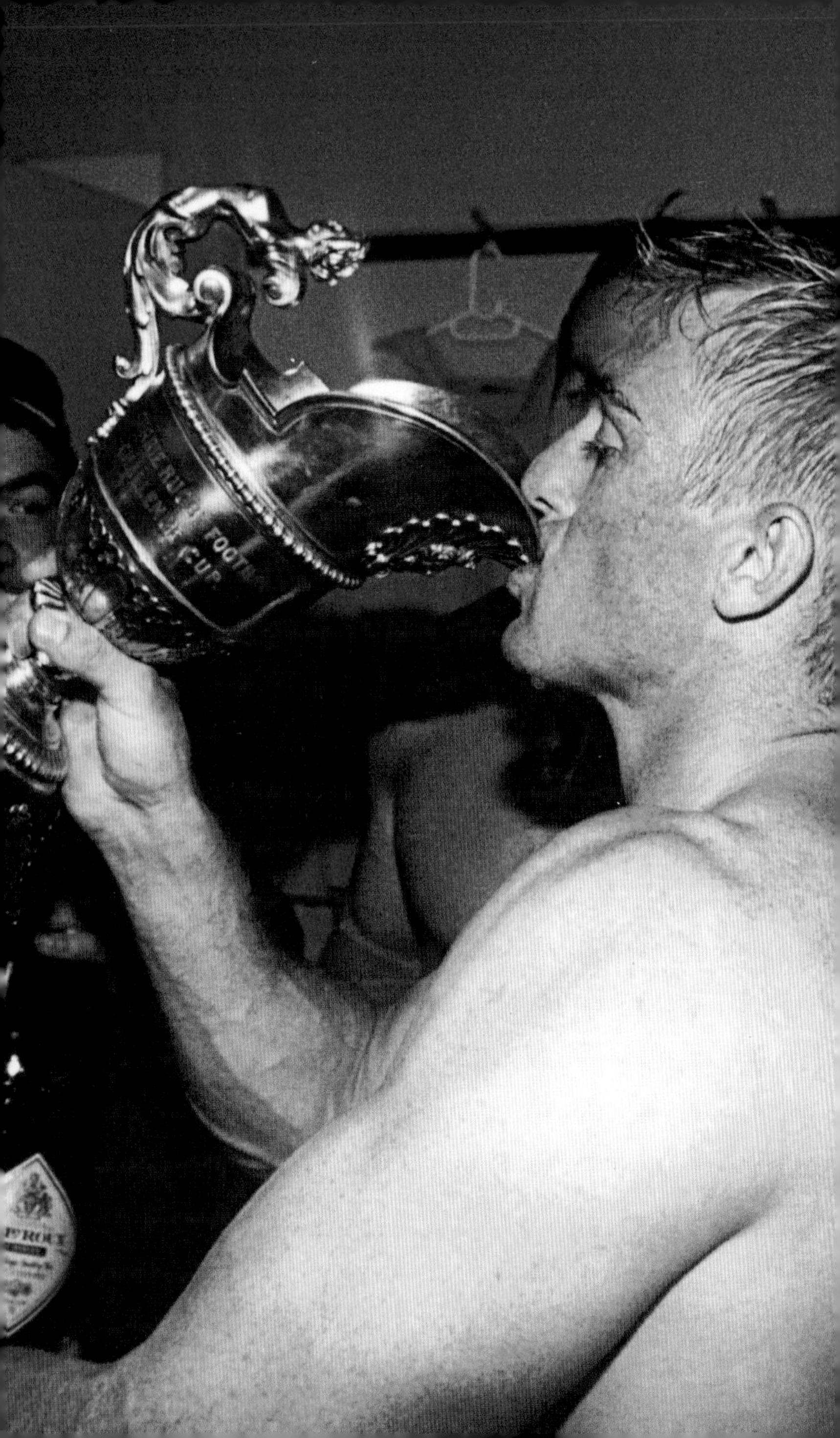

Opposite page: Drinking from the famous Currie Cup after we beat the Sharks.
This page: In the Stormers change room with Pieter Rossouw and Breyton Paulse – we formed a successful back-three combination; a larger group of us that includes Braam van Straaten, Robbie Fleck, Andy Marinos and Dan van Zyl.

This page: Two of my more colourful team-mates, Robbie Kempson and Robbie Fleck.
Opposite page: In the Bok change room with Pieter Rossouw and Stefan Terblanche; having a drink with Christian Stewart and James 'Bullet' Dalton on the 1998 Springbok end-of-year tour.

HEWLETT
PACKARD

This page: A post-match celebration with Justin Swart, James Small, Werner Swanepoel, André Snyman and Pieter Rossouw during the Springboks' end-of-year tour in 1997.
Opposite page: Travelling in the Stormers bus with Hottie Louw and Robbie Fleck; chilling out with Bob Skinstad after a game, with Werner Swanepoel and Os du Randt in the background.

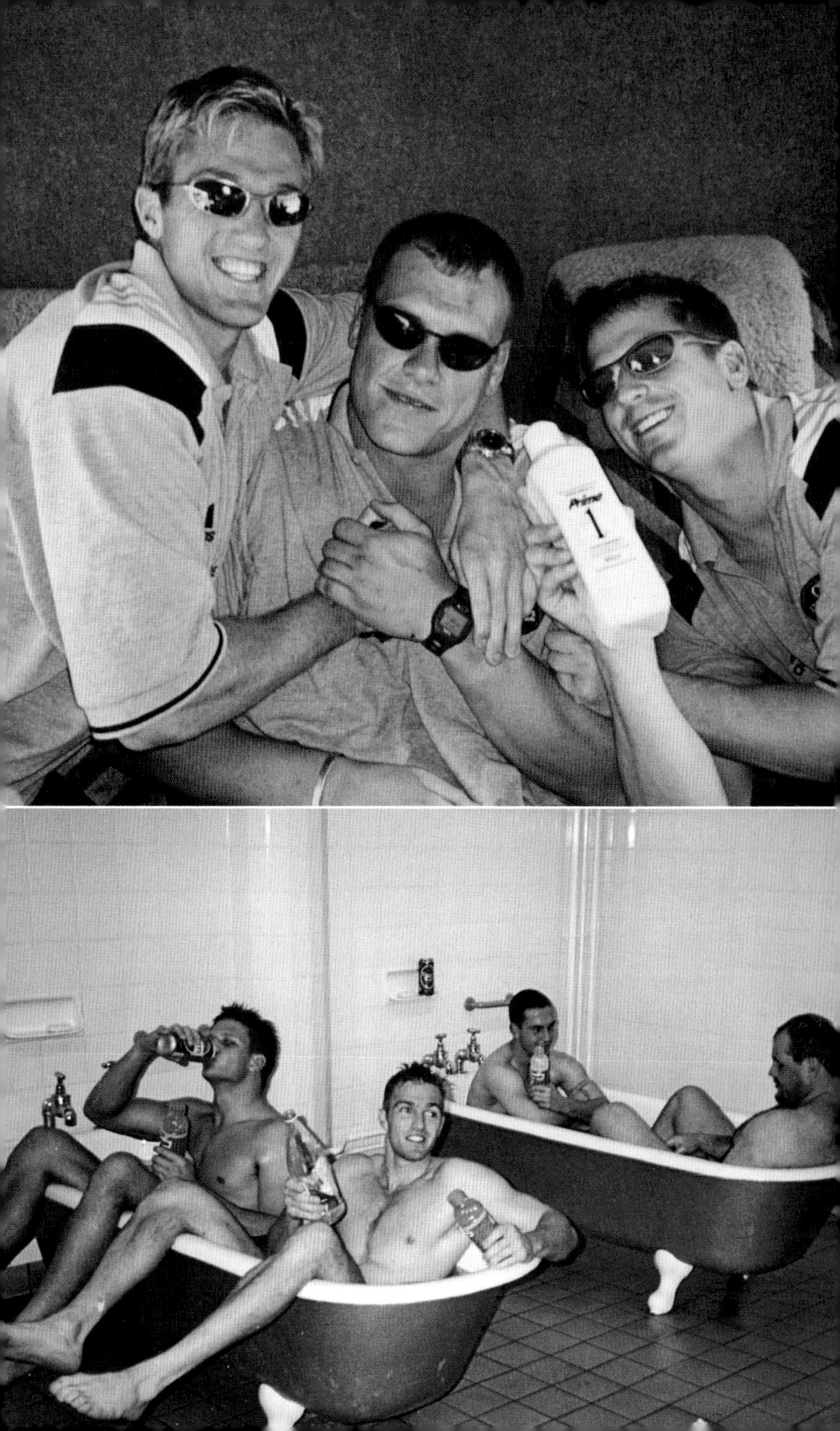

13

Clockwise from left: Getting my Springbok tattoo in Perth during the Boks' Tri-Nations tour in 1997; All Blacks coach John Hart congratulates Bok coach Nick Mallett after our 13-3 win in Wellington; taking a high ball in that match with All Blacks centre Frank Bunce looking on.

There were jubilant scenes after we beat the Wallabies 29-15 at Ellis Park in 1998 to secure the Springboks' first Tri-Nations title. Here I am with Bok captain Gary Teichmann *(top)* and Pieter Rossouw and Stefan Terblanche *(below)*.

Louis de Villiers would write in his summary of the tour, it was Montgomery's first and last mistake in four matches of Bok brilliance. De Villiers – one of the characters of the South African rugby-writing scene and in my view, the most colourful and entertaining when it comes to writing about the sport – raved about Montgomery's defence at fullback, stating that if Joubert was the Rolls Royce of fullbacks and Justin Swart's speed and presence made him a Ferrari, then Montgomery's explosiveness and work ethic made him the Mustang of fullbacks. Montgomery, flattered at the time, said he preferred to aim for being the Ferrari as it was his favourite car. De Villiers, after the Boks had embarrassed France 52-10 in Paris, saw off England 29-11 at Twickenham and humiliated Scotland 68-10 at Murrayfield, rated the back-three trio of Montgomery, Small and Rossouw the most dangerous in the game and on departure, took aim at the British media. 'The same Brits who laughed at Montgomery during the Lions series would be having nightmares about the prospect of facing him in 1998.'

Montgomery, the Man of the Match against Scotland, was one of the best players on tour and the South African media were unanimous in their approval of his status as a Test player. Not only had he won their favour through his performances, but his gesture in gifting Small a try that would make him the Boks' record try-scorer made headlines. Montgomery, at Murrayfield, could have walked over for a try but passed the ball to Small instead to break the record of 19 held by former Bok centre Danie Gerber.

'It is not like I had much of a choice,' jokes Montgomery. 'James was screaming for me to pass the ball to him. We were all aware he was one try away from the record and I knew what it would mean to him. It would have been incredibly selfish of me to have scored myself and in the circumstance, passing the ball to him was the obvious thing to do. When he scored, he told me I'd have many more opportunities to score Test tries. I took that as a thank you.'

Montgomery scored 26 points against Scotland, including two tries, but his recollection is of the kind of rugby the Boks played and the interaction between backs and forwards. Viljoen's WP team had played a similar brand of rugby, with an emphasis on offloading in the tackle and providing the passer with several support running options. It may sound simple, but no other South African team was playing that way and the South African style was to seek out a target, make contact and go to ground in setting up the next phase. With Viljoen in the Currie Cup and then Mallett on the end-of-year tour, the Boks, with so many Province players in the side, destroyed the opposition with the pace at which they played the game and the space they were able to create through offloading in the tackle.

'It was a great tour, made greater by the players on that tour and by the attitude of the management,' says Montgomery. 'At the time, we knew something special was happening and the core of that team went on to equal the world record of 17 successive Test wins. I didn't think beyond what was happening in that month because I was just so happy to be part of a Bok team that was winning, loved by the public, appreciated by the media and happy with themselves. I'd known the other side of Bok rugby in my first five Tests and I enjoyed the last five Tests of 1997 a lot more. I was playing for South Africa and in the position I had played most of my life, which made it that much more enjoyable and easier, but the success of that tour was who was playing around me and how they helped me develop as a player. It also makes things that much easier when you are winning and everyone rates you and the coaches aren't fighting for their careers. Every Test win on that tour was good, but one of the best memories I have is the French crowd giving us a standing ovation after we had put 52 points past their team in Paris. That was an incredible sight and as a player, it was an amazing feeling.'

The tour was not without hiccups and prop Toks van der Linde was sent home after being red-carded in a midweek match, but it was the manner in which everything was dealt with that impressed Montgomery the most.

'There just wasn't any crisis management and no one was being blamed for anything. Gary's leadership was strong and he had guys with lots of experience around him. Nick made the decision that Henry Honiball was his flyhalf and the player who toured Europe was commanding in everything he did, whereas on the Tri-Nations tour he was being treated as a backup player. I got to see then why Henry was rated so highly and how the players responded to his actions on the field because he was never a player of many words and didn't say a heck of a lot. He just played and Nick gave him the confidence to be the playmaker he was at the Sharks.

'Having a lot of WP players in the touring squad also helped and I think having midweek games made the tour easier because everyone was getting game time. Nothing is worse than going on a long tour and within the first week, you realise you aren't needed and you spend the month as a tourist or duty boy. Only the 2007 World Cup experience in France would beat how I felt on this tour. I loved being there, whether in the midweek or Test team, and we played some of the most unbelievable rugby.'

8

KNIVES, SOLDIERS, JAMES SMALL AND THE FULL MONTY

It was the year of *The Full Monty*, the hit British movie about a bunch of local misfits turned strippers in their home town to raise funds for laid-off miners. According to the ad agency of DStv (South Africa's, and later Africa's, multi-channel, digital satellite subscription service), the Cape Town-based Ad Makers, it was a no-brainer to link the movie, which won global acclaim, with Percy Montgomery, who on the Boks' 1997 tour of Europe had indeed been the 'Full Monty' in running, passing, tackling, scoring and kicking. Montgomery's mentor and friend, HO de Villiers, negotiated the advertisement endorsement on behalf of the player. There was only one small hiccup when Montgomery was approached to show off his array of talents to a TV audience – he did not want to take off his shirt, let alone his rugby shorts.

Montgomery was wary of the public backlash to his pretty-boy image. Having endured a season of torment and then triumph in 1997, he didn't want to give the conservatives any more ammunition to have a go at him in 1998. In the end, he was convinced that people would see the advertisement as a play on the movie, his surname and his rugby achievements but, for the ad to work, he had to show off his body. Ad Makers' managing director Duan Coetzee, in an interview with *Rapport* on 19 April that year, said they wanted to portray DStv as the full package and that Montgomery was the perfect fit. They then got a professional male stripper in to coach Montgomery, but after one song and one routine, the bloke told them the rugby player was a natural and the ad was shot. When it was initially shown to a working forum of women, they all commented on Montgomery's body, but none of them could remember what the ad was about.

'We had to tinker with the script to ensure that not only did the viewer see his body but they got the message that to subscribe to DStv meant they would be getting the full package,' said Coetzee.

The advertisement had the expected impact and it was then that De Villiers withdrew the casual management arrangement and suggested Montgomery find himself a professional agent to manage his affairs.

'HO took no commission and wanted nothing financial in return, but he advised me to get an agent and I linked up with the biggest sports agents in the country,' says Montgomery. 'Back then I was naive and as a young player it was also pretty cool to tell whoever wanted to speak to me about a business opportunity, to speak to my agent. In time I would realise that I never needed an agent, but what I needed was people I could trust to look after my finances, manage my commitments and give me professional advice where necessary. I had a bad experience with my agent, which only came to a head near the end of my career, and my advice to any young player is to think carefully about why he wants an agent and why he would want to give up 20% of his salary on pre-determined contracts in which there is little room for negotiation. Invest in an agent who wants to chase a commercial opportunity on an ad-hoc basis, but always surround yourself with people you can trust and whose primary interest is your well-being.'

In 1998, though, Montgomery was a kid on the professional rugby block and he walked big steps with a swagger that annoyed many people only too keen to see him slip on that golden surface.

'I saw the big city lights and enjoyed being in them,' he recalls. 'But not at the expense of my rugby. I worked bloody hard and I took nothing for granted. The Bok end-of-year tour to Europe had been brilliant, but even from my school days, I knew how quickly it turned against you. One day you can do nothing wrong and the next it seems you can do nothing right, so it was never a case of me getting a big head and ignoring my rugby. I trained like never before and I wanted to make an impression in the Super 12 because when I first played there in 1996, I felt out of my depth, physically not up to the challenge and a bit player in the squad. I was more a menace to the team as a duty boy than I was to the opposition, so I wanted to do well playing for the Western Stormers two years later.'

Initially, the 1998 Super 12 produced the sizzle Cape fans had missed when Western Province failed to qualify for the 1997 competition. Regionalism had made its debut in 1998 and WP, now able to select Boland and South Western Districts players, were playing as the Western Stormers. The opening game was against the Wellington-based Hurricanes, who included All Blacks superstars Christian Cullen and Tana Umaga. The Stormers lost a ripper of a game 45-31 and Montgomery scored 21 points – made up of two tries, four conversions and a penalty. However, he was playing at outside centre again, much to the annoyance of Springbok coach Nick Mallett who said he would only pick him as a fullback.

Mallett and Stormers coach Harry Viljoen disagreed on Montgomery's best position. Viljoen said Montgomery's pace was suited to outside centre in Super 12 rugby and that it made sense because in Justin Swart he had a fullback who six months earlier had been the premier fullback in South Africa. Mallett, in no position to demand Montgomery play at fullback, never avoided the topic and was vocal in the media about the wasted opportunity in not playing Montgomery at No 15 in a tournament that featured some of the game's best players.

'I could never insist on him playing there and I accepted Harry's explanation but that did not mean I had to agree with it,' says Mallett.

Viljoen, described by some players as a visionary and by others as a naive romantic, believed the Super 12 was the perfect stage for his style of rugby. He wanted a game in which tries were scored and players off-loaded in the tackle and ran into space (not directly at the opposition). He wanted a game which saw crowds entertained and not frustrated. The businessman in Viljoen had the ideas, but when the execution failed, there was no place for the coach to hide. A year earlier Viljoen, in his first season as WP coach, had won the Currie Cup, but the Super 12 was unknown territory and Montgomery remembers the campaign as one that fizzled and then fell apart. Outside of the shocking regional jersey – a combination of WP, SWD and Boland's colours – the Hermanus pre-season camp was a taste of what was to come in the season when team-mates James Small and Toks van der Linde had fought. Small tried to get at the big burly prop with a knife before being restrained by captain Dick Muir. Four matches into the competition, the inspirational Bob Skinstad broke his ankle and with Viljoen and assistant coach Alan Solomons divided on rugby philosophy and their off-field relationship in trouble, the tour of hope turned to one of helplessness.

'It got messy the more we lost,' says Montgomery, who alternated between outside centre and fullback. 'Harry was taking strain, there were injuries and we were playing some of the best teams in the world. All I remember of that tour is getting a hospital pass from our scrumhalf, Jopie Adlam, stretching high to get it and finding myself flat on my back, winded and struggling to breathe. No one has ever tackled me as hard before or since the day [Blues centre] Eroni Clarke benefited from Jopie's generosity in the pass,' jokes Montgomery.

Robbie Fleck, Montgomery's friend and room-mate on tour, had the closest view of the Clarke tackle, and it was only when Montgomery saw the team video that he realised why the crowd had gasped in awe at their demolition man.

'Monty took the ball and I carried on running in anticipation of the pass. I went 3m forward and he went 3m back. It's one of the biggest hits I've seen,' recalls Fleck. 'To his credit, he got up after what seemed like an hour and continued playing.'

Montgomery laughs about it now, but in 1998 at Eden Park all he wanted to do was breathe.

'I had been winded only once at school and I've never been winded in a rugby game again from a tackle. In more than 300 first-class matches, I remember that tackle as much as I remember anything else.'

The Stormers scored first against the Super 12 champions to lead 7-0 but they would lose 74-28. 'The Blues had a great side and Jonah Lomu and Joeli Vidiri were beasts on the wing. We knew it would be tough, but it turned to embarrassment after our first try,' says Montgomery.

Christian Stewart, former Canada and Bok midfielder, was on that tour and he played against the Auckland-based side. 'Don't ask me about it,' he jokes. 'Ask Monty about the tackle and Fleckie about the tackle on Justin Swart!'

Fleck remembers either Lomu or Vidiri picking up the 95kg Swart and spear-tackling the hapless player into Eden Park's cricket pitch. 'I was about to get stuck into them, but then I heard the two speak for the first time on the field and all that was said was, "Well done, bro". I thought it safer to keep my distance,' jokes Fleck.

Socially, the boys had a good tour, but before they left New Zealand, Dick Muir had indicated he would not play again and the players sensed Viljoen was not going to hang around for the Currie Cup season.

'It was disappointing because after WP won the 1997 Currie Cup, we knew there was so much we had to offer the competition as players and if our first match against the Hurricanes had a buzz about it, I remember the last one of the season against the Cats [now known as the Lions] at Ellis Park as being a shocker,' says Montgomery.

Viljoen and Solomons, after a disagreement during a European skiing holiday at the end of 1997 to celebrate WP's Currie Cup success, were hardly speaking as head coach and assistant coach, and the Cats – a franchise made up of Golden Lions and Free State Cheetahs players – cashed in 40-7. Poor old Jonny Trytsman, an honest solider if ever there was one, captained the Stormers that night, but it is not one he'll be telling his grandchildren about.

Small, a disciple of the Viljoen way, was disillusioned at the pending changing of the guard and he believed Solomons did not rate him as a player. Montgomery remembers Small leaving the field in disgust near the end of the game, pulling tape from his hand and screaming to Solomons: 'Where are your fucking soldiers now?' Viljoen would resign as coach, Solomons would be appointed as WP and Stormers coach and Small would never play again for either side. Solomons, contrary to reports, *did* rate Small as a player but he was not prepared to risk a new team dynamic with Small's behaviour, which Solomons felt had the potential to disrupt a team more than it would bond.

'I was sad to see James go,' says Montgomery. 'He was only ever good to me and he helped me a lot in 1997, at WP and with the Springboks. I always enjoyed his passion and his way, even though I know a lot of people did not agree with who he was or how he conducted himself. But he had always told me to be myself and I respected him enormously for being himself. I saw him when some of the 1995 World Cup winners presented us with our jerseys before the 2007 World Cup final and I liked him as much then as I did in 1997. He spoke passionately to me and the boys about earning the right to win the World Cup and that winning it was different to playing in it. He said we had played in it and played brilliantly, but that now we had to finish the job by going out and earning the right to win it. I also remember him asking me to take my boots off the table before the team photo because it was bad luck. I told him that I put my boots on the table before every Test and it was my ritual. He said boots on the table could only spell trouble and so I put them on the floor. You could have sworn I'd scored a try he was so relieved.

'It was good chatting to him and he has lost none of his presence as a person, but I did tell him I was disappointed he didn't keep in touch. He said our lives had gone different paths and that it was my time in the sun and that I had to enjoy it. I'll always enjoy James Small because rugby is supposed to be about characters and not robots and he was a character, both in 1997 and 10 years later. When I saw him in Paris, he was as fired up as we were about us winning the World Cup.'

9

TATTOOS, CHASING THE RECORD AND THE TORTURE OF TWICKENHAM

The events leading up to Perth and Wellington in 1998 seem trivial for Percy Montgomery, but what happened afterwards is matched only by the Springboks' 2007 World Cup-winning campaign in France and two very special days against the All Blacks in 2008. The Springboks, described as the best team on the planet at the end of 1997, had won in Perth against the Wallabies and a week later would become the first South African team since 1981 to beat the All Blacks in New Zealand. They would go on to win the Tri-Nations with the most stunning of comebacks against the All Blacks in Durban before shutting out the Wallabies in Johannesburg.

Montgomery, like the Springboks, was flying at a height South African rugby had not known since the 1995 World Cup success, but every flight has to end and the landing on this occasion was always going to be more agonising than the take-off. More is the pity that it had to happen in

London, against a team the Boks respect but whose media they despise.

As with all things new, there was no pressure or expectation on Nick Mallett's Boks at the end of 1997, but with each success came talk of a world record of 18 consecutive Test wins. With every win came greater introspection of the vulnerability of a side that for 12 months had inspired their fans and crushed the opposition's. Even when the Boks appeared to play badly, they won by 20 points, and what really grated Mallett was the 20-point wins were no longer considered good enough. On the Grand Slam tour of 1998, I bagged the Boks' performance in beating Scotland 35-10 at Murrayfield. Mallett, overhearing me talking favourably of the Wallabies' away win against France that same day, crapped on me and said the South African media needed to find some perspective and that it was unrealistic to think the team could win by the record-breaking margins of a year earlier. He also asked me to consider the peaks and troughs of any player's season and to give some credit to the mental strength of players who had got up for the biggest game of their career in New Zealand, won the Tri-Nations and now had to get up again for a Grand Slam tour, which included matches against the four home unions.

As I would later come to realise during my rugby-writing career and three-year stint as Bok communications manager, every Bok player would trade a Grand Slam success and a world record to beat the All Blacks in New Zealand. The only thing bigger for a Bok player is winning the World Cup, and while 1998 is remembered by many for the one failure at Twickenham against England in the match that would have given the Boks outright ownership of the world record for successive Test wins, Montgomery remembers it for winning in New Zealand and for signing up to the Bok club for life.

The Springbok tattoo, on his bum, came in Perth. Joost van der Westhuizen, Stefan Terblanche and Bob Skinstad joined him and it is something he never regrets doing.

'Outside of Tasmin and my children, that would be the symbol I'd want most on my body. It is there for life, the Springbok emblem and the number 15, and when I got it I knew it was going to be a tour to remember. I just sensed there was something very special happening in the Bok team and there was this belief that no matter how good Australia and New Zealand were, we could beat them in their own country.

'We were comfortable playing in Perth because there was big South African support and the Wallabies had never played a Test there. It has changed now, with Australia playing there every year, but in 1998 it did have a feel of a home game to us and we cashed in and got every bit of luck as well. If [Wallabies fullback] Matthew Burke had kicked that late penalty, we would have lost and I still don't know how he missed because he is such a good kicker. But the Subiaco Oval is not the easiest ground for goal kickers and he missed plenty that night, I managed to kick a few over and Joost scored a great opportunistic try. We won by a point [14-13], but it was all we needed to be on the winning side.

'I just remember the buzz in the change room and the celebrations. There was no immediate talk about keeping it calm and that the All Blacks would be a bigger challenge. There was such strong leadership among the players and the coaching staff in Nick and Solly [assistant Alan Solomons] that everyone seemed to know the moment had to be enjoyed, but that there was a bigger match the next Saturday in Wellington. We had taken 50 from the All Blacks the year before in Auckland, but we knew it would never happen with this squad and all Nick had emphasised to the guys was that if we fought for every ball and made every tackle, we'd put them in an unfamiliar position and they'd be vulnerable. That night in Perth was big, but I knew there was a more special one waiting if we kept our focus and trained hard.'

That night came in Wellington after the Boks won 13-3. They defended like demons, repelled every All Blacks attack and Montgomery, in testing conditions, landed three from five goal kicks. When you consider All Blacks flyhalf Carlos Spencer missed five from five, it was an achievement. The Test highlights package belongs to Pieter Rossouw's try, but Montgomery was part of an incredible defensive effort – one Mallett still believes has seldom been bettered. Pieter Müller, in the Bok midfield, was colossal. Gary Teichmann, as captain, was superb and Mallett's substitutions were timed to perfection.

'I thought Jonah Lomu had a really massive game,' says Montgomery. 'He was strong when he had the ball and he put in some crunching tackles, but our guys just went for him and our motto was simple – you just had to hang on to slow him down. If you did that, there would be two or three guys in support to knock him over. It was physical and before Pieter's try they could easily have won it, that is how close it was. During the game, I didn't think of Carlos's misses, but afterwards I really felt for him. He was booed off the field by his own people and I had been through that in South Africa. No player giving everything for his country deserves that and it is something I will always despise from people who call themselves fans but are only there in the good times. Carlos had played some brilliant games for the All Blacks and it was just one of those days when his goal kicking didn't go well. The All Blacks were humble afterwards and congratulated us, and [coach] John Hart came to our change room and applauded the effort of each one of our guys. There was a lot of emotion in the change room and Nick even allowed the press in to soak up the atmosphere. When I think of my career, that afternoon is one I will never forget, but I was also impressed by the reaction of the All Blacks to losing. They don't take it lightly, but they give you respect because not many teams have beaten them at home.'

The Boks, in returning to South Africa, knew they needed just the one win out of two to win the Tri-Nations, and when they trailed the All Blacks 23-5 at half-time, it seemed that win would have to come against the Wallabies in Johannesburg. But the belief of the side refused to accept a defeat was possible and in one of the greatest comebacks by any team against the All Blacks, the Boks won 24-23 and ended the game on the opposition tryline.

The All Blacks afterwards claimed that Bok hooker James Dalton did not score the winning try and was short by a few inches. Durban, as in 1995 when French flanker Abdul Benazzi had been ruled six inches short of knocking the Boks out of the World Cup, had been kind to the Boks. Australian referee Peter Marshall awarded the try and as the charismatic Dalton will remind you, there has never been anything short about his stature. Did he score it? 'He awarded it, didn't he,' Dalton told me before bursting into a chuckle. 'Of course I scored it.'

Montgomery kicked magnificently at Ellis Park a week later as the Boks won 29-15 to clinch their first Tri-Nations title. That completed a 12-month fairytale for him, which started against Australia in Pretoria in 1997 and ended against the same team in Johannesburg in 1998.

All that remained in the year was the Grand Slam tour and the world record, even though the squad tried not to talk about it. But if they were true to their word, the media wouldn't let them forget this tour was bigger than beating the four home unions. Mallett and Teichmann, in media interviews in recent years, have acknowledged that the pressure of the record mentally drained the squad and that physically there was nothing left in the last five minutes against England at Twickenham. Mallett conceded that he could have introduced fresh legs from the successful midweek Boks who won their four tour matches, but counters this argument with his faith in the older players who had got them to Twickenham and had been responsible for winning 17 Tests in succession.

'How do you thank them at the finishing line and ask the next generation to cross it?,' Mallett would tell me in subsequent years. 'I truly believed we would win with the team we chose, but I always knew it would be helluva hard, very close and we'd need the kind of luck we'd got in Perth.'

The Boks lost 13-7 at Twickenham. Montgomery missed a sitter of a penalty and the media blamed Mallett's selection of Bob Skinstad for André Venter as the turning point of the tour. Montgomery disagrees, saying the players gave everything mentally and physically and that they couldn't have given more.

'I really felt sorry for Bob at the time because no player picks himself and recently when I watched footage of that tour in SuperSport's *Springbok Saga*, I felt sorry for him all over again. But I don't believe it can ever be as simple as saying we lost to England because Bob was picked and André was dropped. If you argue that, then what of Bob's effort against Ireland the week before when we may have lost had it not been for him [the Boks won 27-13]?'

The rugby played by the Test team was disappointing, but even more disconcerting were the whispers of players indulging in recreational drugs during the tour and of late night revelry that included boozing it up and visiting nightclubs in the middle of the week. Montgomery's name was on that list, but he says talk of Boks doing recreational drugs on that tour was bullshit. 'There were some big nights but I don't know of a player who was doing recreational drugs on the tour and I certainly wasn't.'

Montgomery had got closer to Dalton, Rassie Erasmus and Werner Swanepoel during the Bok tour. The team management, especially Solomons, who was also the Stormers coach, were concerned Montgomery was being led astray by blokes with stronger and more dominant personalities. At one point on tour, Mallett and Solomons cautioned Montgomery to be careful and Teichmann spoke to him about taking care not to do stupid things.

'I think Gary and Solly's reaction was more out of concern for me than it was about having a go at Bullet

[Dalton], Smiley [Swanepoel] or Rassie. I told them there was nothing to worry about and I knew who I was and where I came from. I asked if they could fault my commitment at training or in the match or if my fitness levels had suffered. They couldn't but it didn't stop them from telling me to watch myself.'

Christian Stewart, mentor and friend to Montgomery, was the Springbok inside centre on tour. He also spoke to him about the perceptions of some senior players and team management.

'Monty's one of the sweetest guys you'll meet and I felt he could be influenced at that stage of his career, but it was not my place to lecture. I was also young once and team management often expressed fears about my sanity on tour. I just told him to always remember the hard work that got him into the Bok squad and not to jeopardise it through doing anything foolish. I thought Bullet and the boys were treating him a bit like a court jester, but he refuted this.'

Montgomery told everyone there was nothing to be concerned about, but when he mentioned he was joining Dalton on a boat holiday to South America after the tour, the concerns only intensified.

10

BLEEP TESTS, TASMIN AND WORLD CUP DROP GOALS

Alan Solomons, Stormers coach between 1999 and 2001 and Springbok assistant coach from 1997 to 2000, has a way with words. He also doesn't mince his words, given his legal background. If he had been worried about Percy Montgomery's potential to go off the rails on the Springboks' 1998 end-of-year tour to Britain and Ireland, he let Montgomery know his concern now amounted to a caution that if he did not get his fitness right, he would be pissing away his rugby career.

Montgomery had returned from his South American holiday with James Dalton as one does from a holiday, unfit and too relaxed for Solomons. So unfit was Montgomery that he failed the bleep fitness test for the first and only time in his career. Solomons called him in and told him, in Solly-speak, that the world of commerce was not waiting with open arms for him, that all he had invested in for a profession was rugby, and that he had better get with the programme very quickly. When I remind Montgomery of this exchange, he blushes. When I ask him about the three-week holiday with Dalton, he just laughs.

'It was wild. Let's leave it at that. Solly got stuck into me when I got back and in a couple of weeks, I was back to full fitness and doing my bit for the Stormers. When I think of that month, I prefer to focus on how my fitness improved and not my fitness when I got to training.'

Those in South Africa won't need an introduction to the Stormers of 1999 and the Bobby mania in Cape Town during the Super 12. For those unfamiliar with it, the Stormers, under Solomons, changed their playing strip from the 'Christmas tree' regional colours of 1998 to black, and dropped the 'Western' from their name, becoming simply 'the Stormers'. Solomons, a favourite with the Province players and one of the great servants of Cape rugby through his 20-year association with the University of Cape Town, believed in the enthusiasm and brilliance of Bob Skinstad. He appointed Skinstad his regional captain and Corné Krige his provincial captain, in an obvious attempt to manage the egos of two players who were as competitive as they were friendly with each other.

Solomons had picked up the leftovers of the failed 1998 Stormers campaign and within a few months guided Western Province to the 1998 Currie Cup final in a tournament that showcased the talents of Skinstad, Breyton Paulse, Pieter Rossouw, Montgomery and Christian Stewart as a flyhalf. Province had lost the final to the Blue Bulls at Loftus Versfeld, but they had also come within a pass of winning it when referee André Watson ruled the final pass to Chester Williams to be forward. Solomons had no regrets about the final and was just pleased his team could be competitive after the chaos of the Super 12, but he had aspirations of winning the regional competition because, in his view, the Stormers were one of the strongest squads and had the advantage of being written off because of their failures of 1998.

Kitted out in black and playing to the tune of 'Men in Black' – the theme song from the movie made popular by Will Smith – the Stormers produced the most incredible league season. They beat the Hurricanes and Waratahs overseas, had a great home run, and finished second on the log – on points difference – to the Queensland Reds.

Cape Town was a sea of black, visiting teams were treated like royalty off the field and beaten to a pulp on it, and in just a few months Cape Town's rugby scene was inspired like no other Stormers team has managed since. Skinstad crashed out of the Super 12 when he drove his car into a wall in the early hours of a Monday morning after the Stormers had beaten the Canterbury-based Crusaders in a Sunday match at Newlands. What followed was speculation that Skinstad had been kicked in the knee by Crusaders scrumhalf Justin Marshall during a pub altercation between the two, a story the Kiwi trashes in his autobiography, *Justin Marshall*. Skinstad has never spoken publicly of the evening and the build-up to the crash. Whatever the story, Skinstad was out of the competition and many still believe had Skinstad played through the competition, the Stormers would have won it.

Those are ifs and buts – what was closer to reality was when the Stormers embarrassed the veteran Sharks team 34-19 in Cape Town, which for Bok coach Nick Mallett signalled a changing of the guard and the end of Sharks captain Gary Teichmann's hopes of a World Cup place. Robbie Kempson had joined WP that season from the Sharks and, for those who know Kempson, he parties as hard as he plays. Once the game was over, he had a house-warming party, which was attended by most of the Stormers and Sharks players. It was there that Teichmann and Solomons spoke and when Teichmann left the party, he knew that Skinstad had leapfrogged him for the Bok No 8 jersey. It is also something Teichmann admits to feeling in his autobiography, *For the Record*, although Solomons did not say it outright. Skinstad, though, would get injured a few weeks later and when

Mallett picked him for the World Cup, despite injury doubts, there was no place in the squad for Teichmann, a decision the coach would regret in later years.

Despite being part of the Stormers' 1999 Super 12 season, the Tri-Nations and the World Cup, the most significant thing that happened to Montgomery did not involve rugby. He is adamant that the day he saw Tasmin Tobitt he believed she would be the woman he would marry. He had spotted her at the Baxter Theatre in Rosebank, Cape Town, where they had both attended a show, and he was determined to find out who she was. Through a mutual friend, well-known South African rubber duck racer Mark Louw (the younger brother of former Springbok Rob Louw), the two were introduced and the pursuit to win her over began. Montgomery says it was tougher than any Test, firstly to get a look-in and then once play started.

'She had her independence and she had her career as a model. She didn't watch rugby and didn't know the players. When I first got her number and asked her out she said no. Then friends of ours arranged for us to meet at their place – I knew she was coming but Tasmin was not aware I would be there. She never pitched, but I wasn't going to give up that easily. When I first saw her, I didn't know if she was involved with anybody else, but I found out she had been through a very difficult marriage and had a young boy, and had been divorced for a few years. In those first six months, she was guarded, wouldn't let me get too close and, if anything, we were more friends than boyfriend and girlfriend.'

Tasmin tells a similar story, but says she did not want her son, Nicholas, to be exposed to someone who could be out of her life before the end of the rugby season. She was not impressed by the bells and whistles of the rugby scene and found the whole Stormers mania to be over the top. She also admits to being a jealous girlfriend and at the time she was not prepared to fight the attention all the rugby players were receiving in Cape Town.

'I had married young and it was not the easiest of relationships and I didn't want to make that mistake again. I definitely liked Monty because I found him quiet and shy and adorable because of his simplicity and boyish charm. Right in the beginning of us getting to know each other, he invited me to watch Mark and him ride these jet skis, and while they were out in the water bragging with their toys, he got knocked off his, and I had to help get him out of the water. When I took his wetsuit off, I have to admit thinking, "Now this guy has got a bod". He was all dazed but full of bravado and said there was nothing wrong but nowadays he tells the story how Mark's jet ski had clipped his head and knocked him out. At the time I was hesitant to fall for this guy because I was scared of the celebrity world he moved in and I found the environment too intense and hectic for me. I preferred to stay away and I wasn't comfortable to commit to anything.'

The chase for this love of his life excited and frustrated Montgomery, although it had no effect on his rugby and he was playing well enough for Mallett to describe him as 'easily the form fullback in South Africa' at the start of the international season.

According to best friend, Grant Hinckley, some things had changed and his view is that Montgomery had started to believe he was a superstar in the fishbowl of Cape Town after the Stormers' 1999 season.

'That year, everyone was talking about the Stormers and the Men in Black,' says Hinckley. 'These guys had gone from being the duds of the competition the year before to celebrities the next. They were playing brilliant rugby, had an amazing thing going in Cape Town around every match and the players were put on a pedestal. I don't blame any of them for starting to believe everything that was being said about them, but it wasn't how I knew Monty. We went out the Saturday night after the Springboks played the All Blacks at Loftus – the Test when André Snyman broke his ankle.

Monty had invited me along and a lot of the other Stormers' Boks were there. We were at this club and I just couldn't stand what I was seeing. I thought they were all playing it up and I thought Monty was making a toss of himself. Eventually I told him he had become a chop and that if he wanted to call me when he was the oke I knew, he could do so.'

It took Montgomery a few months to call, but when he did, he introduced himself as Monty and the two have never had another altercation since. Montgomery's Stormers and Bok team-mate Robbie Kempson says the night Hinckley refers to would have been the exception and not the rule around Montgomery during those crazy Stormers days, and defends his mate as not being part of the Skinstad-Robbie Fleck-Corné Krige trio that dominated the media.

'Monty is friends with everyone and Fleckie and him roomed together a lot, but Fleckie and Skinstad were far more outgoing than Monty ever was. I found Monty to be introverted and shy and that was the year he met Taz. He'd keep to himself and as a mate and team-mate, I didn't think he had changed. I know he has always been very emotional in terms of his relationships, but the Monty I first played rugby with is the same bloke I know today … unassuming and someone who has never been too big for the game or the company he keeps.'

The modesty Kempson refers to is perfectly illustrated in Montgomery's recollection of saving Bok wing Chester Williams from drowning during the Boks' 1999 World Cup training camp in Plettenberg Bay. In Williams's biography, *Chester*, he tells how he hated any water-sports activity because he couldn't swim and during one exercise at the camp he panicked, was about to blank out and thought he was drowning. Montgomery, when asked about the incident, says he helped a team-mate out of the water who was in a bit of trouble. Montgomery, as comfortable as a fish in water, loved the experience of Plettenberg Bay but says there was a lot of resentment among senior players over Gary

Teichmann's omission from the World Cup squad and there was always an uneasy tension, even in days when everyone laughed and seemed in good spirits.

'Somehow, there always seems to be controversy around Bok teams and I deliberately tried to ignore a lot of the sideshows and the stuff that was out of my control, but no one is blind and deaf and you see and hear what is going on. I just wanted to go to the World Cup and do well because Nick had stuck with me during the Tri-Nations and Solly had always been there for me at the beginning of the year.

'When we lost to the All Blacks at Loftus, I'd taken a beating from the crowd. Having Andrew Mehrtens send me from one side of the field to the other, like a guy runs his dog around with a stick at the beach, didn't help. I rate Mehrtens the most difficult flyhalf I have had to contend with from fullback because of the length he gets on his kicks and his ability to work a fullback around the field with the accuracy of his kicks. That day, he had lots of fun while I just chased ball after ball. The media wanted me dropped and it would have been easy for Nick to drop me to ease the pressure on him because the Boks hadn't won in more than a month. Nick kept faith with me for the next Test against the Wallabies in Cape Town and defended me to the media. He said I had played poorly at Loftus but he also said he knew I would play well in Cape Town.'

Montgomery did exactly that and produced a superb performance as Robbie Fleck scored the only try of the match and the Boks won 10-9. Montgomery and Mallett were relieved at his performance and more comfort came in a fax sent to Montgomery from 1995 World Cup-winning fullback André Joubert. In an interview with *SA Rugby* magazine in August 2008, Joubert said, 'He didn't play badly at all [that day], but it seemed the crowd thought he was going through a nightmare, and the media were critical the next day. I told him in the note to back himself, to believe in himself, not to listen to the well-meaning advice of others.

I reminded him that only he knew what he was tasked to do for the team, what his job was, and whether he was succeeding or failing. Supporters can be fickle, but you have to remain true to yourself, and true to the team goal.'

Montgomery's memory of the 1999 World Cup is about drop goals, the death of the Springboks' challenge against Australia in the semi-final and having to deal with the death of Tasmin's ex-husband Terry Tsoukas. He died in a car accident on the night Montgomery kicked two drop goals as the Boks beat the All Blacks 22-18 in the play-off for third place.

'Jannie had kicked those incredible five drop goals in the quarter-final against England to win us a game, where no one, except for those of us in the squad, had given us a chance. A week later, Stephen Larkham's freak drop goal and Matthew Burke's brilliant goal kicking at Twickenham would put us out of the World Cup. I loved the intensity and the drama of both games and even though we lost [27-21] in extra time to Australia, I was very proud of how we played as a team and the rugby we produced in the play-offs after the torrid build-up we had to the World Cup. But there was no great celebration after beating the All Blacks because Tasmin called me to say Terry had been killed and there was no question I had to get on the first plane and be with her. I got permission from Nick to leave Cardiff on the Friday before the World Cup final [between Australia and France] and I stood by her side at the funeral.'

Tasmin says it took massive balls for any guy to walk into that funeral as a support structure for her, more so when he had a profile as public as Montgomery's.

'This was a Greek funeral and a Greek family who weren't happy that Terry and I had got divorced in the first place and here I was with another guy,' she recalls. 'But it was the support I needed most and he was there for me, and he was there for Nicholas in those early years when he wanted to know what had happened to his dad and how he had died.

In the last nine years, there have been so many emotional moments that Monty has had to deal with when it comes to Nicholas and the early loss of his father. Nicholas has never been anything but a son to Monty and he has always treated him as his own, but he has never denied Nicholas the memory of his dad. Often he would sit in the room and comfort him while he cried as any boy would do who has lost his dad. People who know Monty know his compassion and it hurt the most when I would read stories about him that were so hurtful, spiteful and full of lies. And all because of a perceived media image that he is the pretty boy from Cape Town who has always had it all.'

The media lies about Montgomery extended to Tasmin and him as a couple. In December 1999, the *Cape Times* reported she had stolen possessions of her ex-husband's and that Montgomery, as her boyfriend, had been an accomplice.

The story, first featured on 15 December, quoted a family member of Tasmin's ex-husband as filing theft and housebreaking charges against Tasmin, but the *Cape Times* on 23 December reported that 'a senior prosecutor in the Cape Town regional court had declined to prosecute Tasmin Tobitt, who was accused of stealing possessions belonging to her late ex-husband, because there is no case'.

The report also claimed that 'Sue Katz, the sister of Tobitt's ex-husband, had contacted the *Cape Times* with information and said she had laid charges of theft and housebreaking against Tobitt at the Camps Bay police station. But Tobitt, in a signed statement, supported by copies of letters sent to Tsoukas's attorneys, said that since her divorce three years ago, she had retained the keys for the house in Clifton, as well as his green Cabriolet.

'"I did so with Terry's knowledge and permission," she said. "Terry always permitted me to come and go from his house whenever I wanted. There is no truth in the allegations that I broke into Terry's house or that I unlawfully removed his vehicle from the airport."'

The report continued: 'On Sunday, 12 December, Tobitt telephoned her attorney Mark Elmes to seek his advice about the car which apparently had been parked at Cape Town International Airport for three months. "On the advice of my lawyer I, together with my boyfriend [Montgomery], collected the vehicle from the airport. I retrieved the vehicle from the airport solely for the purpose of protecting an asset in Terry's estate and not for retaining or using it for my own purposes."'

Neil Lazarus, SC, who was advising Tasmin, reiterated to the newspaper that his client had never been charged and that the senior prosecutor came to the conclusion that there was no case to prosecute.

'It was the most awful month for us,' says Tasmin. 'I'd lost an ex-husband and, despite our differences and the break up, we had shared a life and Nicholas had lost his father. I thought it was insensitive and sensationalist that the media should involve Monty, whose only connection to it all was that he was there to support me as a friend. Monty should have returned to South Africa in 1999 to applause for giving everything to the Springboks, but instead he came back to a Greek funeral very much an unwanted guest and an outsider. I'll never forget his bravery the day of the funeral because it again showed me what a man he is.'

11

PLATINUM PERCY, CURRIE CUP DOUBLE AND TROUBLED TIMES

On the surface, 2000 and 2001 should have been among Percy Montgomery's most cherished memories. Western Province won successive Currie Cup finals against the Sharks, in Durban in 2001 and at Newlands a year later. Montgomery played Test rugby for the Boks and in both years he excelled for the Stormers in the Super 12. But the on-field successes don't tell the story of the off-field roller-coaster ride that emotionally was tearing Monty apart.

The player concedes he was not the victim but the culprit in relationship woes during 2000 and 2001, but he says he was part victim to the social evils that would trip him up in those years.

'I think I owe it to any young player out there to caution him against the hangers-on, the lure of the bright lights and the ease at which you start believing all the hype around you and start living a social life that can never be a part of a professional sportsman's make-up. I'll never judge a young player who goes off the rails or who gets sucked into the sideshows because I have been that young player, who got mixed up with the wrong people, hung out with the wrong crowd and did a lot of wrong things. But I would tell that player to identify who has always been there for him, long before he made it as a rugby player, and ask if those are the people being alienated. It is easier said than done – you don't see it at the time because you are the centre of attention. You don't see how those around you are manipulating who you are and feeding off who you are. When those who care about you point it out in an attempt for you to see the situation as it is, you turn on the caring ones.'

Montgomery admits to turbulent times on the party scene and to indulging in that party scene, and says it is a miracle his rugby in 2000 and 2001 did not suffer more.

'The consistency in my game has tended to be there when I am settled in a relationship and there aren't off-the-field issues. Those two years are the exception because there was a lot of chaos going on in my life away from rugby, but somehow I kept it together on the field. I believe it had a lot to do with the quality of individuals in the side I played in during that period and because of the type of coaches I had at Western Province, the Stormers and Springboks in Gert Smal, Carel du Plessis, Alan Solomons and Nick Mallett. All of them are different coaches, but all of them backed me with selection and while I thought I was playing well enough to make those three teams in 2000, I knew that I had to find more balance in my life away from rugby.

'But having identified I was in troubled company and in a danger zone did not mean I rectified it. I was young, had some form of fame, and had a wonderful girlfriend in Tasmin and was learning to be a father to her son, Nicholas. But I was also out on the town, hanging with a group of people Tasmin did not agree with, and not prepared to change my ways. It spelled trouble on every front at home and in those two years, I unintentionally played a dangerous game and could have lost everything from Tasmin to my rugby career.

'I was never out of control, but I knew I was going down the wrong road and the worst was I couldn't stop it. I continued to do stupid things socially and put myself in vulnerable situations, but the fact that I was playing decent rugby and the teams I was playing in were winning, probably clouded the issues and made me ignore how seriously I was messing up.'

Tasmin says the two of them were struggling as a couple with Montgomery's revelry and with the immaturity of being a glamour couple in Cape Town, a glamour city.

'My memories of Cape Town during that time are awful,' says Tasmin. 'It was such a troubling time for Monty and me in our relationship and both of us were immature and incapable of dealing with a lot of things. I did not approve of people he called friends and he did not approve of friends in my social group. I was blaming his so-called circle of friends for trouble in our life and he was doing the same thing with certain people in my life. We constantly seemed on a collision course and it seemed aggravated by Monty's admission that he wanted a more settled home life, but socially he was living like a single man in his mid-20s. He couldn't have it both ways, and that was a stumbling block. I was also very wary of the crowd he was keeping because of their social habits. I don't blame things only on the social crowd, because in my view Monty was big enough to make the right decisions. I felt the reason he was not divorcing himself from that social crowd was because he didn't want to.'

Montgomery's father, Percival Senior, told me he never addressed the 'hell-raising' years with his son, but spoke to Tasmin about his fears Monty was losing perspective and throwing away his career. Montgomery Senior and his wife, Lillian, had moved back to Cape Town after nearly 20 years in Namibia and Montgomery Senior was concerned at the direction in which Monty was headed.

'Lillian and I had been in Namibia for most of Percival's schooling at SACS, but we had both been back in Cape

Town for the last 10 years, and I've seen the professional highs and lows of Percival's career. In 2000 and 2001, I was worried about my boy because there were too many distractions away from rugby and he seemed incapable of recognising the situation. Tazzie runs most mornings and I vividly recall one conversation we had when I went for a jog with her, in the hope of her talking some sense into Percival. I was worried about what I was seeing in him and told her I was not stupid and could see the damage he was doing to himself. I felt he was being sucked into a world where there was too much money, too much drinking and too much snorting, if you know what I mean. There were too many little *varkies* [pigs] in his social group. She knew what I was talking about. I didn't think she was blameless in their relationship because both of them were young, strong willed and had high-profile careers with many temptations, and I said so, but my issue was more with Percival.'

Monty isn't specific about the crowd he was hanging with that time of his life or just what the social vices and evils were, only to say that you don't need to be a rocket scientist to figure it out.

'They were dangerous times for me and my saving grace is I got through those two years with minimal damage. What kept me afloat most of that time was the rugby, especially with the Stormers and Western Province.'

Province, in both years, won the Currie Cup, and the Stormers were always a contender for the Super 12 play-offs during Alan Solomons' three years in charge.

Mallett selected Montgomery in 2000 but dropped him for the first time in 33 Tests when the Boks played Australia in Sydney midway through the Tri-Nations. Mallett told the media Montgomery had been poor the previous week in the 25-12 defeat against New Zealand in Christchurch and privately was annoyed at what he believed was Montgomery's lack of courage under one particular high ball, when the player let it bounce and attempted to fly hack it into touch.

'I don't know if he heard Jonah Lomu's breathing but I didn't know him to be a player who ever ducked out of any physical confrontation,' Mallett told me at the time. 'Monty was never the biggest player, but from the first day I picked him for South Africa, he had put his body on the line every time. I didn't think he had done so that day in Christchurch.'

Mallett, who had defended Montgomery's Bok selection throughout 1999, told the media that he did not believe there was anyone better to play fullback for the Boks than Montgomery, but in 2000, new options had emerged, among them Golden Lions fullback Thinus Delport.

'There were calls for André Joubert, but I really didn't think he was a player for the future for me. This should be seen as an opportunity for Delport's career rather than the end of Monty's career. I definitely haven't written Monty off.'

Mallett would never get to select Montgomery as a starting Springbok again because he was fired at the end of the 2000 Tri-Nations, despite the Boks beating the All Blacks 46-40 at Ellis Park and losing 19-18 to the Wallabies in Durban when Australian centre Stirling Mortlock kicked an injury-time penalty after Corné Krige infringed at the breakdown.

Harry Viljoen, who adored Montgomery as a player when he coached him in the successful 1997 WP side, replaced Mallett as the Springbok coach, and had no hesitation in selecting him for the Boks' end-of-year tour to Argentina and Britain, with Montgomery one of the best players in the Currie Cup that year.

Montgomery had responded to his Bok axing in 2000 by dying his hair platinum and while the public and opposition ridiculed the new look, Viljoen had no problem with Montgomery's hair colour as long as his performances were of the same description. They were, and when Viljoen picked Montgomery to start at flyhalf for the Springboks against Argentina in Buenos Aires and instructed him not to kick a ball, it was as big a compliment as could be paid to

Montgomery's ability as a rugby player. Jake White, World Cup-winning coach of 2007, was the Boks' technical adviser on that tour, and the guy running the line with instructions to the players during matches. White recalls the Argentina Test for the outrageous approach, in not kicking the ball, and for Montgomery's absolute faith in Viljoen's instructions.

'Monty's was one of the most incredible performances I had seen from a guy who was playing flyhalf for the first time in a Test and who had 60% of his game taken away before kickoff with the instruction, he was not allowed to kick. Monty's boot is one of his strengths and he is a player who loves to play to structure and build a game against an opponent with strategic line kicking and by playing field position first. Monty is a thinker of the game and only when you have coached him do you realise how well he knows the game. He knows the difference between right and wrong on the field and here he was told to run everything, no matter when and where.

'They kicked off, Monty got the ball and, under instruction, ran it 20m from his own tryline and we were caught in possession and penalised. Three-nil to the Pumas. One minute gone and it had already gone wrong, but Monty did not panic for a minute and not once did he ask me if he was allowed to kick the ball because the situation was unmanageable. He kept on with Harry's instructions and in the next 38 minutes, along with his team-mates, played brilliant rugby. We didn't have the fitness to last that type of game and in the latter part of the second half, the Pumas had taken control of the match and were within a point of taking the lead. We were 34-33 ahead and we had a lineout a few metres from our tryline. Fortunately it was our put-in and Harry finally gave me the instruction to tell Monty to kick the ball. I screamed this to him from the side of the field. He was standing near the dead-ball line and the rest of the backline was beyond the dead-ball area. Monty screamed back if I was sure that I meant for him to kick it. "Just kick the fucking thing as far as you can!" I screamed back. We won the lineout, he kicked it for the first time in the 73rd minute of that Test and a late Braam van Straaten penalty gave us a 37-33 win.'

Montgomery, who also wore the No 10 jersey against Ireland and Wales, describes the early weeks of that tour as exhilarating because of Viljoen's mindset and desire to play a different game.

'Harry, like he did with Western Province in 1997, made an immediate impact with the players. He wanted us to wear the best clothes, stay in the best hotels and play the best rugby. I felt reinvented in those first few games, but as the conditions worsened in Ireland and Wales, and as [Springbok assistant coach on the tour] André Markgraaff promoted a more conservative and structured game plan, our performances became more subdued and the tour became more of a strain,' says Montgomery, who ended the tour playing fullback in the 25-17 defeat against England at Twickenham.

'It was the only match we lost on tour and I still believe if Harry had trusted his philosophy and modified it to go with the difficult playing conditions, we could have been more successful playing a more complete game. I was disappointed with the result against England, but the tour did finish on a high when we beat the Barbarians in Cardiff in a memorable game.'

The Springboks' 41-31 victory was against a star-studded Barbarians backline that included Matthew Burke, Chris Latham, Brian O'Driscoll, Christian Cullen, Carlos Spencer and Agustín Pichot. The Boks trailed 31-13 at half-time before turning to a forward-based game to dominate the second half.

'It was a great way to end the year and I was confident the Springboks were going to be something very special in 2001, especially with the way Harry was talking and all the ideas he had for the players. Harry had only had the job for a few weeks before this tour and by the time the international season started in 2001 I was convinced we were in for adventure and success.'

Montgomery, or 'Platinum Percy' as the newspapers had dubbed him in 2000, was lauded for his performances on the Bok tour and the South African media nominated him as one of the five players of the tour. He had played flyhalf and fullback and excelled in both positions, but not for the first time his versatility would count against him. Stormers coach Alan Solomons saw him as a fullback, who could play any other position, and WP coach Gert Smal shared the view. WP assistant coach and former Bok coach Carel du Plessis, who initially picked Montgomery as an outside centre in 1997, also felt the older Montgomery was best suited to fullback in a Province back-three axis completed by wingers Pieter Rossouw and Breyton Paulse.

Solomons, Smal and Du Plessis all felt the Montgomery-Rossouw-Paulse trio to be the best in the country as a combination and Solomons, in particular, did not want to break up what had worked for him in the past. Solomons also believed in the value of Van Straaten at flyhalf, but after discussions with Viljoen, agreed to compromise and give Montgomery some game time at No 10 in the Super 12. As it transpired, Montgomery would play most of the competition at fullback, and play very well, while for the Sharks, Butch James had emerged as Viljoen's new favourite at flyhalf.

When Viljoen announced his Springbok squad for 2001, James was the No 10 and Montgomery the No 15, and it was how they lined up for the first home Test of the year against France – a match that would start sensationally with Paulse scoring after 20 seconds, but end with a 32-23 defeat, despite Montgomery kicking six penalties.

'There were so many ideas and so much enthusiasm going into that first Test and then it all fell apart,' says Montgomery. 'Harry dropped me after that Test and I played a few minutes in the next Test as a replacement centre. He then picked me again at flyhalf against Italy in Port Elizabeth, where I thought I went well, and then he played me at fullback against the All Blacks at Newlands.'

Montgomery, according to all the newspaper reports, was outstanding at fullback against the All Blacks, but he missed three from four penalty kicks in a Test the Springboks lost 12-3 and Viljoen dropped him for the remainder of the Tri-Nations.

Privately, Montgomery couldn't believe he had been made the scapegoat for the defeat, but publicly he said all the right things and added he could only go back to Western Province and prove himself all over again. The relationship with Viljoen would never be the same because even though the coach selected him in the back-up squad for the Boks' 2001 end-of-year tour, the two hardly spoke. What only a year previously seemed a fairytale ride for Montgomery under Viljoen, had turned into a horror show.

Smal, at the time, defended Montgomery's ability as a player and said his availability could only strengthen Province's defence of the Currie Cup.

'I view Percy as the most skilful player to emerge from South Africa in the last 10 years – the kind of player who has an incredibly positive effect on the sort of game I like to put together,' Smal told *Cape Times* rugby correspondent Stephen Nell.

Smal was not wrong and Montgomery would play outstanding rugby in the next few months as Province beat the Lions 43-22 in the Currie Cup semi-final before beating the Sharks 29-24 at Newlands to claim their second consecutive domestic title.

'The 1997 and 2001 Currie Cup wins are two of the big rugby memories for me because we won both finals at Newlands, and it is always special doing it in front of your home crowd. Personally, it also felt in 2000 and 2001 that Province was my family and in both years I got dropped from the Boks. I went back to WP, and played some of my best rugby under Gert and Carel. They were very supportive of me on both occasions, took pressure off me and just kept on reinforcing why they thought I was a good player. I knew my role in that team and I also knew the players so well and it helped that they were an incredible bunch of guys.'

The WP squads of 2000 and 2001 included Pieter Rossouw, Breyton Paulse, De Wet Barry, Robbie Fleck, Werner Greeff, Gus Theron, Braam van Straaten, Chris Rossouw, Dan van Zyl, Neil de Kock, Bolla Conradie, Robbie Brink, Corné Krige, Bob Skinstad, Hendrik Gerber, Adri Badenhorst, Hottie Louw, Selborne Boome, Quinton Davids, Robbie Kempson, Charl Marais, Pieter Dixon and Faan Rautenbach, who were Boks or would soon become Boks. Stuart Abbott, among the back-up centres, would go on to play for England and claim a 2003 World Cup winners' medal.

'The only provincial squad that I have been in since 2001 that could match the Province side of that year for quality on the field and class of player off the field was the Sharks Super 14 squad in 2007,' says Montgomery. 'I enjoyed those provincial years the best, but the only difference in 2007 was that I was a mature and settled family man whereas at the end of 2001, I was still fighting too many off-the-field demons that were threatening to destroy me and my career.'

12

MONEY OR THE BOKS? IF ONLY IT WERE THAT SIMPLE

Percy Montgomery describes the months leading up to his move to Welsh club Newport as among the worst he has ever known. He was convinced he would never play rugby for the Springboks again, there was uncertainty about his relationship with fiancée Tasmin Tobitt and he was angry at what he believed to be unfair treatment from Springbok coach Rudolf Straeuli.

The 2001 international season had ended poorly for Montgomery after then-Springbok coach Harry Viljoen dropped him as his first-choice fullback during the Tri-Nations. Montgomery, no longer a starting option, toured with the Boks at the end of 2001 as part of the back-up squad. But his game time was restricted to a handful of minutes as a centre replacement against France in Paris and a right wing appearance in the last few minutes against Italy in what was his 50th Test. Viljoen had picked Conrad Jantjes as his run-on fullback for the last three Tri-Nations matches and Jantjes would start all four of the Springboks' matches on the end-of-year tour.

Montgomery, his contribution against France and Italy minimal, warmed the bench the following week against England at Twickenham but the most taxing thing he had to do was the pre-match warm-up drill.

Montgomery, once a disciple of Viljoen's management style when the two enjoyed Currie Cup success at Western Province in 1997, had lost faith in the Bok coach, who in turn had no confidence in Montgomery. The two hardly spoke a word in six months. Viljoen was bitter that Montgomery had missed three penalty kicks in the 12-3 defeat to the All Blacks at Newlands in the Boks' first Tri-Nations match of the year. Despite selecting him for the 2001 end-of-year tour, he no longer saw Montgomery as a 2003 World Cup investment.

Viljoen made this obvious to the player in November 2001 by releasing him to play for the Barbarians against Australia in Cardiff on the weekend the Boks were playing the United States in Houston, Texas. Montgomery was at a low and he felt he had no future in South African rugby with a national coach who no longer rated him.

In that week in Cardiff, he started negotiations for a move to Newport once his Western Province contract finished at the end of the 2002 Currie Cup. Before the start of the southern-hemisphere season, it was common knowledge Montgomery would be heading overseas, even if the signing was only made official on 29 May. In between Montgomery agreeing terms with Newport and officially signing with the Welsh club, Viljoen had resigned as the Bok coach in January and his replacement, Sharks coach Rudolf Straeuli, had declared past international performances would count for nothing in his first squad selection. Straeuli, who was also represented by Montgomery's agent, Craig Livingstone, refused to speak first hand to any player in the months preceding the first Test of the season because he was still involved with the Sharks' Super 12 campaign. This only enraged experienced Boks like Montgomery who wanted clarity on his international situation before committing to an overseas contract. Viljoen, in December 2001, had ended Montgomery's premier Springbok contract and, despite Viljoen quitting in January, there was no revision of the contracts. Montgomery was among those who played the Super 12 without a national contract and the financial blow influenced his decision to consider overseas options.

Straeuli, knowing the insecurity of the players, still felt it unfair to speak to any player and by the time the Super 12 was over in mid-May, Montgomery had already verbally committed to a three-year contract at Newport. Straeuli privately considered Montgomery the best fullback in South Africa and his Super 12 form with the Stormers had been consistently good, but Straeuli, in his first year of the national coaching job, was not going to allow any player to dictate terms, starting with a 50-Test veteran. What followed was an ugly spat after lead stories in Cape Town newspapers on 14 May 2002 reported that Montgomery had quit Test rugby because he did not have a long-term Bok contract.

Straeuli hit back and accused Montgomery of lacking the fight to stick around and make the team because he was the best fullback in the country.

'Players for the first Test against Wales on 8 June will come out of the national trials. He has not backed himself to make the Bok team and to get a contract in South Africa and that is extremely disappointing when a player is not prepared to stick it out and fight for his place in a national team.'

Straeuli told the media that Livingstone had contacted him a week earlier suggesting that only a 2003 World Cup contract would keep Montgomery in South Africa.

'I told Livingstone that my door was open to Montgomery. The player never came to see me and last night [13 May] the agent called to tell me Montgomery would be signing overseas and the player later left a message on my phone's voicemail. I called him back and we spoke for the first time about the situation. He told me he was not prepared to play in the trials. I asked him if that was his final decision and he said it was. I informed him that I would be looking at contracts after the trials. I asked him again if he was sure he did not want to be considered and again he said yes.'

Montgomery, six years later, confirms the content of the discussion but says the significance of the discussion went beyond one trial match. Viljoen had dropped him from an 'A' Bok contract to nothing and there was no guarantee that even if he played in a trial game, at the expense of taking up an overseas offer, he would be given a Bok contract.

'It had nothing to do with not having the fight in me,' says Montgomery. 'I've always given everything to play for the Boks and I've always been prepared to get up and start again and take on the challenge. I've never taken a place in the Springbok team for granted and I think I have shown the Boks are bigger than I will ever be in wanting to come back and make the team in 2008. What angered me at the time was the statement I would not fight for a place. It went beyond fighting off the challenge of another player.'

On 14 May, *Die Burger* led its front page with a story that Montgomery was leaving because of quotas and the source of the story was Livingstone.

'The quota system definitely influenced his decision. There are currently two coloured fullbacks in Ricardo Loubscher and Conrad Jantjes in competition with him at fullback and there is enormous pressure on coaches to accommodate these players and therefore it is highly unlikely Percy will be selected ahead of them.' Livingstone also cited a possible curbing of foreign imports in the British game and felt the player had, in his opinion, made the right decision.

Rugby writers in South Africa blasted Montgomery's decision to leave, with Andy Colquhoun, in the *Weekend Argus*, and Louis de Villiers, in *Rapport*, condemning the player's supposed lack of passion for the jersey in exchange for the British pound. Sports minister Ngconde Balfour told Colquhoun in a separate interview that players like

Montgomery, who left because of the quota system, were unpatriotic and inherently racist.

'Players like Montgomery are free to leave if they so wish but they must stop hiding behind excuses. It is an inherent racist claim to lay the reason for their departure at the door of transformation. In this specific instance, the player knows that for a long time he was kept in the Bok side, not because he deserved to be there, but at the behest of coaches who had their own agenda.'

Straeuli, encouraged by Balfour's comments and the rugby media's support on his decision not to award Montgomery a contract, played on the public emotion of a player who took cash over the jersey.

'The player is going because of the cash incentive. He told me as much. He wants the financial security that he feels the British pound [at 15:1] will give him. He does not want to play for South Africa any more. It means more to him to earn pounds than it does for him to play for the Springboks.'

Montgomery, in conversation with Straeuli in 2002, and still today, denies transformation or the fear of losing his Test place to a black player ever played a part in his decision to leave South Africa. He maintains he had committed overseas because of the uncertainty over his Springbok future and because of the need to refocus his rugby and his life. Straeuli, despite his media attack on Montgomery, never had an agenda with the player and wanted to pick him in 2002. But he was not prepared to make a contract exception for Montgomery, believing it would send out the wrong message in his first year as national coach.

WP and Stormers coach Gert Smal, who a year later would assist Straeuli at the 2003 World Cup as forwards coach, tried to save the situation. Smal, who first coached Montgomery at U21 level, did not want to lose Montgomery to any British club and he believed the player was the best fullback in the country. On Smal's insistence, Straeuli met with Montgomery and Smal at Sarfu's offices, but little was achieved as Montgomery left even more disillusioned and Straeuli even more frustrated. Montgomery wanted the comfort of knowing he would have a national contract and be in the national frame and Straeuli was not prepared to commit to it unless he played in the national trial game at the end of May.

'Straeuli was playing a power game with me and he insulted me when he said I had to prove myself to him in the trial game,' says Montgomery. 'I had played well in the Super 12 and had played 50 Tests for South Africa. He either rated me or he did not and one trial game was not going to change his opinion of me.'

It was a stalemate and Smal's priority later in the month then turned to keeping Montgomery in South Africa until the end of the 2002 Currie Cup season, despite Montgomery requesting an early release to Newport. Montgomery, at the time, had not yet signed with Newport but he told Smal that after the meeting with Straeuli, he had given the club a verbal undertaking he would be signing and he said he could not renege on his word. Newport had already suffered the embarrassment of former Springbok captain Joost van der Westhuizen signing and then reneging on his contract a year earlier and Montgomery said the club would never invest in another South African player if he also failed to honour his commitment.

Smal, a huge influence on Montgomery's career since 1997 at provincial and national level, refused to give the player an early release and insisted he play out the 2002 Currie Cup with Western Province, which Montgomery did, producing consistently good performances.

'I knew he was hurting and angry at the time, but I also knew there were issues that went deeper than rugby,' recalls Smal. 'He was going through difficult times in his relationship and he had things to sort out. I told him to take out his anger on the field and to channel the emotion into his rugby. I urged him to make a rugby statement before leaving, which I feel he did. He played his heart out every weekend and I know he was shattered by not being involved with the Boks. He was very important to the success of Province and had won the Currie Cup in 1997, 2000 and 2001. I felt he needed to leave WP with his dignity intact because he owed the province as much as it owed him. Once I explained it to him like that, he was happy to play every match for me.'

Montgomery admits the anger was about more than rugby disappointments.

'It was a very difficult time for me in my relationship as I had things to figure out about Taz and myself. These were complicated by my affection for her son, Nicholas [from a first marriage], who I had been a father to since 1999, when he lost his father in a car accident. Rugby usually gave me an escape, but when I got dropped from the Springboks halfway through 2001, I was crushed and I struggled to come to terms with it. I was depressed and had to do something to get out of the depression as each week in Cape Town was just getting darker for me. Taking on a new challenge overseas, which would also give me the financial security of a three-year contract, and just getting out of South Africa, if only to try and clear my mind, was an answer at a time when I was struggling to find answers. I was going through so much stuff emotionally at the time, was hanging with a crowd that only complicated things in my relationship with Taz and I was having difficulty accepting friends in her life. We were at a delicate stage of our relationship, having spoken about getting married at some point, but everything was going wrong for me, in the relationship, and on the rugby field.'

It was in Newport that Montgomery found the answers missing in South Africa, although the script was not conventional. Within seven months of joining the club, he thought his rugby career was over when he was found guilty of assaulting Welsh touch judge Peter Rees in a club match against Swansea at the St Helens Ground. Welsh rugby's regulations allow for a lifetime ban for any assault on a match official and Montgomery admits the two-year ban he received, 18 months of which was suspended, was more a career saver than a career breaker.

'I know I could have got a life ban and the moment I shoved the touch judge, I knew my career could be over, but I was at such an emotional low that I didn't care. I remember not even looking back to see if I was being sent off because I just knew it had happened. Once I had shoved him, I just carried on walking to the tunnel, absolutely numb about the action and the consequences. I remember getting to the change room and feeling absolutely nothing. One of our blokes, Mike Voyle, who had been sent off a few minutes earlier for using his boot on a Swansea player, was showering and he asked me what I was doing there. I told him I had pushed over the touch judge. He said, "Fucking hell ... what happens now?" I said I didn't know and I didn't care. There was absolutely nothing in me at the time.

'I know it sounds like a contradiction to say I wish it never happened but I am also glad it happened, because something had to give in my life. That night in Swansea forced me to confront everything in my personal relationship and it also made me re-evaluate everything about my career. I had to be honest with myself, take responsibility for my own actions and commit to changing things about myself and my relationship if I wanted the happiness I need to function properly as a person and as a professional rugby player. I am a person who has to have emotional stability in a relationship otherwise I am a mess and, consequently, so is my rugby. When I look back on my career, the highs have coincided with me being at my most content and happy in my relationships. The converse is when there have been issues and emotions, I have been all over the place.

'I have never experienced such a hard emotional time in my life. Tazzie was in South Africa at the time and the long-distance relationship thing was not working. We seemed to be on and off on a weekly basis. She was coming to Wales and then it was not possible. We would talk about marriage and then we would not speak for days. We have an intense and passionate relationship and before our daughter Taneal was born I guess there was a lot of passive aggression in the way we communicated. When I look back now, there seemed to be some sort of power struggle going on. I was a successful rugby player and she was a successful model and neither was willing to step back for the relationship or to give up a personal identity for a new identity as a couple.

'When I got to Newport, I was spending a fortune on phone calls, and being away from her and Nicholas made me feel hollow and unhappy. We both had issues to sort out as partners and we both had to decide whether we would be capable of surviving in a partnership that would always have a media spotlight on it. Then there were our jobs. I had my career and Tazzie had hers and both of them took us away from each other because there is a lot of travel in rugby and modelling. In South Africa, the situation had been compounded by us always being the focus of the media, whether we chose to be or not, and that was proving destructive to us as a partnership.

'I never admitted it to myself at the time but I was not mature enough to handle the pressures that come with being a high-profile sportsman in South Africa and wanting the simplicity of a home life with Taz and Nicholas. Despite all the relationship uncertainty during my first few months at Newport, we had agreed to still go ahead with our wedding, which was scheduled for Cape Town in the latter part of 2003 – the venue was booked and invites were sent out. But more and more, we seemed to be at each other about everything, and we were doing it all by phone with me in Newport and Tazzie in Cape Town. It was an awful situation and I was all over the place, struggling to come to terms with a new environment and rugby culture, but mostly the prospect of losing a woman I knew from the moment we met I wanted to be my wife.

'On the afternoon of the Swansea match, Taz and I had argued on the phone and she said she couldn't go on like this and that she didn't want to get married. I was numb and couldn't believe there would be no wedding. All the preparation had been done and the last thing I was going to do was listen to sound reasoning as to why she didn't want to marry me. I was beside myself.

'Newport had a match to play that evening. I should have withdrawn because I was in no emotional state to play the game, but I didn't and I took that anger onto the field. I was an angry guy out there and the match, despite starting well, went from bad to worse. Decisions went against us, the Swansea crowd was getting stuck into us and there were verbals flying everywhere on the field. I remember them scoring and me turning to run back to our tryline. As I turned, the touch judge was telling me to fuck off. I let him have it back and as he came past me, I shoved him. I completely lost it and I felt like everything in my life came to a head in that moment as he was abusing me. I am told it looked a lot worse than it actually was and as it turned out, he was not swearing at me but at my team-mate Shane Howarth, who I did not know was behind me. Shane testified at the disciplinary that he had heard the swearing of the touch judge and knew it was directed at him, although the touch judge denied he swore. There was no defence to what I did and I told Tony Brown, the club chairman, as much.

'When I met with Tony, I told him I was having relationship issues and that it had contributed to my volatility and vulnerability. He said he knew it was out of character and that the club would support me regardless of the outcome of the disciplinary, but he also made it clear how seriously he viewed any attack on a match official, whether it was verbal or physical. I knew I was in trouble and I feared the worst. I resigned myself to the possibility of a life ban and knew that I had to get my relationship sorted out because my rugby looked like it was over and I couldn't afford the same to happen with Taz and Nicholas because they meant everything to me.'

Andy Marinos, captain of Newport at the time, and an inspiration to Montgomery at the club, recalls Montgomery's explanation to Brown as being blunter than relationship issues. But it also endeared the player even more to the man whose benevolence had ensured Newport could afford overseas professionals like Montgomery and, before him, Springbok captain Gary Teichmann.

'When Tony asked him why, Percy said, "Sexual frustration, Tony ..." He then spoke about his relationship and what Taz and Nicholas meant to him and how he needed to sort his shit out and get them to Newport. Tony understood and as much as he sympathised, he told Monty it was not a good enough reason for lifting a hand to a match official. He then comforted Monty by telling him the club would continue to pay him in the event of a short-term suspension but if the ban exceeded his contract term, it would be a problem.'

Marinos, a team-mate of Montgomery's at WP and the Stormers in the mid-1990s, believes that night in Swansea was the watershed moment of Montgomery's career and possibly even his life.

'I played with him, but I did not know him well socially as we were in very different phases of our lives back then. He was one of the pin-up boys of South African rugby and I was a young father in a very settled home life. He seemed to live for the big lights back then. All I wanted was the peacefulness of suburbia, so we never mixed socially and I only really got to know him in Newport where I was very fortunate to witness his evolution from a boy to a man. When he got to Newport he had played 50 Tests, but as a person, he did not have emotional maturity. That night in Swansea forced him to grow up and the change in him as a person since has been incredible.'

Montgomery's £15 000 fine and two-year ban, of which only six months was enforced, meant he missed the

2003 World Cup after Straeuli had belatedly announced Montgomery would be an asset for the Boks in Australia. But the finding of the disciplinary committee was not a popular one among local referees who felt Montgomery's international profile had been to his advantage when it should have counted against him. They believed an example should have been made of him and at the very least, he should have been made to serve two years and not just six months. The Welsh media also believed Montgomery got off lightly and noted that Leicester's Neil Back was banned for six months for pushing over referee Steve Lander during the 1996 English Cup final against Bath, but added the punishment for such offences was harsher a decade into professional rugby.

Examples were sought to illustrate how serious the charge was and around the same time as Montgomery's case, Kiwi prop Pene Fotuaika was banned for 10 years for attacking referee Fred Barwick, whose nose was broken and mouth and eye were cut in the attack.

In the build-up to the disciplinary, the Welsh media speculated that an extreme case was a life ban and the minimum punishment was two years. They expected a five-year ban for Montgomery and when he got the minimum, of which 18 months was suspended, the perceived leniency was condemned by the Welsh Society of Rugby Referees (WSRR).

The BBC quoted the secretary of the WSRR, Hugh Banfield, as saying referees were let down by the verdict. 'It has been sacrosanct in rugby that a player doesn't touch an official,' Banfield told BBC Sport. 'That has now been breached. We have to ensure if it happens again, a player will suffer the right consequences.'

The Wales Rugby Union (WRU), through general manager Steve Lewis, defended the disciplinary committee's decision. 'There is no way the WRU will tolerate players laying their hands on match officials. We accept that this incident was out of character for a player with an exemplary disciplinary record but the suspension reflects the seriousness of the offence.'

At the time, Montgomery issued a statement through his solicitor Thomas Shepherd and apologised to Rees.

'People may regard my sentence as lenient, given that the IRB recommends a suspension of between two and five years for laying hands on a match official, but I will be hit financially because of the rugby I will be missing,' he said. 'I feel I have been dealt with harshly but also fairly. It may be that I never again play at the level which marks the pinnacle of a player's career. There were mitigating circumstances for my action, but I accept that ultimately there are no excuses for such behaviour and I apologise to Peter Rees for what happened.'

Montgomery, out of the game for six months, still had a future at Newport and in rugby, but he knew he had to sort out his future with Tasmin.

'I knew I loved her and I knew how much I loved Nicholas and how much I wanted them to be my family. I had to find a solution.'

13

SNAKESKIN SANDALS, NEWPORT AND THE DAY JAKE WHITE CALLED

In August 2003, Percy Montgomery phoned his best friend, Grant Hinckley, and told him the wedding would be in Durban. Hinckley responded that he wasn't paying for another two plane tickets only for the wedding to be called off again after Montgomery and fiancée Tasmin Tobitt had cancelled their wedding, scheduled for Cape Town in June.

'We aren't all professional rugby players,' joked Hinckley, whose own professional rugby career was ended by injury at 22. 'Some of us now have to work for a living.'

Hinckley and Montgomery had met in the WP U21 squad in 1994 and Hinckley is quick to dispel the romantic notion that two opposites instantly found a connection, saying it was more a case of pity than cosmic poetry that inspired him to start talking to Montgomery.

'Monty had great rugby pedigree in that he was a SACS boy who had played for WP Schools and SA Schools in 1992 and 1993, so when it came to the rugby side of things he was very sure of himself on the field. Away from the rugby I thought he was a confident guy in his own way, but I felt sorry for him as he seemed to be on the periphery of everything in the squad and I pitied the poor oke. He was quiet and very private and because I considered myself a bit of a boytjie back then, and a jovial one at that, I started joking with him and initially taking the piss out of him. I quickly discovered he could laugh at himself and give as good as he got. Humour – and laughing a lot – was our connection and it still is today because for all that he has achieved as a Springbok he laughs a lot and has never taken himself too seriously.

'He has a great sense of humour, so I had to make sure that talk of another wedding date was not a set-up. I told him, "China, I am not paying to fly anywhere only to have you tell me you or Taz have had second thoughts". He said the tickets were his treat and had already been booked and paid for. He assured me the wedding was on and that he would see me on Saturday morning, 31 August. He picked me up at the airport and we had breakfast. I then went with him to get his wedding outfit, which was typically alternative and Monty-like – a white suit with snakeskin sandals – and then it was off to Zimbali for the ceremony. When we got there, I couldn't see anyone else and I asked him where all his mates were and he said, "You are it, bugger".'

Tasmin says Monty had arranged everything while she was away on a shoot.

'We had spoken telephonically about the wedding when I was in Costa Rica and while I was excited I didn't actually know whether it could work. When I cancelled the original wedding date in June, Monty was very angry. At the time, he was in Newport and I was in Cape Town organising the entire wedding and as it became more and more hectic, I kept thinking, "I'm not ready for this". I had married at a young age and it had been a difficult marriage, which ended badly. I was wary about committing to someone for the wrong reasons. The commitment is so big and both have to give so much, and I had doubts which were mainly caused by the constant absences of Monty in my life because of his rugby commitments. I'd known him since 1999 and in four years, he had probably been away more than he was at home. I knew I loved him and was *in* love with him, but I was scared to go through a second marriage that did not work and there were so many unresolved issues between the two of us.

'He had left without me for Newport at the end of 2002 because we were fighting and then the relationship was off, back on and off again. In the first six months of 2003, I had spent two weeks in Newport visiting him and the rest of the time I was in Cape Town. I wasn't sure we had sorted out our issues and built a strong enough foundation for a marriage. Obviously it was not what he wanted to hear on the phone and it freaked him out. He says it contributed to him losing it and pushing that touch judge.

'I also didn't know at the time that he had taken this monumental decision to tattoo my name on his stomach as a symbol of his commitment to me and to express to me that he wanted to be with me for life [it was a gesture she would reciprocate with Monty's name]. I also wasn't aware of what he had put himself through before making the decision. But I did know he was not in a good space in Newport in those first six months and he had still not dealt with the probability of his Test career being over. The suspension also came at a time when there had been talk in the media he was going to be picked for the Springboks' 2003 World Cup squad and he figured he would never play for them again. You have to be a team-mate of Monty's or live with him to know what his rugby and the Springboks mean to him, but when I called off the wedding, it was because I was not sure if I could spend the next few years being secondary to his rugby. He and Nicholas had built this amazing bond, but just as it seemed Nicholas had found someone, Monty was away on another trip.

'I was also unhappy with his social crowd because they were more bad than good for him and that also caused friction in our relationship. His response was to blame some of my friends for being disruptive to our relationship and that is how it went, on and off, for the latter part of 2002 and in the early months of 2003, when he was at Newport.

'When I cancelled the wedding, I had not seen him for five months, and even though he came to Cape Town for a few weeks in June while he was suspended from rugby, we didn't resolve much in terms of our relationship. He again left for Newport unhappy and I stayed in Cape Town, resentful that we weren't finding a solution within the relationship or moving on. It was a messy time, emotionally, for both of us. Monty was incredibly down because of what had happened in Newport and very unclear about the future and I knew there was too much going on in his head and as much uncertainty in mine. When I told him that was why I would not commit to a marriage, it made him even angrier. He then went back to Newport and we spoke regularly on the phone, but with neither of us committing to anything.

'I told him that I would be doing a shoot in Costa Rica and Nicholas would be staying with my cousin, Liane, in Durban while I was away. Monty and Liane have a very good vibe and he said he would visit as he wanted to spend some time with Nicholas. Monty had been in Durban for about three days when I left for Costa Rica and he moved in with Liane to look after Nicholas. Apparently it was then that he decided there would be a wedding and he would make it work. While I was away, Liane and Monty arranged for my wedding dress to be sent from Cape Town. He booked the venue at Zimbali, arranged the reception, got the rings and did everything. Liane picked me up at the airport and took me to my dad's apartment. I was jet-lagged, tired and now overwhelmed. I didn't know how to react. A part of me was so excited at the chivalry of Monty and the obvious passion but I still doubted whether it could actually work. Liane, blonde, beautiful and an amazing woman in every way, could easily have been the one getting married she was that excited. She rushed me off to my dad's apartment and gave me my wedding dress. I was getting married!

'Monty had made a decision on the guest list as well. Grant and his wife, Kiara, my best friend Lisa and her partner Neil, Liane, our son Nicholas, Gerry Connor, who sang our wedding song – Josh Groban's 'You're still you' – and Doc Shiela, who married us. That was it.

'What followed was incredible. When I arrived at Zimbali and saw Monty and Nicholas standing next to each other beaming at me, they both looked so handsome and happy and it all seemed right. I thought, "If it works, it works and if it doesn't, it doesn't." I knew I loved him, but I also knew we would have to work through the insecurities both of us had, which were made more intense because of the public profile of our relationship and the constant public intrusions into our private space. I wanted a husband to myself and a father for Nicholas and I didn't want to have to share him with the world all of the time. But none of that mattered when I looked at the two of them standing next to each other. I knew I wanted both of them in my life and that I didn't have the answer as to whether or not it would work, but I had no doubt at that moment that I was willing to give it a go.'

Montgomery credits team-mate Andy Marinos as being an important voice amid the turbulence of 2003 and also significant in him returning to Newport to play out his contract at the Welsh club after his ban.

Marinos helped Monty through a treacherous time when he sought solace in the comforts of family life and personal meaning. Marinos had been a friend to him when he first arrived in Newport in 2002 and by his own admission, it took months to gain the trust of Montgomery who, besides being homesick for Cape Town, was socially introverted by nature and did not easily open up to club mates about the emotional demons he was attempting to conquer.

In his first year at Newport, Montgomery stayed with the Marinos family for a while, settled into a family routine and watched how Andy, his wife Lea-Ann, and the children coped, and he liked what he saw. It gave him a sense of purpose to go home to warmth and to the energy of children. It made him miss his relationship with Nicholas even more and convinced him Tasmin and her son were worth any fight. It also made him accept that if he was staying in Newport then it meant they had to be there and he had to compromise if there was to be any such demand. As for compromise, says Tasmin, there wasn't any. She wanted the sanity of a normal existence, away from prying eyes and she wanted a partner who was going to be a part of their daily life and not someone Nicholas read about in newspapers or saw on TV.

It wasn't quite the house with the white picket fence, says Marinos, but it was pretty close when Montgomery eventually settled on the outskirts of Newport with Tasmin and Nicholas. He could have stayed in a luxury apartment in Cardiff Bay, but he chose a quiet suburb outside Newport and home to the Montgomerys was an understated house in a cul-de-sac with neighbours who remain friends.

Tasmin and Nicholas's daily presence and the birth of his daughter, Taneal, on 9 March 2005, combined to give Montgomery a home environment he had never before experienced. As he admits, his recollection of home is more that of a boarder at SACS than a family life in Namibia, because it is at SACS where he spent the majority of time in his formative years. Perhaps he saw something of himself in Nicholas, and what drove him to give Nicholas love and stability meant Tasmin was only going to get the best of him if she committed to the relationship.

'It was not hard to love Monty,' she says. 'It was working out how to negotiate the demands of his life as a professional sportsman, the media intrusion and all the lies that get told and the nonsense that gets written. We had lived through so much hurt in South Africa because of this unrelenting pressure and I had to be sure we were both equipped to deal with it better in Wales.'

Marinos, respected as a senior player at Newport, says he never lectured Montgomery about a set way of life. All he could do was show him what suburbia and family life was like with a young family.

'Monty was adamant of his love for Tasmin and for Nicholas. I don't think love was ever the issue in the relationship's early years, but he seemed emotionally incapable of dealing with the responsibility of fathering a young boy in a relationship in which two very strong individuals were trying to establish some kind of platform. Both of them were also forced to deal with some serious emotional baggage and their public profile, of him being a Springbok and Taz being a model, only made it harder. He wanted it to work, but I don't think he knew how to make it work.

'I remember him being very involved with family stuff when he stayed at our house. He washed dishes, helped tidy the house and contributed easily to conversation and seemed to enjoy the simplicity of it all and how much focus was on real life issues. There is no pretence about parenting and I think he saw first hand that there was no rule book or right way of doing things. I also think he enjoyed having the children around and the topic of children is something we often spoke about.

'I remember telling him how special my kids were to me and how they dominate your life because you want them to be the priority, and how it doesn't matter whether he played for the Springboks or was famous – all he would ever be for Nicholas and any other children he may have is a dad. That is all they ever saw.

'I told him how I experienced the most powerful realisation of this when I was chosen to start for Wales at centre for the first time. When [Wales coach] Graham Henry called me and told me the news, I got in my car, raced to my son Tristan's school and couldn't wait to tell him. He got into the car and I said I'd be starting for Wales against France. He smiled at me and then beamed as he said he had just been cast as Joseph in the school play. That day I knew what my priorities were and it was about him and not me. I said to Monty that no one can teach you to feel that and he would know it himself in whatever guise it happened.

'He loved that story as much as I loved telling it. I know he adores his children but back then, he needed to understand it was OK to want to go home to that kind of simplicity and with the simplicity of this home life came an improved rugby player and a rejuvenated professional career. Monty, in the initial stages of his Newport career, never played poorly, but once he and Tasmin settled in Newport, he became very good as a player and an exceptional asset to the club, on the field and off it. His performances were consistently good and he excelled at outside centre as much as he did at fullback.'

Marinos says Montgomery earned the respect of the local players with his work ethic, humility and willingness to adapt to the way of Newport.

'In those first few months, they would rag him about the fake tan he was trying to keep among all those pale Welsh legs and arms. They would give him heaps about his hair, but in doing so, it was a sign of acceptance that he was one of them. As for his rugby, there were only ever compliments and he certainly was worth the salary.'

Marinos, in 1999, had played centre for the Stormers when Montgomery was fullback. At Newport, they spent many matches torturing the opposition, in defence as much as on attack. Marinos, as a player, was noted for his defence and he says it was Montgomery's defence that won him the respect of his Welsh club mates.

'Everyone knew what a great rugby player he was when he got here, but obviously, in a new club, the local lads want to see if a foreign import, who comes at a price, will play for the jersey and put his body on the line. He showed them from the beginning that he did not shy away from contact and physically he made an impact. He often won the award for biggest hit of the day and his defence was as much a part of him as his ability to create tries or score points. The Newport boys spoke of Monty with a similar reverence to Gary Teichmann, even if the two played at the club at very different stages of their Test careers.'

As manager of national teams at the South African Rugby Union (Saru), Marinos was as influential in ensuring Montgomery's return from Perpignan to South Africa, in 2008, to play out his career. There were many similarities about Teichmann and Montgomery's respective spells at Newport, but the major difference was Teichmann played out his career in Wales and Montgomery reinvented his.

'I learned what it meant to be a professional in Wales,' says Montgomery. 'I also learned what it means to be a family man, to go home to a family and to *want* to go home to a family. Even though I missed the sunshine of South Africa and playing in front of huge crowds in the Currie Cup and Super 12, my time at Newport will always be very special because of the life changes I made and the people I met. I grew up in Wales and the people of Newport allowed me to do this and they also allowed me, Taz, Nicholas and Taneal to be a family.'

Afternoons and mornings, says Montgomery, were long in the winter and the kicking sessions were lonely when mates and friends were not around.

'Taz and Nicholas would come down to the field when they could and kick balls back for me or just be there running around and doing their own thing. It was so important for me to know they were close by. When Bob Skinstad came over to Newport on a short-term contract, he would come down to the field and kick balls back to me. I would tell them all how much I loved being at Newport, but how I missed playing for the Boks and how much I wanted to play for the Boks again. I remember Bob telling me I would play Test rugby again because my form was too good to ignore and I was too good a player not to make it. He encouraged me to never stop believing in myself and that all the lonely kicking sessions would be rewarded when I played Test rugby again. Bob's always enthusiastic and believes anything is possible and, at the time, I needed to hear those words. I guess I needed others to believe that being a Springbok again was possible and not just my dream. The passion to play for the Boks never went away and it never will.'

Marinos will testify to that and he tells of Montgomery's pain at not being involved with the national side.

'He hadn't been at Newport for long and we were at my house, about to watch the Boks play. The South African anthem was being played and I looked over at Monty and he was tearful. I asked him what was up and he said he couldn't watch because it hurt him too much not being there. I knew that being dropped at the end of 2001 had knocked him but that day, I saw just how much the jersey meant to him. After the anthem was over, he wanted to leave because it hurt too much. I said he owed it to himself to watch every Test involving the Boks while he was in Newport because it would only add to his motivation to get back there and be a part of it one day. "It must hurt, Monty," I said, "and the more it hurts, the more you will want to win back the jersey".'

Marinos says the only other time he saw tears from Montgomery was when the family left Newport to return to South Africa in 2005.

'The people they met, especially neighbour Phil James and his family, remain their close friends,' says Marinos. 'The farewell that day in their cul-de-sac was something no one will ever forget. Everyone was in tears, those staying and those going.'

Marinos believes Montgomery's three years in Newport extended, instead of interrupted, his international career.

'I don't know what would have happened to Monty had he stayed in South Africa in 2002, and not dealt with his relationship issues and continued to drift further away from the national rugby scene. But I don't think we would be celebrating the career of the most capped Test Bok or the relationship he has with his wife and children. I think the three years Monty spent in Wales gave him three more years as a Test player and the chance to win rugby's biggest prize.'

Montgomery agrees, and says his life changed in Newport, even if the obstacles seemed insurmountable in his first year at the club.

'I learned to be at peace with myself. I got my head sorted out and my rugby naturally improved because of it. I redefined my goal-kicking approach and understood the value of my career and the need to be in the best possible emotional shape, otherwise all the physical conditioning in the world was never going to be enough.'

Mike Ruddock and Alan Griffith, head coach and backline coach respectively, added to Montgomery's euphoria at Newport, both embracing the personality and talent of the player. When the duo left to coach Wales, it was never the same again for Montgomery.

'I loved playing under Mike and Alan. They were excellent coaches and they were human beings as well. They had character and I found them inspirational because they thrived on what a player and team could do and not what they necessarily wanted you to do. It was always about the players for them and their motivation came from how the players would benefit. When Chris Anderson arrived, it was clear he didn't have the same compassion or working relationship with players and I thought he didn't have the basic background in rugby union to be effective.'

Anderson, the former Australian Kangaroos rugby league coach and a rugby league World Cup winner, had never coached in rugby union and his appointment was either going to be a spectacular success or a flop. The fact that his one-year contract was never renewed did not surprise Montgomery, who says the league coaching legend was out of his depth.

'Rugby union and rugby league are different codes and they require different skills in players. I never thought he could appreciate that and for me he tried too hard to be one of the boys to ever get my respect. He had a different way of doing things that I don't relate to. I don't get motivated by a coach screaming at me or challenging me with his fists or questioning my toughness as a guy. He did this and it riled me because I felt his tough-guy attitude was an attempt to cover up what he didn't know.

'We had a couple of confrontations and one day I told him to "fuck off" on the field because he didn't know what he was talking about. It is the only time in my career I have ever sworn at or shown disrespect to a coach, but he knew so little about rugby union he had it coming. His response was to want to take me on and "sort it out like a man". He challenged me in front of the other players and not only did I think it was childish, I thought it showed just why he was a failure as a coach at Newport. I just walked away because I wasn't going to get into that kind of nonsense. Maybe it worked like that at the rugby league clubs he coached, but that's not the kind of rugby schooling I ever had. My apprenticeship as a schoolboy came from a Springbok great in HO de Villiers and even when I was a 16-year-old schoolboy, this famous guy treated schoolboy players with dignity and respect. I was not going to take this tough-guy thing from a rugby league coach many years later, no matter how revered he was in that code and especially after the working relationship I had with Mike Ruddock and Alan Griffith.'

Newport had settled Montgomery and revived his career, but from a rugby perspective, it was time to move on. When new Springbok coach Jake White asked Montgomery and Tasmin to meet him at the Marriot Hotel in Cardiff in 2004, she feared the worst and Montgomery expected the best. They were both thinking the same thing, which was that White wanted Montgomery to play for the Boks.

14

WHITE'S KNIGHTS AND LOFTUS LOUTS

Going back to South Africa in 2004 and playing at Newlands against Ireland was bigger than making his Test debut for Percy Montgomery. Back in 1997, when he started for the Springboks against the British & Irish Lions in Durban, he did not believe he could fail. He was a youngster, who couldn't even believe he was a Springbok. Just being there was a success story for Montgomery and he admits he played his first Test on adrenalin. Not too much thought went into the magnitude of the occasion because testosterone and tenacity made a good enough cocktail to survive the examination of the experienced Lions midfield of Scott Gibbs and Jeremy Guscott.

Seven years and 50 Tests later, the pressure was different because it came from within. Montgomery had lusted after a 51st Test cap for three years while reinventing himself in Newport, Wales. He had played 36 times for Newport, served a six-month suspension, watched enough agonising Bok defeats on TV, got married and settled down.

New Springbok coach Jake White had selected him as one of two foreign-based players, the other being flyhalf Jaco van der Westhuyzen, who was playing for the Leicester Tigers.

Montgomery's form had been good for Newport, but in his final match of the season, in Ireland against Leinster, he had fractured his left hand and arrived in South Africa unable to play in the first Test against Ireland in Bloemfontein. White was criticised for investing in Montgomery, but the coach was defiant in his defence and generous in his praise of a player who would prove so influential for White in the next four years.

'Not enough South Africans appreciate how good this guy is,' White told me at the time. 'He has played 50 Tests in four different positions and he has won a Tri-Nations and played in a World Cup. He is also a better player now than when he left South Africa in 2002 and I need the likes of Percy Montgomery to be playing well if we are to become dominant and win the World Cup in 2007. I know how good he is and that is why I brought him back. Ideally, I want him playing his provincial rugby in South Africa, but if he doesn't, I will still pick him.'

Montgomery would eventually return a season later to the Sharks, but in 2004 he went from playing for Newport to playing for the Boks and back to playing for Newport. The schedule was demanding, but nothing compared to the emotional intensity of that first Test back.

'Jake did not want me playing with an injury on my return and did not want to risk me underperforming in Bloemfontein because the pressure there was on him for bringing me back,' says Montgomery. 'He wanted me in a good head space and confident in my ability. He also thought that playing at Newlands would be the ideal reintroduction to Bok rugby for me. It was the ground at which I had played most of my professional rugby and it was as good as home. The supporters at Newlands had always been good to me and he felt all those secondary factors would help settle

From top to bottom: I really love to hunt. Here I am with my son Nicholas on his first hunting trip; I've also been hunting with the Cronjé brothers – Jacques and Geo, and Bok video technician Willie Maree; another one of my trophies.

Clockwise from left: I'm a really big fan of Leon Schuster's music; Tasmin and I with my best friend Grant Hinckley and his wife Kiara; my sister Haley and I; having a festive lunch at my neighbour Phil James's house in Newport.

Clockwise from left: Taz and I early on in our relationship; getting to grips with Taz's pregnancy; spending time with Taz's parents, Craig and Maureen; Taz, Nicholas and my parents.

This page: I wore a white suit and snakeskin sandles to our wedding at Zimbali. *Opposite page:* Flying back to South Africa from Newport in 2005; Taneal and I with my folks.

This page: Taz and I on holiday in Mauritius; on the beach at Camps Bay, Cape Town. *Opposite page:* Nicholas and I share the same birthday (15 March) and on this one we were given surfboards.

RUSTY

Opposite page: Newport Stadium is covered in snow; braving the weather before training. *This page:* Playing for Newport; running the dunes during pre-season training – the toughest, and best, I've ever experienced.

Scottish Amicable

Opposite page: In the Barbarians change room with Joost van der Westhuizen, Jonah Lomu and Friedrich Lombard; having a Guinness or two with Tim Horan, Pita Alatini and Ofisa Tonu'u. *This page:* With Alatini, Christian Cullen and the Big Fella; in the Baa Baas bus with Thomas Castaignède, Alatini, Mark Robinson, Christophe Dominici *(back row)* and Liam Botham and Pieter Müller *(front row)*.

August 2004

Dear Monty,

Today your experience will be seen by all. Enjoy the moment. Talk on defence help the players around you. Run hard, maybe today the world will see what I believe you are a Springbok Legend

Best wishes

Jake.

This page: A special letter from Bok coach Jake White during the 2004 Test season; my first Test in three years was celebrated with Nicholas at Newlands.
Opposite page: With this penalty kick against the Pacific Islands I surpassed Naas Botha as the Springboks' leading point-scorer; with the Bok mascot after being named Man of the Match.

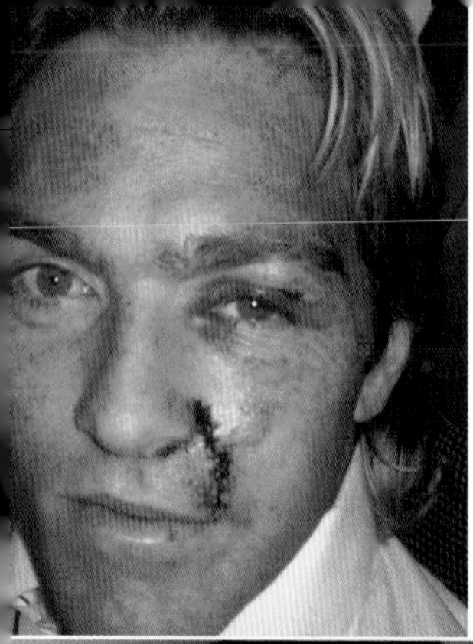

The pain and the passion of the Tri-Nations. I got this cut after getting an accidental boot to the face from Matt Giteau in 2005, but I looked a lot better in 2004 when we won the Tri-Nations after beating Australia in Durban.

whatever nerves there might be. However, I don't think he realised just how nervous I was and it rates as the biggest Test I played in because of the pressure I put on myself to succeed. I did not want to let myself down and I certainly did not want to disappoint Jake. He had been bold in bringing me back and talking me up and I simply had to reward him with a quality performance.'

Ireland – arguably the best of the Six Nations teams in 2004 even though France won the title – were hammered 31-17 in Bloemfontein, but their captain, Brian O'Driscoll, spoke of Newlands being similar to Lansdowne Road in Dublin and the visitors were confident of squaring the series 1-1.

'I'd played against most of those guys in the Celtic League and I knew they had underperformed in Bloemfontein,' recalls Montgomery. 'O'Driscoll is a class player and I felt their pack would present a greater contest because of the playing conditions at Newlands. But I was more worried about delivering for Jake and the team than I was about how good the opposition could be. We were a young side and I was one of the most senior guys. That week I tried to instil in the boys the need for each player to set his own standard as this would be a sign of respect for what Ireland had done in the Six Nations and the threat they posed. The win in Bloemfontein had been good, but Ireland were always going to be better in Cape Town and mentally, if we were not switched on, we would get beaten.

'I also had to settle my own nerves during the week. Being back in Cape Town was huge for me. I loved being in my city again and the familiarity of everything, and I was desperate to do well. There is no better experience for me than playing Test rugby at Newlands and this was shaping up to be the biggest game of my Test career.

'When I got my 51st Test jersey, it felt like I had never had one before. It was huge to know I was back again and that the challenges of the last three years had been overcome. I remembered the lonely times on my last tour with the

Boks and the desperation I felt in that first year at Newport because I was no longer a Bok. I remembered the heartache of watching the Boks on TV and not being a part of it. In my first 50 Tests, I had never taken one of them for granted and I had never assumed I would be there for the next one. But not taking it for granted and not being there are different things. I had always felt I appreciated the privilege of playing for the Boks, but I learned what appreciation meant when I was not there. I had made my 50th Test appearance as a replacement wing against Italy, but that was not how I wanted to get to that milestone because I did not contribute anything to the Test. It felt like a handout and I don't believe anyone has the right to a free minute of Test rugby. Each minute has to be earned and on that 2001 Bok end-of-year tour, I felt like a spare wheel. I always hoped my last memory of being a Springbok would not be that of a player feeling he wasn't wanted or needed.

'In Cape Town, before facing Ireland, it all felt right again. I had earned my selection and I was determined to prove Jake right. When we had met in Cardiff earlier in 2004, I said I could make a big impact on the squad, but that I also had to be managed if I was going to make it to the World Cup in 2007. I did not want special treatment, but I wanted to be treated as an adult in the team environment and I wanted to be given the opportunity to be a leader. My game thrives on communication and I wanted reassurance that the environment would allow for me to talk without the management thinking I was full of myself or bigger than the team. I also wanted to play a big part in ensuring the Bok traditions were upheld and that players coming into the squad were educated about the privilege and tradition that goes with being a Bok. Jake said the success of the World Cup campaign would be in how the senior players responded to the pressure of leading and that if there were to be any restrictions then he shouldn't have picked me. He was insistent that the safeguarding of tradition was not up for debate and he was pleased I felt so strongly about it. But most importantly, he told me to go out and show South Africa through my performance how I had matured in Wales. And I did that in a Test that will always be among my most memorable because of what it symbolised for me. It showed that if you want something badly enough, you can get there and that there is always hope in moments of despair. When I left Cape Town to go to Newport at the end of 2002, I was suffering emotionally and I was an angry person. To be back two years later at the rugby ground I love the most, playing in front of the fans closest to me, was incredible. In the next four years, there would be more memorable and bigger games, but none as significant to me as our 26-17 win against Ireland at Newlands on 19 June 2004.'

Montgomery kicked two conversions and four penalties in an afternoon in which he missed just one penalty attempt. White was beaming at Montgomery's performance, but as the coach and player would discover a few weeks later, it would take more than a match-winning performance against Ireland to convince the Loftus crowd in Pretoria that Montgomery was a Springbok with soul and substance.

The Springboks, in Harry Viljoen's first home Test in 2001, had lost to France at Ellis Park and afterwards, the players were making their way to a Bok team bus decorated with images of the squad. Two Bok supporters, dressed in Bok jerseys, were pissing against the bus, aiming specifically at Montgomery's photo while the player, along with team-mates, looked on. Once they had urinated against the bus, they then abused Montgomery as he got onto it. Some players wanted to beat the crap out of the two but Montgomery did not even respond to the taunts.

Montgomery was disgusted, not so much at the actions of the two, but that they called themselves Bok supporters. He had been used to abuse at Ellis Park in Johannesburg and Loftus Versfeld in Pretoria when representing the Cape-based Stormers and Western Province, but he could never understand the lack of loyalty to the Bok jersey and the refusal to support any player wearing it.

'Our rugby is very provincial and there are positives to that, but the negative seems to be when people can't look past the provincial identity of a player in a Test match. You've got 15 South Africans out there playing for the Springboks and supposedly in a home Test, you have supporters wanting the Boks to win. But I never felt that at Loftus in a decade of Test rugby. The supporters there have always been on my case and it has soured my experience of playing at what is one of the best grounds in the world. It is a goal kicker's dream and the facilities are first class, but the support for the team is erratic and in my case it has pretty much been non-existent.'

Montgomery's worst experience at the ground has been the jeering of his name when the teams have been announced to the crowd. He has often been booed during the game and in 1999 against the All Blacks, he took an inordinate amount of abuse from the crowd during the game, which his Bok team-mates afterwards described as disgraceful.

'You dismiss it as a player but it hurts,' says Montgomery. 'You are playing a home Test and your own people are booing you and then you go out and indirectly play for these people and your performance influences how their evening is going to be. I've never gotten the resentment they feel towards me and I don't buy the stuff about peroxide hair and white boots. Many of the players up north have dyed their hair and in the last 10 years, I've seen all sorts of colour boots on players at Ellis Park and Loftus. I guess I have been stereotyped as a *soutie* from Cape Town's southern suburbs when in fact, there has always been a very strong Afrikaans presence in my life through my father.'

Nick Mallett felt that during his time, Montgomery may have fuelled the dislike by refusing to conform to the norm when playing a Test up north. 'It didn't bother me what hairstyles the players wore or the colour of their boots. I was interested in how they played and influenced the match, but there were occasions when I spoke to Monty and said he wasn't making it easy for himself,' says the former Bok coach. 'I knew what kind of abuse he got because of this perception that he was a spoiled English kid from a private Cape Town school. When I coached the Boks, I used to get a vulgar mouthful most times when we played a Test in Bloemfontein, Johannesburg or Pretoria, but I knew how it could negatively impact on a young player. Monty was very unfairly made the scapegoat regardless of any Bok performance. I would urge him not to give the crowd ammunition but he would say he wasn't going to change who he was to please people. In his mind, all that should have mattered was that he was putting his body on the line for the Springboks.'

Montgomery says when he first made the national squad, James Small encouraged him to not be afraid to wear his heart on his sleeve and to be true to his own identity.

'James was a free spirit and asked only to be judged by how he played his rugby. I liked that in him and that has been my attitude throughout my career. If I am not playing well, I will be the first to admit it, but I also know when I have done my job and helped the Boks win Tests. I wasn't going to try and be something for the people in Cape Town and another thing for those who watched our games in the north. And if I made mistakes as a youngster then it was part of growing up, but I never wore white boots to irritate supporters and I certainly didn't plan what hairstyle or what colour it was going to be whenever I played at Ellis Park or Loftus. I can tell you if I had worn black boots and had black hair they would still have got on my case. At least that's my experience of playing Test rugby at Loftus.'

The vitriol against Montgomery can't be based on performance for the Boks. In 10 Tests at Loftus, he has only ever lost twice, against the All Blacks. He has scored 105 points despite only being the goal kicker in six of the

10 Tests and scored 31 points against Wales in 1998 after a year earlier scoring two brilliant tries against Australia in the Boks' 61-22 win. Yet the cursing has never stopped and it disgusts Bok captain John Smit, who, despite his strong Pretoria background of playing for the Pretoria Boys' High 1st XV and the Blue Bulls Craven Week team, has also taken a verbal beating when captaining the Springboks.

'If they want to have a go at me, then fine, but when there is so little respect shown for a guy who has done so much for South African rugby then it is not on,' says Smit. 'Monty holds nearly every Springbok record there is but I felt embarrassed to witness the kind of abuse he got during the England Test in 2007. He had been courageous under the high ball and kicked brilliantly all day. Yet when he was given a rest with 10 minutes to go and we had just gone past 50 against England, South African supporters close to the subs bench just wouldn't let up. Their spite was despicable and sadly the action of this minority overshadows the goodwill of others at the ground.'

White says he often debated whether to rest Montgomery for the Loftus internationals during his tenure as national coach, but too often, the quality of the opposition did not allow it.

'You want to put your best team out whenever possible, and in the context of our side between 2004 and 2007, he was the best option at fullback. I always found it ironic how well he played at Loftus, despite the uncontrollable elements within the crowd, and in my time, I can only recall him ever playing one poor Test, against the All Blacks in 2006. I subbed him because he was not playing well that day and was physically drained after three years of back-to-back northern- and southern-hemisphere rugby. Monty even came to me afterwards and thanked me for recognising it was not his day and sparing him even more abuse.'

Montgomery remembers the match and speaking to White afterwards about being replaced mid-match.

'He promised me in Cardiff in 2004 that he would manage me and that match was one example of it. Jake got the best out of me as a coach because he believed in my ability, but he was not blind to times when I struggled, and that day at Loftus, I struggled. But I take comfort from the eight wins in 10 in which I know I played a part.'

Montgomery, within two matches of being back in South Africa in 2004, had been reminded what he disliked about South African rugby, but more importantly, what he had missed.

'For me, it doesn't get better than being a Bok in a Test at Newlands, but I'll take the abuse at Loftus or Ellis Park any day if it means I am getting a chance to represent South Africa. I will never deny how much it hurts when my home crowd gets stuck into me, but ironically, I have good memories of the rugby at Loftus.'

In 2004, Montgomery would also have great memories of playing in Durban because it is where the Boks would triumph in the Tri-Nations, with White singling out his goal kicking as the difference between coming first and second.

The small town of Gosford, outside of Brisbane, would also be significant for Montgomery.

15

SCRAMBLING DEFENCE, WHITE ARM BANDS AND NAPPIES

On the eve of their first Test against Ireland in Bloemfontein, in 2004, Jake White asked his Springbok squad if they believed they could beat England at Twickenham later that year. When they said yes, he wanted to know why anyone could then believe they could lose to Ireland in Bloemfontein.

White also tells the story of not being able to coach a team to scramble on defence. Players, he said, chose to scramble, and in sides where players cared about each other, you usually found scrambling defence and players who refused to be beaten. White had worked with 1995 World Cup-winning Bok coach Kitch Christie, whose team ethos was based on that of a close family. Christie also taught White that being a good selector is as important as being a good coach. He said there is no such thing as the right selection, but there is such a thing as the right selection for what a coach envisages to be the right way. In rugby, it is said, you can assess the closeness and bond of players in the way they defend and this is why White knew what he had in these Springboks after their impressive win against Ireland in Bloemfontein.

'When Bakkies Botha turns, chases back and makes a brilliant try-saving tackle after one of his team-mates has missed a tackle, you know you have something special in a player,' says White. 'When the others are doing the same thing, you quickly accept you've managed to identify a very fine bunch of rugby players. I knew when we beat Ireland 2-0 in that series that we were onto something as a squad. We had a wonderful mixture of experience and youth and we had what I believed to be some of the finest talent in Bok history.

'I had identified what I felt was the right captain in John Smit and there was immediate recognition of his leadership from the players. Smitty also cared about the players. Part of his appeal as a leader was that he was motivated by what was good for the team and not what was comfortable for him or any individual. It was important to surround Smitty with senior players who were loyal to the Bok jersey and that was why Monty would be so significant to the evolution of the squad.'

Montgomery, who had last played in South Africa in 2002, was immediately struck by Smit's presence as a leader and also by the unity within the squad.

'I wasn't at the 2003 World Cup and when I got to Bloem for the Bok warm-up camp at the end of May 2004, it was obvious that no one was looking backwards. This was a new era, with a new coach, captain and squad. Jake spoke of tradition and respect for the Bok jersey. He made sure every player knew that the jersey was on loan and no one owned it. I liked that because I have always felt that way about playing for the Springboks. It is a privilege and not a right and you have to earn every Test cap. Smitty also wanted to move on from the 2003 World Cup experience [the Boks lost 29-9 to the All Blacks in their quarter-final]. Both him and Jake were clear that the squad was about to start a four-year journey, but that part of the journey was about restoring Bok pride. The Boks were ranked No 6 in the world and had taken some beatings on the field and off it. It was up to us to take the team back to No 1 and everyone felt they were lucky to be involved in such a challenge. Jake told the squad in Bloem that in an ideal world everyone would be in Paris in 2007, but more realistically, the goal had to be that the core of that first squad made it through to 2007. We could only do this if we were winning and clicking as a team. I have always been big on the family thing in a team context and so is Smitty, so from the beginning we created a mood in which friendship within the team environment was encouraged and one in which guys played for each other. It was also the first time I'd played in a team with Schalk Burger and his energy on the field was incredible. He does the job of two players and I don't think Ireland had experienced that kind of intensity from one player. Schalk was magnificent in that series and his urgency and work rate were an inspiration for the rest of the team.

'In 2002, I'd left South Africa feeling so down, but to come back and be a part of something so new and exciting was a great feeling. I also knew exactly what was required of me and there was an instant recognition within the team from the younger guys for what I had achieved as a Springbok. To me that was important because it showed they respected what had gone before them and it certainly helped having a Bok coach who emphasised the importance of tradition. I believe you can only achieve something if you are aware of the history that goes with it. It wasn't that the guys showed me respect, but that they showed respect to the 50 Test caps I had. I came from a Bok era where few players, no matter how good they were, made it past 50. The high turnover of Bok coaches had a lot to do with that, but my experience of South African rugby before I left for Wales was that the coaches, media, public and administration often "retired" a player at 25 years old and looked at someone younger. There wasn't much emphasis on experience and there were many Boks who left South Africa feeling disillusioned and unwanted. They played good rugby in Europe for another two or three years when they were still good enough to play for the Boks. Jake was big on experience but he was also prepared to pick any youngster he thought was good enough for Test rugby. He showed that in 2004 with Schalk and in 2006 with Frans Steyn.'

If the rugby environment excited Montgomery, what dulled the senses was the on-going issue of national contracts. When he had left for Wales, he'd cited financial security as the most powerful influence. Back then, he believed in a fixed national contract, if you were good enough to be in the Springbok squad, and a long-term contract if the coach trusted a player's ability to last three years at that level. In 2002, Bok coach Rudolf Straeuli initially refused to commit to a national contracting system and it expedited Montgomery's signing for Newport. Now the Boks were in a similar position, with some of the players guaranteed security on existing contracts and others told they would be rewarded only by match fees.

The situation was not ideal with White trying to build a family unit, but not being able to treat all the players as equals in terms of contracting. Smit, supported by the senior players, took up the fight with the South African Rugby Players Association (Sarpa). What followed was weeks of intense negotiation between Sarpa and SA Rugby, the professional arm of Saru. Smit, in South Africa, had initiated meetings with Sarpa to explain the Bok squad's position. This was a player fight and Smit kept White and fellow management out of the meetings.

The team left for a historic one-off Test against the Pacific Islands (a team made up of the best players from Fiji, Samoa and Tonga) in Gosford, Australia, followed by the standard Tri-Nations commitments in New Zealand and Australia.

However, the contract issue did not go away, and Smit continued to fight the players' cause, through e-mails and phone calls.

'It was a very testing time, but it was also very necessary that we stood together as a unit,' recalls Smit. 'Some of us were guaranteed contracts, but you can't expect every player to put his body on the line when he is thinking, "Hang on a second, I am not deemed an asset but the other guy is". We couldn't have division in the squad because of money and contracts and if this was going to be a journey to the World Cup, the players had to trust each other and know we were all backing each other. It was also very important that the younger and newer players saw that the senior players were prepared to fight for the rights of the entire squad.'

Montgomery's reflection on the Pacific Islands Test match is more about the stand the team took on the national contracting issue than the 38-24 victory and the penalty kick which took him past Naas Botha's Springbok record of 312 points in Test rugby.

'We needed to make a statement, but in a non-threatening way because fighting the administrators was going to resolve nothing. Smitty was very particular about the players keeping their focus on the match and he also made a point that if we did not play well and lost it was hard to make financial demands, no matter how realistic we believed them to be. [Bok loose forward] AJ Venter had the job of going out to buy the white tape that we would wear as armbands. The most difficult thing was hiding it from the coaches and management because we couldn't put it on until just before kickoff.

'Smitty had handed Jake an envelope and told him only to open it once he was in the coach's box. In it was a letter explaining what statement we were making and that it was necessary that the players stood together as one. He also wrote that it was not a management issue and it was something the players would sort out themselves.'

The media reported afterwards that the white armbands were in memory of someone who had passed away, but Montgomery and Smit say the players would have worn black ones if that had been the case.

'It was a statement made by players expected to win Tests for South Africa to the SA Rugby administration that we were a team and not a bunch of individuals in which some had it easier than others,' says Smit. 'But we had to walk the walk and that meant winning. It was a long road and winning the Tri-Nations helped with getting a resolution. We eventually found the common ground on contracts that was necessary in order for the squad to be united in our World Cup challenge.'

Montgomery believes the wearing of the white armbands was significant in pulling the players together and growing the trust and belief in each other. His record-breaking kick was secondary.

'We won and I went past Naas's record, but it was a night when the team stood up for each other. We showed we were all in this together, and that meant more to our World Cup aspirations in 2007 than an individual record. Having played in some very good teams and in ones that have struggled, I could sense something very good was coming together with this Bok squad.'

South Africa were narrowly beaten in both of their away Tri-Nations matches. They lost 23-21 after a try from All Blacks wing Doug Howlett in the last movement of the game in Christchurch. A week later, a late try from former SA U21 captain Clyde Rathbone gave the Wallabies a 30-26 win in Perth. But the Boks would not lose again in the Tri-Nations, crushing the All Blacks 40-26 at Ellis Park and seeing off the Wallabies 23-19 in Durban. That left all three teams with two wins each, but the Boks' two bonus points achieved overseas gave them the title.

Montgomery's goal kicking was pivotal to the Boks' success, especially in Christchurch where he kicked three touchline conversions to ensure the bonus point, and he also kicked well in Perth. But according to White, it was his penalty kick against the Wallabies in Durban, in the last act of the first half, that was the most telling [the Boks trailed 7-3 at the break].

'We weren't in the game in the first 40 minutes, but somehow we had managed to limit the damage to just one converted try. Monty's kick, from 40m and into the wind, changed the flow of the game and the mood in our change room was one of hope and not the despair of the 39 previous minutes. We played fantastic rugby in the first 20 minutes of the second half and this was where we won the game and the tournament.'

Smit and Montgomery agree that the Boks were good enough to win all four of their Tri-Nations matches, but too many in the squad lacked the conviction to believe the All Blacks could be beaten in New Zealand.

'It was only when we pushed the All Blacks so close in Christchurch and led for 79 minutes that the guys actually looked at each other and knew it was possible,' says Smit. 'Jake was very good in speaking to the players after that defeat. He told them to feel disappointed but also very proud because we had shown how good we were physically. We proved we could score tries by outscoring them by three to one. Once we accepted how good we were, no one would beat us. It was a turning point in the mindset when playing the All Blacks, but it was helped by the fact that it was a quality Bok team with the potential to be even better the more we played together and the more experienced we became.'

However, Montgomery describes the 22-16 win against the All Blacks at Newlands in 2005 as even more satisfying than the win against them at Ellis Park in 2004.

'To score 40 points was a huge achievement, but there was a lot of talk that they had injuries and that many of their players were either on their way out or stop-gaps for better players not available for the game. You only play who is in front of you, and that was our approach. On the day, they were considered the best 15 players in New Zealand and not many teams have scored 40 points against the All Blacks. You take any win against them but when they beat France [45-6] in Paris at the end of the year there were 10 changes to the team that lost to us. So as a player I took more from beating their strongest team a year later. They'd beaten everyone in Europe easily in 2004 and smashed the Lions 3-0 in the 2005 Test series. All of their top guys played in Cape Town. We knew this would be a defining match for us and for them in the build-up to the World Cup.'

The Boks, having blown their Grand Slam tour of 2004 – by controversially losing 17-12 to Ireland and 32-16 to England at Twickenham – had to prove the 2004 Tri-Nations success was not a once-off. Beating a New Zealand team described in the British media as the best ever, was one way of doing this.

In between the wins against the All Blacks in 2004 and 2005, Montgomery had experienced the most incredible rugby high in South Africa. But he had again wondered if there would ever be acceptance of his personality from the South African media.

Tasmin tells of the hurt her husband felt after reading an article, supposedly written by himself, in the popular weekly magazine *You* and its Afrikaans sister publication *Huisgenoot*, which has a total readership of four million. In the article, 'Montgomery' apologised to the South African public for who he was and said he was a misunderstood individual. It was in poor taste and a weak attempt at satire. Tasmin says Monty was initially furious when he read the piece and then just felt hurt. The two were at Sun City for the weekend when he read it and she says he couldn't handle the insult, especially after coming back to South Africa to play for the Boks in 2004 and playing as well as he had done.

'He felt that he could never win in South Africa and that no matter what he did or how well he played he was always the target of insulting media that got very personal,' says Tasmin. 'He was always such a private person and the media perception was so wrong, but it didn't stop them from writing what they wanted about him. It was something that never happened to him or us as a couple or family in Wales and that was one of the things he loved about playing his rugby over there.

'The article made him so depressed that he just wanted to spend the day in the room on his own. But that was the day I wanted to tell him I was pregnant and I didn't quite know how to break the news to him given his state of mind. He was so disillusioned and hurt and asked me over and over what satisfaction people could get from hurting us, and him in particular, like this. He'd never harmed anyone in his life and he couldn't accept how people actually enjoyed ridiculing someone else and got pleasure at their expense. I told him to forget about it, that we would be back in Wales soon and that he had plenty to be happy about.

'I arranged a special lunch for him of champagne and sushi at a private venue that afternoon at Sun City. When we walked into the room, he asked who the champagne was for. I said it was for us and that I wanted him to tell me what made him happy and what made life worthwhile. He spoke of his love for me, Nicholas, his family, his friends and the Boks. He said he was fortunate to be living his dream of playing rugby and that he was blessed because of his health.

'When he was finished, I gave him what looked like an ice-cream stick with a mark on it. He asked me what it was and I said the mark would soon be his child because I'd done a pregnancy test and the mark showed it was positive. His mood changed immediately and he just beamed. He has always been a wonderful father to Nicholas and always treated him as his own, but this was our first child together and it was something he always wanted. It made our return to Wales even more exciting, although selfishly, I would have wanted to be close to my family in South Africa during the pregnancy and especially the birth.'

Taneal Montgomery was born at the Royal Gwent Hospital in Abergavenny on 9 March 2005 and Montgomery was at his wife's side throughout the birth.

'I couldn't believe what pain Taz went through,' recalls Montgomery. 'And all I could do was hold her hand, tell her I love her and encourage her. I felt powerless because there was nothing I could do to make it easier, but it was the most unbelievable moment when Taneal was born.'

In November, the Boks beat Wales 33-16 in Cardiff. Montgomery scored a try and played brilliantly, but he says his biggest victory in Wales was cementing his partnership with Tasmin and seeing his daughter born.

'Taneal will always be my reminder of how good my time in Wales was, what a lifesaver my move to Wales was and how much I grew as a person during that period,' says Montgomery. 'But having gone back to South Africa to play for the Boks in 2004 and then going back to Newport, I knew that I wanted to be playing my domestic rugby in South Africa. Jake was delighted that I wanted to return and I knew Tasmin would love being close to her family again. I felt I had done my rugby time in Wales, gained invaluably from the experience and had given a lot to the younger players at the club. But I am South African and I wanted to help turn South African players into Springboks. I also wanted the thrill of playing in front of big crowds every weekend and not just in Tests. I missed the Currie Cup and Super Rugby and despite all the nonsense that was written about me in the media, I missed South Africa. I am South African and I will never be anything else. I knew I'd eventually end up in Cape Town, which is the city that will always be my home. I just didn't know when I'd get back there permanently.'

Fittingly, Montgomery experienced one of his most memorable Tests in Cape Town when the Boks beat the All Blacks in 2005. The Boks had not done this at Newlands since 1976 and White played on this sentiment in the build-up to the match. He asked former Springbok captain and 1995 World Cup manager, Morné du Plessis, to present the players with their jerseys and to give them a motivational speech. Du Plessis is revered by the modern Boks and Montgomery described his presence in the team room as being very powerful.

'The players have so much respect for him. He was a great captain and leader and if you go anywhere in world rugby, Morné commands respect. He is part of the Springbok tradition and he spoke about the jersey and the responsibility each player has when he wears it. But he also spoke about the supporters we have in South Africa and how lucky we are to have people who are so passionate about their rugby and so loyal to their team. He said that, win or lose, they would be back to support us the next week and he knew we were good enough to beat the All Blacks if we believed it and played to our ability. His speech was motivational but he also spoke about what it would take in rugby terms to beat New Zealand, which was cool heads and physicality in everything we did. That day was huge. Jean de Villiers got an intercept try, I kicked some points and then we just tackled and tackled.'

The All Blacks that day made 18 linebreaks to the two of the Springboks, but each side could only score one try and All Blacks flyhalf Dan Carter, who had been sensational in the series win against the Lions, struggled with the pressure and intensity of the Boks.

'Dan is an amazing rugby player and I have never seen a guy control a series like he did against the Lions, but no player is as good if he is going backwards and if he is constantly being put under pressure,' says Montgomery. 'We knew that to have any chance of beating the All Blacks, we had to be in their faces from the first minute and that we couldn't let up because they are capable of scoring two tries in two minutes. That day we did it from the first minute to the 80th and it ranks as one of the highlights of my career. I have been part of some big Bok wins. Obviously the World Cup win in 2007 and the win against the All Blacks in Dunedin in 2008 were massive, but beating New Zealand in Cape Town in 2005, will always be a big one in my book.'

However, Montgomery's season would end poorly when the Boks lost 26-20 to France in Paris. He fluffed his first three penalty kicks and looked like a man in need of a rest from rugby and perhaps even nappy duties.

'It had been such a big year on every level. I loved having a daughter but it also stressed me out being away from home so much that year because, in my absence, Tasmin was bearing the brunt of everything. We had moved back to South Africa from Wales, I was away for the Tri-Nations, the rugby was non-stop and there was the pressure of trying to balance the rugby with fatherhood. If I loved being in Paris in 1997 and 2007, being there in 2005 was probably a Test too many for me. So much had happened, on and off the rugby field that year, and by the time we got to Paris, I just wanted to be at home with Tasmin, Nicholas and Taneal, doing my bit as a husband and father.

'Jake told the players in the change room after the defeat that we would be back at the same venue in 2007 at roughly the same time and the only difference was that those players who were there would be standing around the Webb Ellis Cup they'd just won. He then asked each player to think hard about whether he was going to be one of those victorious players. That was his challenge to us. "Think about that this Christmas," he said.

'I knew I wanted to be in Paris in 2007 and that I could help the Boks to win the World Cup, but right at that moment I also knew I wanted to be on a plane back to South Africa. I was needed more at home and I wanted to be at home, even if it just meant changing nappies.'

16

SCRAPING THE BOTTOM OF THE BARREL IN BRISBANE

Os du Randt, John Smit, CJ van der Linde, Victor Matfield, Danie Rossouw, Juan Smith, Jaque Fourie, Bryan Habana and Percy Montgomery were colossal for the Boks on 20 October 2007 in the World Cup final against England in Paris. So how did these giants crash so spectacularly to the Wallabies in Brisbane 15 months before that famous night in France?

Montgomery does not have the answer. He says it would be easy to blame the uncertainty around Springbok coach Jake White's future at the time, especially after there were media reports that White would be fired before the end of 2006. In the Test before the Brisbane blowout, the Boks lost at home for the first time since 2003 and White was publicly fighting his employers at the South African Rugby Union (Saru) on issues of selection, transformation and salary. The Bok coach had entertained an approach from England and was seeking an extension of his Bok contract beyond the 2007 World Cup. When the Boks got on the plane for Brisbane, White and the Saru hierarchy were not speaking.

Montgomery, the most senior Springbok in the squad, says the players were aware of the politics at play with White and of the infighting between the game's administration and the head coach, but that was not the reason the Boks failed to score a point for only the second time in Tests en route to their worst defeat against Australia and their second-worst Test defeat (53-3 against England at Twickenham, in 2002, remained the worst).

Flank Schalk Burger's absence because of injury was a factor and so was jet lag, but the combination was not worth 49 points. Montgomery says the players simply did not pitch up for the game and while he doesn't speak on behalf of any of the other players, he says he was mentally drained and that he should not even have been on the tour.

'I put my body on the line that night and was physically committed, but mentally my mind was back in South Africa. I had gone non-stop for two years in both hemispheres, my family had relocated to Durban from Newport and I was away from home more than I was at home. My home life was taking strain because of the travel as I had been with the Boks for three months in 2004, gone back to Newport after the Tri-Nations, linked up with the Boks again for the end-of-year tour and then played out my contract with Newport until May 2005. Then it started over again internationally, there were my Currie Cup obligations with the Sharks, the end-of-year Springbok tour and straight into preparations for the 2006 Super 14 with the Sharks. Then came the home Tests and that Tri-Nations night in Brisbane.

'I know that I was not mentally right for the tour. Physically I felt OK but emotionally I was gone. I wanted to be at home with Tasmin, who was again playing the role of single mother in my absence, but this time to a young boy and a two-year-old girl. Anyone with young kids will know what we went through as a couple and the pressure of parenting a young child was exhausting on the relationship, especially with me being away so much. Tasmin and I were taking strain. Looking back it was obvious that she saw a repeat of how it had been before I left South Africa for Wales in 2002, when rugby consumed my life and I was near burnout. We were not in a good space when I left and the situation was aggravated by the 36-26 defeat against France at Newlands and the negativity around the team. She could see I was mentally finished and in the build-up to the Test in Brisbane we never spoke telephonically. It freaked me out and I couldn't cope with the lack of communication. Physically, I felt strong for the Test, but the mental strength just wasn't there. I don't know why the other guys didn't perform, but I know I was not in the right frame of mind to be playing Test rugby that night.'

Montgomery says that while the Springboks were very bad, the Wallabies were very good. Australia had been hammered by the All Blacks a week before and needed a decent performance to stay alive in the competition. They produced something closer to spectacular than decent.

'They were really aggressive in the tackle and clinical with the ball. Pierre Spies had joined us from the U21 World Championship where he was named Player of the Tournament and Jake started him at No 8. Early in the game he fielded a high ball and I was running a support line off him. The Wallabies players were charging at him and screaming "fuck him up". They absolutely smashed him and that set the tone for the night. I think the next two times Pierre got under a high ball he kicked it back, and that was the story of our night. We gave away possession, were physically dominated, created nothing, fell off tackles and just kept on getting pounded.

'I had never been in such a position in a Springbok jersey before. I didn't have a kick at posts all night and each time I looked up at the scoreboard I couldn't believe what I was seeing. Smitty [John Smit] was doing everything he could to get something from the players, but there was just nothing. Everyone listened, but no one reacted.'

Smit created the only Bok try-scoring opportunity in the match, breaking a few tackles before offloading to Montgomery, who was held up on the line. The movement, in the 49th minute, came with Australia leading 30-0.

Publicly, White questioned Paul Honiss's application of the tackle law, but the referee was not the one who missed 22 tackles in the first half an hour of the match.

'It was ugly,' says Montgomery. 'We were 30 points down at half-time and in shock. Jake was very calm in the change room and told us we had to go out there and salvage pride. The first thing was to try and win the second half and if we did that, it would be an improvement on the first 40 minutes. Jake's strength in the change room was that he never panicked, or if he did, he never let on to the players that he was concerned. He summarised where we were getting beaten and told us what he wanted to see from us in that second half. He then raised his voice and urged us to protect what we had built up in the last three years. He challenged the senior players to take charge as they had done on so many occasions. The truth of the matter is that as the most senior player, my mind was not in Brisbane. We were too far gone and no amount of composure, positive thinking or common sense was going to turn around a 30-point deficit against the Wallabies in Australia.'

The home side added 19 points in the second half and Montgomery says the mood in the change room afterwards was even uglier than at half-time.

'Statistically, there had been an improvement from the first half to the second, but we knew what had just happened was unacceptable. No one tried to make any excuses and the coaching staff didn't offer any. Jake told us we couldn't change the result and that we had to learn from it. He said we would never forget this hurt and that we had to turn that hurt into our favour if we were going to complete our journey that would culminate in winning the 2007 World Cup. There was no ranting and raving in the change room because that wasn't Jake's style. He said what happened against New Zealand in Wellington and the following week against Australia in Sydney would define us because 49-0 was not a representation of who we were.'

For all the talk of positive energy, Montgomery was down and as close to being out as he had ever been. Ideally, he wanted to go home and be with his family, where he felt he would be of better use.

'The squad didn't need a senior player moping around in New Zealand. Most of us were trying to figure out how the hell it had all gone so wrong on the field and I did not want to burden anyone else with my stuff.'

Springbok mental coach Henning Gericke believes White's fighting with the Saru administration had a greater impact than the players care to admit. He also says that several of the senior players had issues at home and in their private lives, and he spent the week in Brisbane doing more one-on-ones with senior players than at any stage in 2004 and 2005.

'The French defeat hit the team hard because they did not believe they could lose at home after nearly three years of dominating every team, including the All Blacks. But the Jake stuff was troubling many of them and there was uncertainty about their futures if he was fired. Jake had also decided to take a more relaxed approach to the Test in Brisbane, believing he needed to do so to preserve his sanity. He was extremely upset at the public and media's reaction to a first home defeat in three seasons and he was angry that he received so little backing from the bosses at Saru. He told me he wanted to enjoy the Tri-Nations and that he had been putting too much pressure on himself. Whatever the players may say, the intensity in training that week wasn't there. We were on dangerous ground but I don't think anyone knew how to deal with it. In three years, this team had not known much adversity. We beat Ireland 2-0 in our first series in

2004, and scored 53 points against Wales. We lost by two and four points to New Zealand and Australia respectively, away from home, before coming back to South Africa and scoring 40 points against the All Blacks and then beating the Wallabies to win the Tri-Nations. In 2005, we had also won in Australia and beaten the All Blacks in Cape Town. We knew good times and were not burdened by too many poor rugby performances, but the sideshows between the administration, politicians and Jake had finally caught up with us. No one ever thought it was possible to lose 49-0, not with this team. What kept our heads above water was we knew we were not 50 points worse than Australia when it came to player ability.'

Gericke, busy in the week before the Brisbane Test, was in demand on the Sunday after the game and Montgomery was one of the first to go calling because he wanted to go home.

'I went to see Smitty and Jake when we got back to the hotel and I said it would be in the team's interests and definitely in mine to be sent home. I didn't believe I could add anything to the side in the remaining two Tests against the All Blacks in Wellington and Australia in Sydney. Jake was sympathetic to how I was feeling but said it would send the wrong message to the squad, the media and the rugby public. As a senior player, he needed me to fight through the emotional strain and to lead from the front. Smitty said he needed me to help with the leadership and it was in these trying times that all the senior players had to show a united front to the younger guys. I am a private person and don't easily share things outside of rugby with team-mates, but Smitty knew I wasn't at my happiest. Both Jake and Smitty wanted me to see Henning, who I trusted. Henning made sure I called Tasmin and explained my mental state to her, but he also encouraged me to stay with the squad and make a difference. What was telling to me, was his suggestion that if after talking to Tasmin, I still wanted to go home, he would ensure it happened. Tasmin told me to stay and turn things around and my mind was made up.'

White and Gericke were adamant that any panic among management would lead to more disaster against the All Blacks. White knew his players had not become bad in a week and after losing to the All Blacks in the last minute in Christchurch in 2004 and by four points in Dunedin in 2005, he always believed he had a team capable of winning in New Zealand.

But White also had to be honest about how the defeat against France had affected him and how the response of people had hurt him.

'As the coach, you have to show strength, but that loss in Cape Town really knocked me. One minute we were leading 23-11 and the crowd in the grandstand at Newlands was turning to the coach's box and giving me the thumbs up. The next we were trailing 36-26 and the game was a minute away from being lost. I walked down to the change room on my own and got abused on the way down by the same people who at half-time clapped when I walked past them. I felt winded and helpless and when I got to the change room, I couldn't handle the situation. I stood there alone and feeling empty, and I just burst into tears. How could we have lost after all the effort we had put in? It was one of my lowest moments in a Springbok change room and while I thought I was alone, I wasn't. Jean de Villiers, who did not play because of injury, was also in the change room. There was a moment when his eyes caught mine and we both knew how much hurt we were feeling. He said nothing, but gave me a reassuring look and went and stood outside the change room while I composed myself. It was a powerful moment for me as a coach because I thought I had shown vulnerability to a player I rated so highly, but he had interpreted it as a display of how much I cared about them as players and the Springboks as a team. In Brisbane, the result was worse than I could ever have imagined, but I knew that I had to pick myself up in Wellington and not allow Saru's administration or the politicians to get to me. That week was dominated by Solly Tyibilika's selection and media accusations that I had insulted Solly by saying I had only picked him because of transformation. Solly's situation added pressure to an already tense situation and the player wanted to know if he deserved to be in the team. I was being crucified in the South African media for picking Solly ahead of Luke Watson, but I felt Solly was the better option and had the advantage of being with the squad for two years. Schalk was injured and I was confident Solly would do the job for me. He had played well against Scotland in Edinburgh and started in the win against the Wallabies at Ellis Park in 2005. Solly was not my concern – it was getting the senior players back on a high after the disaster in Brisbane.'

Gericke's theme was turning adversity into triumph and Montgomery could get across the message to the squad that it was possible to come back from anything.

'We had a team meeting and I wanted to reinforce what was good about the players and what was good about the team. But each guy also had to draw on any individual experience of distress. I asked all the players to write down something particular to themselves that they felt comfortable sharing with their team-mates. The idea was to put up each player's words in the team room so that throughout the week, in their own time, they could read what the others had to say. Monty asked if he could read his to the team.

'"I've been through this plenty of times," he said. "One thing I have learnt is you turn the negatives into positives. People have criticised me my whole career and I have always come back and proved them wrong. I was the scapegoat with my white or silver boots, and long, blond hair. I have been booed at Loftus and sworn at by our supporters. I will never forget it. I can forgive but I will never forget it. That's why I don't give a fuck. I'm just happy to be here [with the Boks]. I've learned there's no point getting upset because they are going to say what they want anyway. Everyone has an opinion. So if you're not happy with your game, you will know. Only you can work it out if you want to."

'There was absolute silence,' recalls Gericke. 'Monty spoke with such emotion about the hurt and then Pierre Spies stood up and spoke about the trauma of losing his father and how he had to fight to overcome that pain. In five minutes, we had the squad's most experienced player and the youngest sharing intimate feelings. A few more players spoke after that and then Smitty urged the guys to look ahead and never allow a repeat of what happened in Brisbane. There were so many strong characters in the squad and now was the time to show our resolve to the world.'

Fourie du Preez would charge down a Dan Carter kick and score after just 17 seconds against the All Blacks but there was to be no miracle in Wellington as the Boks lost 35-17.

The miracle would come a fortnight later when the Boks came within two minutes of beating the Wallabies in Sydney, and while the squad rallied for pride, Montgomery says opinions differed as to whether White should stay as coach.

'There were a lot of strong characters in our squad and these guys had strong opinions, especially Victor Matfield and Fourie du Preez. Victor, in particular, did not have a strong relationship with Jake. While Jake made no secret about the fact that Victor wasn't top of his list, Victor also did not hide the fact that the inspiration in his career was Bulls coach Heyneke Meyer, who he thought should be coaching the Boks. In 2006, Jake was a hot topic at the back of the Bok bus, and for those who haven't been inside a Bok bus, that's where the senior players sit. I defended Jake, as I always will. He is the best international coach I've had because he was the first one confident enough to empower the senior players and to manage players specific to each one's needs. He identified who he wanted and he trusted his judgement and I was one guy he always rated. He was always good to me, in 1998 when he was the Bok technical adviser and for four years as the Bok coach. He had faults, like all of us, and weaknesses and he made mistakes. But he had knowledge of rugby and a passion for the game and he also allowed his senior players to have a voice. I think his best trait as a Bok coach was that he managed the players more than he coached them. Gert Smal did a great job with the forwards and I always rated Allister Coetzee as a backline coach. They did the hands-on coaching and Jake controlled that, but more than that, he trusted the on-field experience of the senior players. I know he rated Victor as the best lock in the world but the two of them never connected and it had a lot to do with how Victor felt about Heyneke.

'The Bulls, in every Bok team I have been involved in, have always been very close to the point of perhaps alienating themselves from the other players. When I first got into the Bok squad in 1997, it was each man for himself and each province for itself. You just had to walk into our team room during breakfast, lunch or dinner to know that. But I definitely witnessed a change between 2004 and 2007, although the first time I felt I was genuinely in a national team room all the time was in 2007. Before that, there were still the factions, although there was never malice and no one ever made it an issue. The senior players chat a lot about things at the back of the bus when going to or coming from training and mostly it was a general chat without anyone getting too emotional. But Vic was adamant Jake's time had come and gone and that we needed something new. I know Fourie was disillusioned because Jake was rotating him with Ricky Januarie. He felt he was playing well enough to keep his place and that he was fighting the politicians as much as the opposition. A lot of players, especially the younger ones, don't read papers or care what is being said or written about them or the team. I've been there and that's probably why I got through my first season of Test rugby. But by this stage of my career I was on the internet a lot and I read the morning papers. I knew that Jake was under pressure. I also knew that he was doing everything to protect the players from the administration and the political interference and I respected him even more for that.'

Gericke, often the man in the middle, says White had issues with Matfield for a perceived attitude that was not necessarily accurate. White wanted a certain type of image from his leading players and Matfield seemed to represent the opposite.

'Nothing ever happened between the two and there was never an incident I was aware of, but Jake, with his school teacher background, favoured conservatism in image from his players and Victor, by nature, isn't like that. I know how highly Jake rated Victor as a player, but he could have been more appreciative of Victor's talents in the media. In turn, Victor could have been more sensitive in speaking up the virtues of Heyneke because it obviously got to Jake. It is a credit to the two of them that they never allowed these differences to affect the team dynamic, although the players knew their relationship had to be stronger if we were to be a united team for the World Cup. In 2007, I arranged a meeting between Jake, Heyneke and Victor where everyone had their say and got everything off their chests. It was an open discussion and Heyneke was very influential in determining the outcome because he made it clear to Victor that while he played for Jake in the Bok set-up, he needed to give him all his support. Heyneke also gave Jake some insight into how he managed Victor and how he got the best out of him. It was a very good meeting and from my perspective, there never was an issue again between Jake and Victor in 2007. When they went to the World Cup, they went very much as members of a team and not as individuals in opposite corners. This also helped with any potential conflict between the Bulls players and the rest of the squad because of the big following and influence Victor had.'

Montgomery concurs that the Bulls players tended to be a unique bunch, but that in 2007 they were united in a common goal, which was to win the World Cup. He also admits to never having had an issue with any Bulls player in his Bok career.

'I like the Bulls players and have always gotten on with them. In my earlier days with the Boks, a lot of the players from other provinces wouldn't mix with the Bulls players and there were split opinions about a guy like Joost [van der Westhuizen], who I never had a problem with and who I got on well with. My dad's Afrikaans, my favourite music is Afrikaans, I am a big Leon Schuster fan and I love hunting and eating biltong. So by all accounts I found it easy chatting to the Bulls guys and they never rejected any interaction with me. I went hunting with guys like the Cronjé brothers – Geo and Jacques – and Danie Rossouw and enjoyed their company. I think they saw me as just another guy who enjoyed hunting and not an English-speaking player from Cape Town. I've always gotten on with the Afrikaans guys and admired the way they play the game. I'd never seen a player as dedicated as André Venter, and Rassie Erasmus and Werner Swanepoel were great Bok team-mates and good guys to be around socially. The Bulls issue, though, was bigger than any English or Afrikaans thing. Some guys thought that their domestic success had gone to their head, but to me they were okes who had done well, enjoyed their rugby but had a different vibe about them and I was comfortable in their company.

'On this tour, though, things got bad and Jake was under pressure. Some guys were angry before the French Test when they heard he might be taking the England job and be coaching against us at the World Cup, but Jake had told the squad he would never do that and it was media speculation. He was as desperate as we were to go to the World Cup and win it and he said so in team meetings. But there was a big lobby for Heyneke, and Victor swears by what Heyneke has done for his career and for him as a person. Victor and Fourie made their case for why Jake should go and I made mine for why he should stay and we left it at that. I want to make it very clear that every guy always gave it 100% on the field and while there may have been likes and dislikes among players and management, once the players got on the field, they were Springboks playing for the country.

'Smitty was always aware of provincial team dynamics, but he never took a side or interfered because he understood the background to the South African professional psyche and the guys knew that. What I enjoyed was that Smitty never made an issue about who sat where or who talked to who, and any integration between player groups was done naturally over the course of four years. It was no different when we left Wellington for Sydney. Whatever the opinions of players, everyone felt we could win in Sydney and the chararacter of the side showed in those few weeks after the 49-0 loss. While no one could give an explanation as to how we got such a *klap*, everyone knew we were a better team than Australia. We had beaten them three times in 2005 and felt we should be beating them in Australia and in South Africa. We believed we could win in Sydney, even though no one outside of the squad thought it was possible. People kept on asking how it was possible to turn around 49 points, but there has never been that kind of difference between the two sides,' says Montgomery, whose try late in the match gave the Boks an 18-13 lead.

White had made five changes from the side humiliated in Brisbane. Butch James at flyhalf for Jaco van der Westhuyzen was significant, so too Du Preez for Januarie. In the pack, he had stuck with Tyibilika as an openside option ahead of Joe van Niekerk, specialist lock Johann Muller replaced utility forward Danie Rossouw and the more physical Jacques Cronjé started in Spies's place.

'I don't know how significant the changes were because the squad was united in the belief that we had the players to beat Australia. With a couple of minutes to go we thought we had won it, but then [Wallabies replacement flyhalf] Mat Rogers scored and the game was level at 18-all. No one likes a draw but I would have settled for that result at that stage because it would have ended our losing streak. I rate [centre] Stirling Mortlock as one of the best players at Test level and he is also a very good goal kicker. His strength is his temperament and he does lift himself for the bigger moments and big occasions, but I still tried to put the mockers on him in my mind. "Please miss. We need the miss more than you need the kick," I thought, and for a few seconds I thought he had. But the kick hit the upright and bounced in. Game over.

'The guys were crushed at that moment because we had come so close to winning. In Brisbane, we were never in the game but here we had a chance to win it. When we got to the change room, we were already feeling more upbeat but Jake wasn't about to applaud defeat. He told us he was proud of us and of the way we fought back in Wellington and Sydney, but he made sure we weren't going to become good losers and accept defeat. It had to hurt, even more than Brisbane, because the match was there to be won.'

White, having taken a beating in the press after Brisbane, told the media: 'All we've heard for the last three weeks is 49-nil, 49-nil ... but this one hurts the most because of how we lost it and because it is also the most consecutive times we have lost as a team and it definitely is the most we have been abused in the media.'

The abuse of White and the Springboks did not stop in Sydney. The 45-26 defeat against the All Blacks at Loftus Versfeld was the team's fifth successive loss and it also proved to be Montgomery's last Test of the year. White substituted him, much to the relief of the player, whose mind and body were finished after 31 successive months of rugby and 84 matches.

That included 38 for Newport in 2004 and 2005, four for the Sharks in the 2005 Currie Cup, 11 for the Sharks in the 2006 Super 14, 30 Tests for the Springboks in 2004, 2005 and 2006 and one non-cap match against a World XV at Ellis

Park in 2006 when Montgomery kicked nine penalties in the Bok XV's 30-27 win.

Having played the first of 36 matches on 2 January 2004 and the last on 27 December 2004, Montgomery would finally be given a break two years later.

'Monty was gone at Loftus,' says White. 'The poor guy had given so much to us over the last three seasons and, in hindsight, I should have rested him a bit more in 2006. But we had so many injuries to players and I needed every bit of experience. I respected the way Monty had battled through Australia and New Zealand and when it started to go wrong for us against the All Blacks at Loftus and the crowd typically started getting on his case, I owed it to him to get him out of there. If those jeering him at Loftus knew how influential he had been to the squad, they would have given him a standing ovation, but that would have been asking too much of a crowd that has never been fair to him.'

The Sharks coaching team also accepted there was no gain in squeezing a few Currie Cup matches out of him and his first competitive match would be for the Sharks against the Bulls in the opening round of the 2007 Super 14.

'When Jake subbed me against the All Blacks at Loftus there was nothing left,' recalls Montgomery. 'My body ached and everything was sore. I also needed to be home and I needed rest. Jake released me for the last two Tri-Nations Tests against New Zealand in Rustenburg and Australia at Ellis Park [which the Boks won]. We agreed that I would not go on the end-of-year tour to Ireland and England [where the Boks would lose in Dublin and share the two-Test series at Twickenham]. If I was going to do anything for the Sharks in the Super 14 and for Jake and the Boks at the World Cup, I had to have a proper off-season. I also had to spend time with my family and get my mind ready for what was going to be the biggest year of our lives.'

17

SPIRITUALITY AND THE SYMBOLISM OF 4, 7 AND 47

John Smit and Percy Montgomery asked Springbok mental coach Henning Gericke to help them arrange a team-building session before the squad's departure for the World Cup in France. Smit had been through the infamous Kamp Staaldraad pre-World Cup camp in 2003 when players were humiliated, starved of food, water and sleep in a misguided belief that it would make them mentally tougher. What Smit and Montgomery, as the two most senior players, wanted before the 2007 World Cup was something that required physical effort from the players and was enjoyable, but also had a singular purpose of further uniting what they believed was a close unit.

They felt the players needed time alone to talk about the significance of arriving in France as a squad and winning the tournament as a squad. Only 15 players could start and every one of the 30 wanted to. Smit, having experienced the disastrous 2003 World Cup campaign, did not want a repeat of a divided squad based on team selections and he knew that the strength of the campaign would come from those fringe players not involved in the play-offs. How they were involved would determine how they reacted to the time spent at the World Cup. He knew that the starting XV chosen for the play-offs had to feed off the energy of those on the bench and in the stands.

'I've learned throughout my career that those guys on tour who aren't playing have to be involved and made to feel part of the starting XV,' says Smit. 'Each one had to know that at any time he could be playing. Jake had left 20 players in South Africa during the away leg of the Tri-Nations and that was a clear message that those 20 would be going to the World Cup. I did not want a situation where some players felt inferior or secondary at the World Cup. When we got the 30 players together after the Tri-Nations, I wanted each one to be comfortable to talk and to give input. I always knew we had the playing potential to win the World Cup, but it was how we gelled as a unit and how we supported each other in France that would win it for us. All 30 guys would get a medal and that meant all 30 had to make a contribution.

'Monty, Henning and I felt there had to be a purpose to whatever we did, but the fun element was just as important. The guys had to enjoy it and it had to be something that could inspire us during the tough times at the World Cup. Henning was brilliant in organising everything and he also guided us in what was needed, so as not to force the situation. I've been on so many team-building exercises in which the players have had no input and subsequently got no benefit. For me, it was critical that this had to be about the players because the coaches in a World Cup final aren't the guys catching, passing, tackling and running for us. When the crunch came at the World Cup, we had to stand together as a squad and we had to commit to that before we left South Africa.'

Montgomery attributes so much of the World Cup success to the senior players and to Jake White's trust in them and his willingness to allow them to dictate terms to each other.

'It had to be our decision as players. We had to agree on a protocol as players and be accountable for it in France. Smitty is an exceptional leader and person but no one leads on his own and you can't lead if the players don't believe in what you are doing. I knew the importance of a united squad. My first World Cup was in 1999 and there were some fantastic players in the side but there was so much unnecessary pressure because of Gary Teichmann's omission and Bob Skinstad's inclusion. Bob's fitness was questioned by some after the knee injury and many players felt that Gary should never have been dropped. It was unfair on Bob because he didn't drop Gary, but some players didn't see it like that. I thought the coaches and management underestimated the impact of team unity and how feeling like a family is so important to the success of a team. People laugh when I talk about the importance of players treating each other as if they are family but when you believe in the guy next to you and care about him, you make the tackle he missed and he makes the one you missed. Some teams I have played in never got that and others got it immediately. It was down to the character of the players. I knew we had that quality among the players in the World Cup squad and so did Smitty and Henning.'

Gericke organised a walk for the Boks, with four stops along the way to coincide with the three World Cups South Africa had played in as well as the upcoming fourth one in France.

'Os had played in the 1995 and 1999 World Cups,' says Gericke. 'Monty had been to the 1999 World Cup and there were quite a few guys who were in Australia in 2003. We wanted to get the guys talking about the experience – about what worked and how easily it can go wrong. We also wanted the players to celebrate each World Cup the Boks had been to and be reminded of the highs, lows and sacrifice. It was important that the guys who hadn't been to a World Cup knew the history of the event. We also needed them to understand it is no one's right to attend a World Cup and you have to earn the right to win it. Some of the game's best players have never won the World Cup and Smitty was insistent that a player's career is defined at the tournament. Smitty and Monty were adamant that it had to be a fun and meaningful day. They felt it had to be just the players because in those crunch moments on the field the players had to be able to look each other in the eye and have a common bond when it came to inspiration.

'My job was to organise the day,' says Gericke. 'In the week before the walk I got all the players to write down the person with the biggest influence on their life and career. Only Monty and Smitty knew that once I got all the names we'd have these people flown to Durban on 25 July and driven to Smitty's holiday house to greet the players at the end of their 30km walk. Smitty also insisted on the three Bok coaches – Jake, Gert Smal and Allister Coetzee – being present. They represented the coaching hierarchy and the leadership of the team and he did not want any form of alienation between the coaches or players. There was so much energy in the squad, but if one player put himself before the team cause, it could be the difference in a final. My involvement was to set up the route and ensure the beers, cool drinks and water were at each stop. The players were told they were going on a team-building walk and there was no secrecy about it because we knew there were enough players present from the 2003 World Cup who had experienced a different kind of team building. The last thing we wanted to create was uncertainty or a feeling that this was 2003 all over again.'

Montgomery says nothing was forced during the walk. Neither he nor Smit made an issue about anything and most of the talking came at the stops and not during the walk.

'Typical of players, they wanted to get the walk done as quickly as possible, but at each stop we swam, joked, sat around and chatted and the stops took longer as the players relaxed more.

'Os [du Randt] was huge in the team environment and I don't know how any informed journalist could ever have questioned why Jake picked him. The young players were in awe of him and we knew the opposition felt the same way. I think the lucky ones among us get to see one Os in our career and I was inspired by what he had achieved in winning the 1995 World Cup as a youngster, struggling with knee injuries, retiring and then coming back into the Bok set-up in 2004. I enjoyed having him in the change room even when he wasn't playing because a nod from Os was worth everything. His type comes along once in a generation. What all the guys loved about him was how low key he was and how little he talked, but when he did talk, you listened. I can't remember Os opening up about 1995 or preaching to any of the guys about how they won the World Cup and it was more the other guys asking him questions about it. They wanted to know what it took to win and what the magic formula was. They also wanted to know how it had changed his life. Os spoke of his respect for [World Cup-winning Bok coach] Kitch Christie, family values within the squad and hard work. He told the boys that if they could be a family they could not be divided, but if we went as 30 individuals we were vulnerable. And he said fitness was non negotiable.

'I spoke about being at the 1999 World Cup and how important it was that each player knew his role and the expectation was defined before the tournament. Jake had been honest with every player, telling him when he envisaged playing him. The players had to respect that and turn it into a positive. There was a pecking order as to who would start the play-off matches but the other XV needed to know they were good enough to win a final if someone was injured or suspended. I thought we had a good enough team to win the 1999 World Cup and we were beaten by a very good Wallabies team who relied on a drop goal from Stephen Larkham to beat us in extra time in the semi-final, but we were never a unified team. There was too much uncertainty in selections and Gary's axing caused unhappiness. Everyone was comfortable with him as captain because while Joost [van der Westhuizen] always led from the front and gave everything in effort, he did not have Gary's calming influence on the players. There were players in the squad who did not relate to Joost. Gary, during my time, always had every player's support as a captain and it was a shock when Nick Mallett dropped him in 1999 because he had been so instrumental in moulding the team that equalled the world record of 17 consecutive Test wins. In 1999, transformation issues and talk of quotas made white players feel insecure and the black players picked as Boks were insulted by being called quota players. But I still think the biggest mistake at the 1999 World Cup was Gary's absence and many of the senior players never got over him not being picked. There were clear divisions in the camp, before the World Cup and during the tournament.

'We couldn't afford that kind of situation in France in 2007 and if a player had an issue he had to talk about it before we left South Africa and not when things got tough in France. I believed we, as a group, were Springboks and not provincial guys playing for the Boks. To me that was our strength and that is what our bond would be in France. I knew we would care for each other and play for each other and if a team beat us in the final they would do so because they were better and not because we had let ourselves down.'

Smit says he never focused on Kamp Staaldraad and neither did the others who were at the 2003 World Cup. Instead, he spoke about doing the right things in France and the fortunate position each player was in because each guy could write his own chapter. Win the World Cup, Smit told them, and you will always be remembered as a winner.

'What was the point of looking back?' says Smit. 'In 2003, we went to Australia hoping to win the tournament but never believed we were good enough or had a strong enough squad to do it. There was just too much going on outside of rugby for us ever to have believed in ourselves. There had never been enough continuity or consistency in selection. I know each guy gave everything, but the preparation in 2003 when compared to 2007 was like chalk and cheese. In 2007, we never believed anyone could beat us and we left for France knowing we could win it and not just hoping for the best. We had that confidence because we had beaten every team in the four years since the last World Cup and that is a confidence the squad of 2003 did not have. We also had a strong group of senior players who had the respect of the young players. Our pool match against England was as big as a final for us and everything we did was in preparation for that match. I knew that we could beat the English because we had won our last three Tests against them in London, Bloemfontein and Pretoria, and we also had much more experience in the 2007 squad than when we played England at the 2003 World Cup [and lost 25-6].

'What was important for me about this team-building exercise was that each guy, in his own time, would sort out his head, and if he needed to fix something with a team-mate he did it during the 30km walk. Don't ask me what each guy thought or had to say that day because no one was keeping notes. It was about cementing a bond that we had nurtured over four years and making sure any issue could be dealt with before we left for France.'

Montgomery describes the fourth stop of the walk, at Smit's house, as 'monstrous' because of who was there.

'The players thought they'd be having a braai at the end of the walk and that would be the end of the day, but when each player saw who was waiting for him, the evening became about that person. I've had wonderful people in my life and I will never forget what they did for me. Simon Perkin [his coach and teacher at SACS] is special. So is HO de Villiers and every coach I've had has added to me as a player. But my dad has always been the biggest influence in my life, even though we never experienced the kind of father-son relationship most guys would take for granted. I was so proud to have my dad there because I know what sacrifices he and my mom had made to give me great schooling and every opportunity to succeed. I am ashamed to admit that as a teenager, there were times I was embarrassed that my parents didn't have the wealth I saw in the homes of classmates and out of ignorance, I couldn't understand why I didn't have the material luxuries others enjoyed. But as I got older, I recognised the shame I felt in having been embarrassed and I wanted to make it right by trying to give as much to my parents as I could. I love them and I know how supportive and proud my dad has always been of my career.

'That night, around a braai and with people who will always be close to me simply because of what we went through and what we would achieve in France, I was honoured to be in a position to honour my dad and to thank him for everything. It was a big moment to hand him a jersey with a personal message on it and it was nice just to have him around. My dad is a private person and he isn't one for sideshows or the hangers-on you get in rugby. He has never been one for trying to live his career or life through whatever I have achieved with the Springboks. He doesn't have to because he was a good player in his day and played for South West Africa. He coached there as well and he was among the first guys to coach a coloured side, simply because he loved rugby and it was an opportunity to coach. He has always been in the background, but he was never further away than a phone call and while he has a big opinion on the game, he has never told me how to play it or tried to play his game through me. He has made suggestions and always been blunt in his observations. If I played badly, he would tell me and if I was good he would let me know. Most of the players had their fathers there, but I know it was a night of joy and sadness for André Pretorius and Pierre Spies, whose fathers had passed away. Lions coach and André's mentor Loffie Eloff was there for him and Bulls coach Heyneke Meyer was the person Pierre had listed as his inspiration to get to the World Cup. But I knew both of them would have given anything to have their dads there, which only made me appreciate it even more that I could say thank you to mine.'

The value of family, says Gericke, was a constant whenever Montgomery spoke to Jake about bringing the players closer together. Montgomery was always the one pushing for greater interaction with family and he motivated why it was important that the families of each player should be involved in the World Cup journey and never feel isolated.

'I had played in squads where it was unfashionable to have your wife and kids or girlfriend around, but I could never understand that because you play your best when you are around those people you love and are important to you.'

Smit, his wife Roxy, Gericke and Bok physiotherapist Clint Readhead had 25 green wrist bands made for each squad member to hand out to family and friends as a symbol of unity and support for the World Cup. Each wrist band contained an inscription: 'Bok family energy – we believe 47'.

The 47, says Gericke, was because of the 47 days the team would be in France and on reflection, it was a number with some significance, at least according to the more spiritual among the squad.

'One of the players pointed out after the World Cup win that when Eddie Jones joined the management team we became 47, that we played four pool games and seven matches in total. And that if you add four and seven, you get 11, which was Bryan Habana's jersey number – he finished as the leading try-scorer and Player of the Tournament. And the religious guys also found meaning in Noah being in the ark for 40 days before releasing a dove which returned seven days later with an olive leaf. As far as the players were concerned, it was meant to be that we would win in France.'

Religion has always been influential in Springbok teams, especially among the Afrikaans-speaking players, but at times over different generations of teams, it had also been divisive.

Gericke says that religion, like language or colour, was never an issue with the 2007 World Cup winners.

'Those who did their Bible readings in groups never made a fuss about it and those who were not religious just did their thing. As management, we always wanted the players to be comfortable and whatever they did was their own choice. But once we got to the World Cup and this wave of optimism followed us wherever we went, the players, even those who had never spoken about religion, started to talk of a greater force guiding this team. Bob Skinstad had told the media all year that the stars were aligned for South African rugby and he was convinced the Springboks would win the World Cup. Even though the players all started to believe that they could not be beaten at the tournament, they also knew that they had to train hard, play even harder and be at their best to succeed. There was never this simplistic belief that God would win it for the Boks. There was respect for the opposition and Jake kept on repeating that it takes seven games to win the World Cup, but only 40 bad minutes to lose it. No player could afford to think beyond the next game.'

Spirituality had played a big role with the 1995 World Cup-winning Boks, with winger James Small famously saying even he started to pray during the tournament. At the 1999 World Cup the squad was very divided on religion, especially because Mallett detested religion and politics being introduced into any team environment, and in 2003, no amount of praying was ever going to save a campaign that was doomed before it started.

'Religion did not dominate team meetings at all during the 2007 World Cup, but I think players were comfortable to talk about things because of the familiarity that comes when you have been together for a long time and most of the squad had been around from when Jake started coaching the Boks in

2004,' says Gericke. 'It was more about players having a sense of spirituality than religion and channelling their energy into a common goal, which was to win the World Cup.'

Montgomery says he has never experienced a will as strong as the 2007 world champions and that the desire to be successful meant players put the team ethos above all else.

'The only rule we had among players was an unwritten one and it was that we would all do what was necessary to win the tournament. Players couldn't be selfish and they had to be accepting of team selections and game plans and they also had to take responsibility for their own off-field behaviour. We didn't have to speak about the commitment on the field as every guy knew that was a given. When Jake left 20 of us out of the squad for the away leg of the Tri-Nations in 2007 and sent us to Cape Town on a two-week conditioning programme, it showed confidence in the players and bonded the leadership of the team even more.

'Cape Town was a bit like a trial run for the World Cup, even though I don't think Jake ever intended it to be that. The senior players, as they would have to do in France, had to manage the player dynamic and we fended for ourselves. We made decisions and if we felt like having a pub session or a good night out we did it, but the next day we worked even harder in training. The senior guys wanted the responsibility and when it came to the sprint drills, I was insistent that we always go beyond what was expected of us.

'There was one particular drill when we'd do five sets of sprints from the tryline to the 22m line. We'd get a minute's rest after the completion of the set of five and then we'd do four sets and continue the count down to one. It is one of the more gruelling drills and when the boys finished the five sets I screamed out "Five. Four. Three. Two. One," which meant we go again. From that day in Cape Town, it became a call everyone used during the World Cup when they felt we needed to put in even more hard work. We had to be the fittest team there and we also had to be the strongest mentally. The senior players agreed that we had to train as if the play-offs were potentially 100-minute games, so we would cope if we were forced to go beyond the 80 minutes.

'I had experienced extra time against Australia in the 1999 World Cup semi-final and everything felt different because we were conditioned to play 80 minutes. The senior players spoke about the necessity of being strong at the finish of games and in all our World Cup matches, we felt capable of going another 20 minutes if we had to. We also spoke about chasing every tackle and that even a lunge at a guy could be the difference in the final. As it transpired, Danie Rossouw's desperate tackle on Mark Cueto, when Danie refused to stop running and just managed to get a shove in, was enough to put Cueto into touch and deny England a try. The kind of stuff every player did at the World Cup was stuff we talked about often in the build-up to the World Cup. It was OK to make a mistake, but it was even better to acknowledge it and fix it the next time.

'In those two weeks in Cape Town, the senior players did a lot of talking among themselves about the campaign. We all felt there had to be balance to how we spent our time in France, but that we could never allow the sideshows to distract us and if we wanted to be treated like adults then we had to behave as such. We did not want to be governed by rules and we certainly did not want to be accountable to a manager for whom there was no respect.

'We all knew [new Springbok manager] Zola Yeye was a political appointment and I thought he added no value to the campaign. Anyone who gets selected for the Boks, whether a player or management member, has to earn respect. Zola, in one of his speeches, had called Ruan Pienaar, Francois Pienaar, and had also refered to Wynand Olivier as Wynand Claassen. The players never let him forget that and every time the team bus would leave Jaque Fourie would call out that Francois Pienaar and Wynand Claassen were not on the bus and that we couldn't leave until they arrived. The players took the piss out of Zola because of those kinds of mistakes, which the manager of the Springboks should never make.

'He also alienated himself with players by putting himself before the team. An example of this was when we used to book in our luggage at an airport. The players and management would queue with their luggage and he would walk past everyone, drop it in the front and expect Mac Hendricks, the operational manager, to sort it out. It may seem petty of me to mention this as an example, but within our team dynamic what he did was simply not acceptable. Jake and Zola also did not get on and the players knew this. Jake had no confidence in Zola as a manager and neither did the players, who learned to tolerate him. But he never had my respect because he did nothing to earn it, and I did not know of any player who felt he was an asset to the squad.

'It was because of this kind of situation that the senior players accepted how crucial their role would be at the World Cup. Jake had always empowered the players and we did not want to change what had previously worked because it was the World Cup. We had to treat it as another tournament and keep our routine. We were not going to stop players from having a night out or having a few drinks in their rooms. We were not going to judge any player on whether he drank a milkshake, a whisky or a few glasses of wine two nights before a match. Each player had to be accountable for his own actions and take responsibility for the consequences. We would be judged on our results at the tournament and for the players to perform at their peak, they had to be comfortable and happy.

'We also had to be mature about the team dynamic and accept that some players had stronger friendships within the group, but as team-mates we were all equal. As players, we wanted to be in a position to talk about issues and sort them out and not have management do our thinking for us. Jake had identified his senior players, whom he had faith in as a group, and we knew our actions had to be our words to the younger and less experienced players.

'The senior players had to work the hardest and during those two weeks in Cape Town, we trained as hard as I've ever experienced in a Bok squad. Os had emphasised how fitness played such a big role in their 1995 success and I had experienced the additional pressure of having to play extra time in a World Cup play-off. We had to be the fittest team in France and we had to have a routine that would sustain this fitness during the tournament. Jake's message to the team was to live the World Cup, enjoy it and leave France as better people, but we also knew that the main reason we were in France was to win the World Cup and not to be tourists. Physically, we had worked hard in Cape Town, socially we had enjoyed ourselves.

'The only frustrating thing for me was learning to speak French. Jake insisted the squad take French lessons so we would be more comfortable during our stay and at the very least, he wanted us to be able to string a few sentences together by the time we got to Paris, so that we could also appreciate the culture and interact better with the locals, but I found them difficult. I have never professed to be an academic and anyone in my class at SACS will tell you I was born to play sport and not be in a classroom. I hated having to go to the lessons and I struggled. I know I wasn't the only one who found it draining, especially because the physical training was so intense and the last thing I wanted to do was go and learn a new language. One day, during a French lesson, I lost the plot completely. I was battling with a sentence that I had been asked to say out loud and the boys were onto it like a flash. I was seated between Butch James and Jean de Villiers and both of them consider themselves stand-up comics, who can be as irritating as they are funny. They're very smart and quick with a chirp and unrelenting when they're together. I probably would have handled the situation if it had been one or the other, but with the two of them going at me from left and right I exploded and threw a punch. Unfortunately for Butchie, he was sitting on my left and my right hand throws the stronger punch. Butchie and I are good mates and if I had to choose between the two I would have decked Jean, but Butchie felt the full force of my frustration. Butchie had been silenced, Jean got the message very quickly and there was a brief pause from the squad before the French lesson continued.

'Jean, in the last year, has matured a lot and I believe it is because of the additional captaincy responsibility with the Stormers and Western Province. He is a fantastic player and he is proving to be a very good leader, whose feel for the game is one of his strengths. He is a fun guy, who in the past could take things too far, but my experience of him in 2008 was that there was more balance to his humour and a far greater understanding of what it means to be a senior player. He will be one of the superstars of Springbok rugby, but in 2007, just before the World Cup, his jokes, wit and mocking were too much for me, and poor Butchie just happened to bear the brunt of it.

'I felt terrible that I had hit Butchie and that evening when I apologised to him, I was nearly in tears. But Butchie, as he tends to do, laughed it off and admitted the chirps had been a bit excessive. It was something that had been sorted out between the two of us and the senior players were happy that was the end of it. No one mentioned it again and it was another example of how close the squad was and how private they were willing to keep things. I know from previous Bok tours and campaigns that if a Bok player had punched another one, no matter the circumstance, it would have made it into the newspaper because someone would have phoned a journalist. In this side, we dealt with it as players and moved on.

'There were two other punching incidents at the World Cup, when Ashwin Willemse hit Wayne Julies and Gary Botha hit André Pretorius. Wayne, like Jean and Butchie, is never lost for a word and he got on Ashwin's case one time too many. Gary's sorting out of André came after the narrow win against Tonga. André had not kicked well and it had influenced Jake's decision to send on a lot of the experienced players early in the second half to try turn things around. Gary was one of the guys substituted. I have never asked Gary why he hit André but I reckon it was out of frustration. There were so many fringe players, including Gary, who were desperate to do well, and with opportunities so scarce, perhaps this was the reason. As with the other punches, it was dealt with in-house and never got into the newspapers. That showed me how tight this team was. There was no malice in any of the three incidents and no one held a grudge. They were isolated incidents but the refusal of anyone involved to make it public proved to me that the team came before the individual and no one wanted to do anything to harm the team. There have been times in my career when players have used the media to further their cause at the team's expense, but at the 2007 World Cup, this never happened and it is a tribute to Jake's management of the players and the trust he put in the senior players to sort things out first.'

When I interviewed White for this book, I mentioned the three punching incidents, and he did not even know about them. White also said he did not know the details of what the guys had been up to in Cape Town while he was in Australia and New Zealand with the back-up players.

'The feedback was they were busting a gut and had the fitness statistics to prove it and they were looking after each other. That's all I wanted them to do and I did not need to ask any further questions.'

White confirms that the senior players, in consultation with him, controlled player affairs.

'The biggest bonus this team had was experience among the coaching and playing staff. Gert had been to a World Cup. Os and Monty had been to a World Cup as experienced players in 1999. Guys like Smitty, Victor and Bakkies went in

2003, and were four years older, more secure in their ability and the best in their positions in the world, while a guy like Schalk hated every minute of being a passenger at the 2003 World Cup. We weren't going to let any young player feel like that at this World Cup. There was honesty among us and that didn't mean we all agreed with each other, but at the World Cup, if I wanted to have a drink, I had one, so why couldn't a player? We all agreed that if someone dropped the ball off the field, they dropped it for everyone. I tell people this World Cup was won before we got there. We'd done all the work and now we just had to play. Sure we needed luck, any team does, but we didn't go to the World Cup trying to find a winning formula or searching for answers. I knew my best XV and they knew I knew it because I had told them. I had told every player what I expected of him and who was numbers one, two and three in every position. I also told them we would reassess everything at the quarter-final stage, so beyond that there would be no guarantee.'

White insists that over four years, a special group of players had come together and the quality of the squad was characterised by those who did not make it.

'Some very good players missed out and that showed the guys who were there how good and how fortunate they were. But we were determined not to make the mistakes of the past. The players asked for balance, but that did not mean a week away for a vacation, or beach sports or less intensity. It meant once we had trained, they could do their own thing, and it was also predetermined when the families came and where they stayed. There was nothing secretive and those players who had signed French club contracts took a couple of days out to visit those clubs during the World Cup. That's the recipe this squad had. There simply was no bullshit and Smitty led a core of strong leaders, who all had an opinion and spoke their minds, but within the framework of the team ethos. When we left for France we'd bonded over four years and not four days. It is why I will never stop preaching the philosophy of building a team because within that set-up, players learn to play for each other and sacrifice on behalf of each other. We were ready for France and we went there believing we could win and never hoping for a win. As a coach, there is a huge difference when your players have that mindset.'

18

AN ARM WRESTLE, A PUSH TO THE BACK AND A GOLD MEDAL

Jake White confesses to being in two minds before playing England in the World Cup final. His ego wanted to put 30-plus points past the Poms again, as had happened in the pool match, and show the world that it was possible to play expansive, extravagant and exciting rugby in a World Cup decider.

The Springboks, so far, had been magnificent. They had scored nine tries in the play-offs, more than any other team. Bryan Habana was the tournament's leading try-scorer, Percy Montgomery was the leading point-scorer and outside of the scare against Tonga and the two-minute terror against Fiji in the quarter-final, the Boks had looked unbeatable. White and his Boks had always targeted the pool game against England as the mini-final, and when they whipped them 36-0, there was a fear among the media and South African rugby public that the Boks had played their World Cup and that against tougher opposition they wouldn't regain the intensity so evident against England. The games that followed had been ordinary, with the occasional thrill overshadowed by a side seemingly in second gear. White told the media not to worry and Springbok specialist coach Eddie Jones (who coached Australia at the 2003 World Cup) said the team, having peaked for the one pool game that mattered, needed to build towards a climax for an anticipated final. If you were in France throughout the tournament, as I was, and followed the Boks around, you believed White and Jones, simply because the mood of the players had not changed from day one until the last day when they won the World Cup. The routine stayed the same, be it Samoa in the opening game or England in the final. All the players admitted afterwards that the only match they felt on edge was the quarter-final against Fiji, and they only felt nervous because the night before they'd seen Australia and New Zealand crash out of the World Cup.

The players and management knew that the hard work for the World Cup had already been done in South Africa. They all agreed the first 40 minutes in the warm-up match against Scotland in Edinburgh was enough for them to know they would not lose the World Cup, but that another team would have to play exceptional rugby to beat them.

There was also this total belief that the Boks would not play the All Blacks at the World Cup. Whenever I spoke to a player or to one of the Bok coaches, they seemed convinced New Zealand would implode somewhere along the line. White, in particular, had seen footage of the All Blacks doing downtime in the waters of Marseilles, so as to not put pressure on themselves. He had read about players getting a week off to refocus between pool games and outside of the first 20 minutes against Italy, the All Blacks struggled for consistency in performance. The Bok coach thought they'd got it all wrong in their approach because they were confusing downtime with a holiday. He told me France would beat the All Blacks in the quarter-final, just like he had predicted Argentina would beat France in the pool stage to set up a New Zealand-France quarter-final in Cardiff. When

White saw the All Blacks team for the quarter-final, he was even more convinced of his prediction and the only time he backtracked was when he was made aware of the French starting XV. 'No All Blacks team can lose to those guys,' he said to me. 'They've picked the slowest centre in world rugby at fullback [Damien Traille] and a one-dimensional flyhalf [Lionel Beauxis]. The French don't believe they can win. This is about limiting the damage.'

As it transpired, the All Blacks would never even look to expose Traille's inexperience at fullback and lack of pace. They would also completely change their approach of the previous four years in trying to batter the French into submission because of an apparent fear of a French counter-attacking game that never existed at the tournament.

Jonathan Kaplan, South Africa's leading referee and the world's most capped Test referee, was running the touchline in the Cardiff quarter-final and he erred when missing an obvious forward pass that led to France's second try. But as Kaplan would point out afterwards, the most telling statistic of the All Blacks' defeat was how they completely disregarded what had worked for them for the last four years and tried a new game for the first time in that quarter-final.

'The All Blacks attacked through pick-and-go and around the fringes four times more than the average over four years,' he said to me when I mocked him about the forward pass. 'They completely changed and ignored what had worked for them in the four-year build-up to the World Cup.'

Kaplan has never denied missing the forward pass, but says any analysis of the New Zealand performance would show they lost because of more than one missed forward pass.

White is another who has no doubt the All Blacks blew it through poor selections and a mystifying game plan in which they seemed terrified to use the ball and the width of the pitch. But more than that, White knew that when the All Blacks went out of the tournament, the Springboks would lift the Webb Ellis Cup.

'We were always confident it would take a very good team to beat us and I think everyone in our squad knew that the only team capable was New Zealand. They'd come from 21-12 down in Durban to beat us 26-21 [in the 2007 Tri-Nations], and while none of our players feared the All Blacks, there was respect for their capabilities. Psychologically the All Blacks would also think they had an edge – that if they beat us in Durban, why could they not do it in Paris?'

White describes the night of the All Blacks' exit as one of the more extraordinary because of how the Boks reacted to the result.

'Normally players watch those kinds of games in the team room, but that night most of the guys watched in their own rooms. Every time France scored there would be a cheer. I remember thinking it was too good to be true and that the All Blacks couldn't be blowing this one. With a minute to go, I thought they'd get out of jail when a French hand clearly played the ball on the ground from the wrong side of the ruck. I closed my eyes – we'd be playing the All Blacks in the final and it would take one hell of a performance to beat them. I was convinced the French would be penalised, the penalty would be kicked and the All Blacks, having won 21-20, would then step up a gear in the semi-final and final. The referee [Englishman Wayne Barnes], God bless him, did not award a penalty and the French won 20-18. When the final whistle went, I knew the tournament was ours. Our players were on the balconies of their rooms, bellowing that the All Blacks were out. I knew we couldn't lose to Argentina, France or England, and although we still had to get past Fiji the next day, I felt we were too good to lose to them, no matter how well they played or how badly we performed.'

Montgomery tells a similar story of the euphoria at the news that the All Blacks were going home.

'They were the one team who had beaten us more in those four years than we had beaten them. With them and Australia gone, it was our tournament to lose, and that is perhaps why we put in such a stuttering performance against Fiji. I think we were afraid to lose instead of focusing on winning and that's exactly what Smitty told us during the game when Fiji scored two tries to level the scores at 20-all. He said our eyes were beginning to look as big and disbelieving as those of the All Blacks in Cardiff – that it was bullshit and we needed to hit back immediately and play the kind of rugby that got us to the quarter-final. He refused to accept we would be leaving Marseilles as the third big team out of the World Cup, and the boys responded with a strong last 20 minutes. JP Pietersen's try-saving cover tackle just after Smitty's talk behind the posts, was also huge in the context of the game – one I was just relieved to have got out of the way.'

White says all the players felt the same after the 37-20 win. Frans Steyn was one of the first to put his arm around him and express relief that he wouldn't have to see another Pacific Islands team at the World Cup – having felt the tackles from the best of Samoa, Tonga and Fiji, and been made to tackle them. And with the best Pacific Islands team at the tournament, the All Blacks, also gone, the Boks knew that if they played to their ability they'd win the competition.

Montgomery says nothing ever changed in their build-up throughout the tournament, with the boys only reducing their alcohol intake in the week of the final (although he won't commit to knowing exactly by how much).

'The only week in which there seemed to be a bit of friction was in Marseilles leading up to the quarter-final, but that was perhaps nervous tension. I read in Jake's book [*In Black and White*] how Smitty and him had a go at each other behind closed doors. None of us were aware of that at the time, but for the rest we trained as we had done all year and we prepared with the same calmness we had done all tournament. England, in the pool stage, was our big game and we didn't believe we could lose to them. When we were leading by 30 points the message on the field was that the other victory was to keep them scoreless. That is why there was such desperate defence in those last few minutes. Afterwards, Smitty was calm when talking to the guys in the change room. He said that we'd known enough disappointment against England in the last few years and that we had earned the right to enjoy the win and to celebrate the occasion. He, like Jake, wanted us to admit what a big win it was and enjoy it for that. There was no talk about the next game being tougher or only celebrating at the end of the tournament. We were entrusted to enjoy it and we did because we knew that most of us would not be starting against Tonga [a match the Boks won 30-25].'

Montgomery says the discipline in the side was because of the lack of rules.

'If you wanted a drink you had one. If you wanted two you had two. Each guy was trusted to know when to stop. It was only in the week of the final when the boys got together and said we should limit the amount of drinking because World Cup finals only come around once in a lifetime for most – with Os [du Randt] the exception.'

Montgomery also says that the key to the build-up was that there was no change in approach from the coaches.

White attributes a lot of that to Eddie Jones's influence.

'With Eddie, he tells you what he thinks and not what he thinks you want to hear. Right from the start, he added value in everything he said. Even when he didn't have the answer he added value because it showed me I wasn't dealing with a guy who thought he knew everything. When we played Samoa in the first game and things weren't going according to plan I turned to him and asked him: "Eddie, what's happening here?" His response, at a very tense time, made me laugh: "I don't know, mate. I've never been in this position. Let's hope they're in the lead by the time we get to the shed and then we can sort it out". I loved that about Eddie at the World Cup. He was no smart arse who had every answer.

'When it came to the semi-final, we knew we had the psychological edge over Argentina because they've never beaten us in the history of the game, and that counts for something in the change room. It is easier to motivate your team when they've never lost to an opponent than it is for that opponent's coach to convince his team they can win. When the Pumas took the ball two channels wide of the ruck and tried to attack us away from our forwards in the opening five minutes of the game, Eddie calmly turned to me and said: "Mate, they don't believe they can beat us and that's why they've changed the way they've played all tournament." He was spot on and we played some outstanding "finals footie" to win [37-13].

'I admit I was eager to blow the English away in the final because I knew we had a team good enough to beat them with an expansive game, but Eddie, in private, questioned my approach. He said he had coached in a losing World Cup final [Australia lost to England in the last 20 seconds of extra time in 2003]. He said to lose the World Cup, you needed one point less than the winner and to win it you needed one point more than the loser. No one, he added, remembered how World Cup finals were won, but they never forgot how they were lost. He stressed that the only coach's voice the team needed to hear in the week of the final was mine and that I shouldn't change what had worked for me as a coach or for the players as a unit. England, he said, could only have a sniff if we played high-risk rugby. If they got an early intercept or a breakaway try and with their passionate support base, they might begin to believe the miracle was on. I'll never forget his description of the final and why it would suit us. "It is going to be an arm wrestle, mate, and they aren't strong enough to win it". He was 100% accurate and when I spoke to the senior players about the approach to the final and about decision-making, they all agreed that England didn't have the ability to play catch-up rugby. When it came to suffocating the opposition, we had the advantage in every aspect to win the game. As a team, we knew it wasn't going to be pretty, but we had come to win the World Cup and in the tournament we'd shown we could also play brilliant rugby. The final was about winning.'

White says the 'arm wrestle' analogy influenced his decision to select Wikus van Heerden ahead of Bob Skinstad among the reserves because he needed cover for Schalk Burger. He and Jones felt this was not a final that was going to be won by a moment of attacking brilliance, but by physicality in the tackle, around the fringes of the ruck, and in defence, as well as through superior tactical kicking.

'There was a reason every selection decision was made at the World Cup and especially in the final. England played better than I thought they would in the final, but we were always in control and the only time they broke our line, just after half-time, was from a pass that went behind [England centre] Matthew Tait and the bounce of the ball beat our defence more than any structured play. We survived that following minute and that was as close as they got.'

Montgomery also singles out Danie Rossouw's desperate lunge on England wing Mark Cueto as a crucial moment in the final (TV replays showed Cueto's left foot had made contact with the touchline and the try was disallowed by Australian TMO Stuart Dickinson). But he doesn't believe the Boks would have lost if England had scored and taken the lead had Jonny Wilkinson added the conversion.

'It would just have forced us to be more attacking and I felt we had the attacking game to break them down if we needed it. But as a team we had agreed that we did not have to put ourselves at risk and play rugby that could be seen as stupid rugby in a final.'

Montgomery's bravery in playing the last 58 minutes of the final with torn knee ligaments has been detailed in the first chapter, but he insists he was never coming off, unless it was on a stretcher. Of the final, he remembers everything, and unlike most Tests, it was not one that passed in a blaze.

'Because there was so much tactical kicking, everything seemed to be done at a slower pace and the only frantic minutes were just after half-time when Cueto nearly scored in the corner.'

Montgomery also couldn't believe Toby Flood, England's replacement centre, was not given a yellow or red card for a cowardly push into his back that forced him to hurdle over the advertising boards and crash into a TV camera.

'The push was unnecessary as there was no way either of us could beat the ball to the deadball line. It was dangerous and could have caused me some serious damage. I could have gone straight into the advertising boards and I was very lucky to escape injury. I hurt my hand on contact with the camera but, like with the knee, the adrenalin meant I dealt with the pain. I saw footage of that push afterwards and if I had done that to a player I'd feel embarrassed. As it was, all I felt that night was elation.'

I bumped into Montgomery sometime between 3 and 4am on the Sunday following the 15-6 victory and the Boks' second World Cup win in four attempts. Jake White, a mate and I were on our way to the coach's room for a photo with the World Cup. Montgomery had come from the team room with a plate of steak and chips. Jake, in the lift, asked Monty if the chips were for his model and vegetarian wife Tasmin.

'You know she doesn't eat meat,' joked Montgomery.

'How is the knee?' asked White.

'Sore,' said Montgomery.

Coach and player then beamed at each other, saying nothing, but screaming acknowledgement that they'd won the World Cup.

Montgomery was too sore to soak up the festivities going on downstairs in the team room and just wanted to be upstairs with his wife. In the morning, he phoned his father. When I asked Montgomery Senior what Monty had said he admitted not a hell of a lot.

'I told him "Well done my boy" and he said, "Hey dad, that's the big one, hey". And then he again thanked me for always believing in him.'

19

WHEN SIX ACTUALLY MEANS 100

'Why would you want to go back to South Africa now? What is there for you to achieve?,' Jake White asked Percy Montgomery. 'You have just had the perfect send-off by not missing a kick in a winning World Cup final, and displaying the most unbelievable courage to complete the game with torn knee ligaments. Why risk that kind of ending to your international career?'

The World Cup-winning coach and World Cup-winning fullback were in St Petersburg, Russia, being honoured at the Laureus Awards – sport's international equivalent of the Oscars. The world champion Springboks were voted the 2007 Team of the Year and Montgomery shared the stage with sporting legend, and arguably the world's greatest tennis player of all-time, Roger Federer.

'I looked up all night and couldn't believe who was sitting around us,' says Montgomery. 'These were the men and women who dominate the sports pages around the world, who get recognised in every country and who are the best in their professions. And here I was – a World Cup-winning Springbok – part of that kind of company. Why, asked Jake, would I want to give this kind of ending up for one that possibly would not go according to plan if I went back and played for the Springboks for one more season? I know Jake was concerned that I'd end up being disappointed in 2008 – that I would fail myself or that I would not be appreciated in South Africa or that I'd break down what I had achieved playing in his side. But I also knew that no one could take away 2007 and there was something in me that stirred at the chance of being a part of a new Bok chapter and, as world champions, beating the All Blacks in New Zealand. I'd won there once in my Test career [in 1998], which was more than most Boks I had played with, but there were so many good players in the Bok squad and I believed 2008 would be a year in which it was very possible the Boks would win in New Zealand. I will always want to give something back to the game and when I was spoken to about a possible short-term Bok mentorship with those players identified to play fullback for the Boks, that was equally appealing.'

And so began the debate within Montgomery's mind. Should he leave France, where he had signed a one-season contract with Perpignan, return to South Africa and fight for a place in the Springbok squad in an attempt to become the first South African to play 100 Tests? Or should he reflect on an international career that climaxed in the most glorious fashion in Paris when the Boks beat England to win the World Cup? Montgomery admits the month that followed the 20 October triumph had been the most frantic and intense of his life, but privately the most satisfying because, for the first time, South African rugby supporters unanimously, without bias and without question, cheered him.

'For the first and definitely last time in my life, I felt like a rock star. I'll never forget the day after the World Cup final when the squad went down to Rugby Town near the Eiffel

Tower to do a signing session, and when we got there people were chanting our names and screaming and waving. We were all South Africans and we were all winners. I was not Percy from Cape Town or the guy who missed a kick, or the guy with white boots. I was one of the players who had brought happiness to people. It was the most awesome feeling. Then when we got back to South Africa, it was even more amazing – at the airport and when we went on the tour of the country. It was the most incredible feeling I have ever known to see such adulation, support and happiness on the faces of people. I've had mixed reviews and reactions in South Africa throughout my career, but during that week when we took the World Cup throughout the country, people celebrated us. Personally, I have never felt so loved by rugby supporters.'

So why go back and risk being booed at Loftus Versfeld in Pretoria or being cursed by the media or being ridiculed by supporters?

New Springbok coach Peter de Villiers and manager of national teams, Andy Marinos, had visited Montgomery in Perpignan. De Villiers had told Montgomery that he did not view him as his first-choice fullback because he wanted to use 2008 to start building the next generation of player who could defend the World Cup in 2011. But he also told him he rated him enough to pick him in his squad and he asked if he was willing to play a supporting role to a less experienced and younger player and share his knowledge. Montgomery was emphatic about only one thing: if he did go back he would have no problem helping whoever it was De Villiers had identified (Conrad Jantjes). He told De Villiers it was no player's right to demand a starting place in the Bok team and that no player had the right to think the Bok jersey was his. He also said he did not want to be picked because of sentimental reasons or emotion, but because the coach felt he had a role to play, be it in the starting XV, the match 22 or the extended squad.

Top to bottom: Enjoying a 'starter' with Bakkies Botha and John Smit; a bit of team building with Bryan Habana and Schalk Burger; and getting into the swing of things with Jaque Fourie, Danie Rossouw and Schalk.

This page: Bakkies Botha and I couldn't go to France in 2007 and not have a French loaf; drinking coffee – French style – with John Smit and Butch James.
Opposite page: Toby Flood shoved me into a cameraman during the World Cup final. I was lucky not to be seriously injured.

RUGBY WORLD CUP 2007
SAINT-DENIS

2007

This page: Bob Skinstad, Bryan Habana and I wearing our special World Cup caps, with Jean de Villiers, the team jester, doing his best not to miss out; Nelson Mandela holds the Webb Ellis Cup, with the Boks all wearing 46664 T-shirts in support of Madiba's Aids programme.
Opposite page: A family photo with a difference – I literally brought the World Cup home.

This page: Taneal and Nicholas with the Webb Ellis Cup. *Opposite page:* South Africans lined the streets in their thousands for the Boks' nationwide tour after the World Cup; the Boks got to meet Roger Federer, arguably the world's greatest ever tennis player, at the Laureus World Sports Awards in 2007. The Boks were named Team of the Year.

SASOL
THE SPRINGBOKS
SASOL

Apart from the green and gold of the Springboks, I've worn seven other jerseys during my professional career: Western Province, Western Stormers and Stormers *(this page)* and Newport, Barbarians, Sharks and Perpignan *(opposite page)*.

KooGa
NEWPORT
DAVID
LEWIS
NEWPORT
Scottish
Amicable

dacom
Percival Colin
Montgomery
100th Test
canterbury
sasol
Vodacom Rugby
goes mobile.

Opposite page: Walking out onto Newlands before my 100th Test was an emotional experience. *This page:* A fan shows his support; my parents cheer me on from Highbury Safika Media's private suite; Nicholas and I thank the crowd, while Taneal looks on.

century

Opposite page: All Blacks captain Richie McCaw offers his congratulations after my 100th Test. *This page:* Saru president Oregan Hoskins presents me with a special gold Bok cap to mark the occasion. I had absolutely no idea that this ceremony had been arranged.

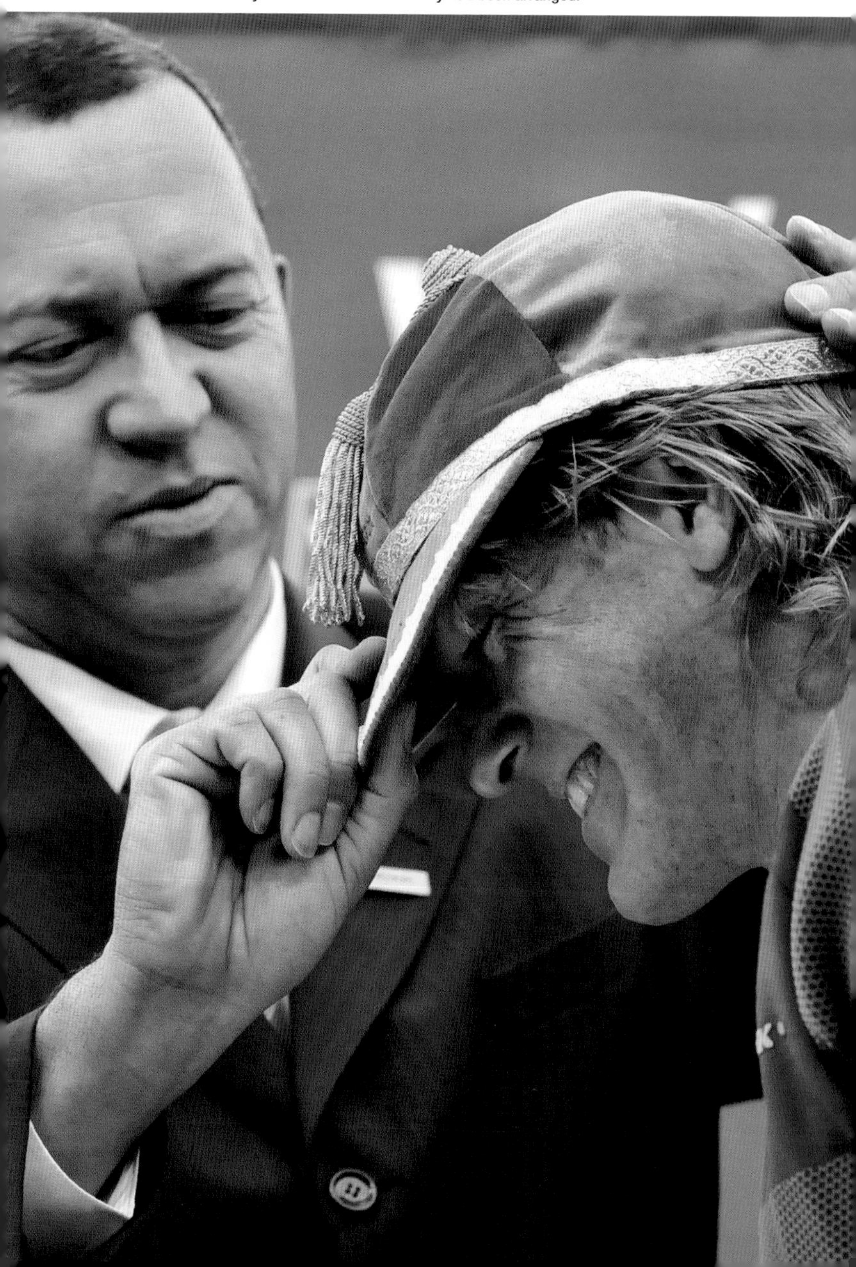

Saluting the Ellis Park crowd after my 102nd, and last, Test for the Boks. We thrashed the Wallabies 53-8 and I kicked two conversions in the second half.

'I looked at this guy, who had played 94 Tests for South Africa and won everything there was to win and all I saw was humility, passion and professionalism,' says De Villiers. 'I could not make the decision for him to come back to South Africa, but I needed him to know there was a role for him to play in my first year as national coach.'

'What would you do?', Montgomery asked me when I visited him in Perpignan to continue the background research for this book. I echoed De Villiers's sentiments that he had a role to play and that I did not believe he would be doing his career justice by playing out his last year in France. I knew he had always wanted to return to Cape Town and that he wanted his son, Nicholas, to be schooled at SACS. I knew he wanted to be close to his parents and that he wanted the familiarity of the city dearest to his heart. I knew it because he had told me it often enough, but for a player who had unintentionally divided rugby opinion in South Africa, there were doubts because he was hesitant to break down what had been achieved in Paris.

'Mark,' replied Montgomery, 'when I feel homesick, which is often, I don't watch footage of the World Cup final. I go onto YouTube and watch footage of our bus rides through South Africa after the tournament. I watch the joy on the faces of people and I get goosebumps knowing I played a part in that. When I think of the World Cup win, I don't think of what I did but of how our team success gave so many people such a high.'

And so the debate that Montgomery had been having with himself about one more go at the Springboks extended to me and a few other people, which included, most importantly, Tasmin, his parents, Nicholas, Stormers coach Rassie Erasmus, Western Province coach Allister Coetzee, Bok coach De Villiers, Bok captain John Smit, Western Province MD Rob Wagner and, critically, Springbok and Stormers assistant coach Gary Gold. Gold had acted as a go-between with SA Rugby (the professional arm of Saru) and WP on behalf of Montgomery, who a few years earlier had dispensed with agents because of his disgust at how his affairs were handled. His father-in-law, Craig Tobitt, now managed his financial portfolio and I encouraged Montgomery to invest in the efficiency of In-Site Player Sport management to give him organisational comfort should he return to South Africa. Former SA Rugby MD, Rian Oberholzer, was a director of In-Site. Another former SA Rugby employee, Jonty Goslett, was operationally strong in the company and was also a shareholder. Both were thrilled at the prospect of assisting Montgomery and as both represented De Villiers, there was also clarity in communication between the coach and player.

Montgomery wanted no favours and De Villiers wasn't prepared to give him any, but he did believe there was value in having him there to hand over the baton to his successor. De Villiers also felt that Montgomery's experience and professionalism would be a factor if the Boks were to win in New Zealand. De Villiers, a big believer in tradition, also felt it was only right that Montgomery played out his Test career in South Africa and not at a club side in France. The money Montgomery would get if he returned to South Africa was a third of his income in France, but the counter-argument to that was he probably had one year left of professional rugby and in any event, no amount of money could buy a player the honour of being the first Springbok to 100 Test caps.

When he asked me again why I believed he should come back, I said he had a part to play, that the Boks would win in New Zealand in 2008 and that he had a coach who believed it was only right for his achievements to be celebrated at Newlands, against the All Blacks on 16 August 2008. I also knew how much he wanted to wear the Western Province jersey again and make a contribution to a generation who were about to start junior school when he first played for the Province senior side. We spent a great week in Perpignan chatting about the Springboks, WP and Cape Town, and he and Tasmin openly discussed the positives and possible negatives of the player's return. The two had been through so much in Cape Town prior to Montgomery's departure for Newport in 2002 and while he makes no secret that Tasmin is the emotional rock in his life, he was not prepared to make a decision that would benefit a personal goal of getting 100 Test caps.

'It had to be the right one for our family. Tazzie had to embrace it and Nicholas had to want it. Taneal, being just three-and-a-half years old, wanted me around and I had to take that into consideration because if I went back, it would mean being away from home for a few months while the Boks travelled. I wanted to go back and fight for those six Test caps, but not at the expense of my family. If Tasmin and Nicholas had said no then I would have stayed in France.'

Tasmin says saying no was never going to be an option when she saw the sparkle back in her husband's eyes.

'He had arrived in Perpignan so determined to do well for the club, but still carrying the knee injury from the World Cup final. He rushed his recovery because he felt guilty about not being able to play immediately when we arrived. He also struggled with the club culture – the way they played and the lack of communication between the coach and himself, mainly because of the language barrier. As a family, we were loving it in Perpignan because we were always together and he was always at home and we could live in absolute normality with no media intrusion. But I knew he was not happy with his rugby. I knew he so desperately wanted to be back in South Africa and I also knew what the Springbok jersey meant to him.'

Montgomery doesn't hide the fact that there was a brief moment when, after reading Jake White's autobiography *In Black and White,* he despised everything about South African rugby on the basis of what Saru had done to White. Montgomery, after reading the book, didn't know if he ever wanted to play for the Springboks again.

'It was a knee-jerk reaction because it had nothing to do with how I felt about the Springboks, but more about the administration. It seemed to me that the administrators, no matter how good or bad they were, survived because of the team performance and that they seemed to dine out on the World Cup win. Naively, I thought at that stage that any help I would give the Springboks meant I was helping these guys survive. I mean, we never saw anybody from the administration when we were at the World Cup and we only ever read about them when there was something controversial being said about South African rugby or the team. As a player, you think you have an idea of what is going on, but when I read Jake's book I was horrified at some of the things that had been happening behind the scenes.

'Throughout my career, I have never criticised the game's administration, because as a player, I could only be harming my career. I took a lesson from Auckland in 1997 when Louis Luyt, in crapping on the Springbok team after we lost to the All Blacks, told James Small to shut up, sit down and remember who paid his salary. Shutting up, I decided, was the safest policy and in any event I was never the guy who would make big statements to the media to stir up controversy.

'For me, it was always about doing what was best for the Boks, but I felt horrible inside and depressed when I finished reading Jake's book. I was down because of what the administration had put him through. I told Taz that maybe it was best that it all ended with that night in Paris. But as the months passed in Perpignan and certain people started speaking to me about possibly playing for the Springboks again, my belief in the power of the Boks took over from my disillusionment about what I had read in Jake's book. I had told the media after the World Cup final that if the new Bok coach ever needed me in any capacity, I was a phone call away, and the new coach had done more than phone – he had come to Perpignan to see me.'

De Villiers, a month before the start of the Test season, reaffirmed his interest in Montgomery. Perpignan, SA Rugby and Western Province all agreed to an early release for the player, with the only proviso that he return for the French Top 14 semi-final and possible final, which he would do on the weekend in June when the Springboks played Italy in Cape Town.

'I have always given everything to every team I played for and if I do have one regret in rugby, it is that the people of Perpignan never got to see the best of me,' says Montgomery. 'The lifestyle in the south of France is fantastic, the people are wonderful and I always got support and encouragement whenever I was out and about in Perpignan. But I know I came back from injury too early and I did it because I wanted to show them I was not a World Cup star over there on a pension payout, but someone who wanted to help them to succeed. We played in the European Cup quarter-final and made it to the Top 14 semi-final and while the low point for me was that I was never in prime form, I will never forget being a part of the Perpignan team that ended Stade Français' unbeaten home record of 62 wins over a four-year period. I kicked well that night in difficult conditions and played well in general and to see what winning in Paris meant to the local Perpignan players was memorable. I also got to play my last game for Perpignan in front of a crowd of more than 50 000 in Marseilles and while we lost to a better team in Clermont [who reached the Top 14 final], I still felt privileged to play in a match of such importance to Perpignan.

'Books are about honesty and, where necessary, apologies. To the people of Perpignan, I apologise for not making more of an impact, but please know that I always gave it everything and the jersey meant as much to me as it did for those guys who were born in Perpignan. The provincial jersey that will always be my most cherished is Western Province's because that's always been my home jersey. But when it comes to commitment, I have always believed that when you put on a jersey, you become part of that culture and you play with the passion that culture demands. I did that at Newport and at the Sharks but unfortunately my fitness and form at Perpignan were not as strong as my passion, although by the time I left, I felt I was playing better rugby. Emotionally, I was ready to fight for those six Test caps, even though I knew there was no guarantee I would get to 100. That was the risk I was willing to take because I was convinced going back to South Africa was the right thing to do, not just for those six Tests, but for my family to settle in Cape Town and for us all to start living away from the abnormality of the life I'd experienced as a professional rugby player.'

Montgomery played 18 matches for Perpignan, scored 118 points and went past 320 first-class games in a 13-year professional career, but when he got on the plane from Paris to Johannesburg, there was no reflection on his achievement. The number he thought most about was six because 94 was a number easily forgotten, but being the first Bok to 100 Tests was an achievement that would always be remembered.

20

RICKY'S RUN, 100 TESTS AND RETIREMENT

Percy Montgomery played 102 Tests for South Africa and Ricky Januarie's match-winning try, against the All Blacks in Dunedin in 2008, is the best Bok try he saw during his career.

'The circumstance – scoring a try with three minutes to go and with the Boks down by five points and down to 14 men – obviously adds to the impact, as does the fact that it was against New Zealand at a ground where the Springboks had never won, but I'll always consider myself very lucky to have been at Carisbrook to watch that try,' says Montgomery. 'It was just an amazing piece of individual brilliance, and while some say Ricky got a lucky bounce, I disagree. He dummied, broke, beat a defender and knew exactly where he wanted that kick to go when he chipped it. Players practise those kinds of kicks, so it top-spins and rolls, and bounces back to the left or to the right. It doesn't always come off, but when Ricky kicked it, he knew his biggest challenge was to be the first one there to collect it. If there was a moment when I held my breath, it was when he dived elaborately because I've seen players lose control of a rugby ball in those situations.

'When people ask me why I came back to South Africa in 2008 after the high of winning the World Cup in 2007, I tell them it was to be in Dunedin and to be part of history – to watch Ricky's sensational try and to be in another Bok team that beat the All Blacks in New Zealand.'

If that day was one of the highs of Montgomery's career then his low was the 2007 Super 14 final at Kings Park – when Bryan Habana scored a try in the last passage of play to give the Bulls a 20-19 victory. The Sharks, who'd earlier become the first South African team to top the log, were shattered.

'When I reflect on the achievements of teams I have played in then that defeat certainly is the only negative I would list. It is a memory I don't enjoy because I believe it could have been so different had Smitty [John Smit] and I been on the field. There is no guarantee I would have succeeded with the conversion Frans Steyn missed or I may also have missed touch in the last movement of the game. But deep down, I back myself to have made that conversion or at least to have been in a position to influence a positive outcome in those final minutes. Smitty and I were the two most experienced players in the Sharks team and I will never understand why [coach] Dick Muir pulled me off with nearly 20 minutes to go. In terms of hollow moments, watching from the sideline as Frans rushed the conversion and missed is right up there with seeing Bryan Habana score the try to win the game.

'Bryan was a very good Bok team-mate of mine, but he shouldn't have been on the field at that stage of the final – he should have been given a red card in the first few minutes for taking me out in the air when I went for a high ball. Outside of being on the end of a spear tackle, I'd say a lineout jumper being sacked by the opposition without his support players there to assist and a player being taken out in the air as he is fielding a high ball are the most dangerous because the falling player is powerless to stop the fall. I am not exaggerating when I say I could have broken my neck when I came crashing down from Bryan's challenge and I was shocked that he didn't at least get a yellow card. I have seen guys being given a red card for that kind of offence and [Wallabies wing] Wendell Sailor was given a yellow card in the 2003 World Cup pool match against Argentina for a similar infringement.

'I was angrier with Bryan than New Zealand referee Steve Walsh. I can understand the referee being reluctant to send off someone in the opening minutes of a final, but it is that kind of inconsistency that troubles players. If that had happened with five minutes to go, I am sure he would have had no hesitation in giving Bryan a card. I actually thought Walsh had a good game, even though we lost, but he should definitely have acted against Bryan. Bryan SMSed me to apologise afterwards and when we met up at the Bok camp a day later, he apologised again. I accepted it, but it didn't make up for my anger at the time or my hurt at how the Super 14 final had finished.

'You could say my match started with a fall from grace and ended with the biggest one when Dickie yanked me. I was probably more hurt than angry. I thought I had played well enough to be on the field and that my experience in the last quarter would be valuable, but Dickie felt differently. It is the one match that I look back on my career and ask "Why?" It was one of the hardest defeats I've known and I sulked that night. Some of the Sharks boys came to my house for a few drinks. I played Steve Hofmeyr's "Ek bly 'n Bul" [I'm always a Bull] over and over again as I drowned my sorrows.'

However, Montgomery prefers to focus on the good times in his career, and one of those was Januarie's try in 2008.

'I was so pleased for him. He had been one of the true characters at the World Cup and despite having to play a supporting role to Fourie du Preez, he was always upbeat and got behind every player with his enthusiasm. It was just reward for someone who has had his fair share of disciplinary problems within the Boks, but can never be faltered for how he plays the game.'

It is the 30-28 win against the All Blacks in Dunedin that made every financial sacrifice worth it when Montgomery decided to return to South Africa from France and try and become the first Springbok to play 100 Tests. He believed the World Cup Boks were good enough to beat the All Blacks. To be part of a team that got a chance to do it in New Zealand could not be matched.

'If we had won in South Africa, then the doubters would have argued we had home-ground advantage, so to win where no Bok team had ever won, with most of the World Cup-winning players, was even more special. To finish off my Test career in New Zealand with a win is something to cherish because so few Boks have experienced that feeling.'

The win made Montgomery the only post-isolation Bok to have won twice there against the All Blacks. The fact that it took 10 years between the first and second illustrates the enormity of the victory in 2008.

'I've played in New Zealand so many times – for Province, the Stormers, Sharks and Boks – and there is no tougher place to win because they have such good rugby players. I don't think it was ever a mental thing or the fact that we, as South Africans, didn't back ourselves. They are just so hard to beat there and when we beat the All Blacks in Dunedin, it was the first time they had lost at home in five years. While Ricky's individuality won the game for us, we fielded a very good side to be in a position to win the game.'

Montgomery's belief in the quality of the Bok players in 2008 never wavered, despite the 19-8 defeat to the All Blacks in Wellington, the 16-9 loss to the Wallabies in Perth and two disappointing Tri-Nations defeats against the All Blacks at Newlands (19-0) and Wallabies at Kings Park (27-15).

'There are such good players in this country and to be given a chance to come back and reach the milestone of

100 Tests in that company is a debt I will always owe to Peter de Villiers. When we spoke in Perpignan, I told him I did not want an emotional handout and he said he would not give me one. It was explained to me that in the way he had mapped out the season, he was going to start me at Newlands against the All Blacks in what would be my 100th Test. Peter was honest with me throughout the season and explained which matches I would be playing in and what my role would be when I was not starting. He also allowed me to impart my knowledge on the younger players. It felt good to be in a team environment where I knew exactly where I stood. I will always be a competitor and fight for the right to start, but it was made clear from the first day I was at the Bok camp in 2008 that I was not part of the next World Cup campaign and that my value to the team would be to help in Peter's first season as an international coach. I was comfortable with that. Peter and I agreed that I would be the only one who would know when it was time to go at Test level, but I would only know for sure if I was playing for the Boks.

'When I was in Perpignan and the talk started about me possibly returning to South Africa and trying to make it to 100 Tests, the one motivation was that I never wanted to look back on my career with any regret and think I should have done it differently. I would have been crushed to watch that Dunedin win on TV in France knowing I had turned down a chance to be part of Peter's first Test squad. What I felt when we beat the All Blacks in Dunedin is right up there with how I felt the night we beat England to win the World Cup. As a player I don't separate the two wins. One was as big as the other.'

If the two wins Montgomery speaks of are the greatest victories in his career, then the greatest day will always be winning his 100th Test cap, although the days that followed the occasion confirmed to him that it was time to go as a Test player. All that had to be determined was whether he went after Test 101 (in Durban) or Test 102 (in Johannesburg), which was the Boks' last Tri-Nations match of the season.

'Any player wants to go out a winner and in the build-up to the Test against Australia at Kings Park I gave it thought that I should go after that match and complete the circle – finish at the ground where my Test career started against the Lions in 1997,' says Montgomery. 'But that would have been selfish and from a squad perspective, it was only right that I gave 100% until the final whistle at Ellis Park on 30 August. I told the coaches and players on the Saturday night after the Durban defeat that the Ellis Park Test would be my last, but I asked everyone not to say anything to the media and not to make a fuss about it because I felt it would distract our preparations. We had lost three Tri-Nations matches in a row, and didn't need any sideshows or distractions.

'It was a strange week knowing that I'd never experience the occasion again as a Bok player – that the ritual of the midweek team dinner would be my last and that the post-match team *kontiki* [fines meeting] would be the last I'd chair as the most senior player in the squad. It was a very emotional week because every time I did something, I knew there wasn't going to be another week in which I would be a Bok player. It was so different to the one in Cape Town before my 100th Test because Cape Town was a celebration of something that had never been achieved and in that week in Jo'burg, I knew I was bringing closure to my Test career.'

Montgomery's 100th Test, at Newlands on 16 August, with 50 000 people chanting his name, was described in the media as bittersweet. Some even suggested it was not a match he would want to remember because the Boks lost to the All Blacks, he missed two penalty kicks and there was no fairytale script. But Montgomery says it was the most incredible day of his career, win or lose.

'That entire week was just so big emotionally, but the reason I missed two kicks at goal had nothing to do with the occasion. There was very little wind during the warm-up and I kicked everything over, but once the game started the wind had picked up and I overcompensated for it with both kicks. It was that simple and I think [All Blacks flyhalf] Dan Carter did the same when he missed three penalties and a conversion from pretty much the same position in the first half. Naturally, I wanted to be on the winning side, but the experience of the week is something I will never forget and the achievement is something that can never be taken away from me. I had downplayed what the 100th cap would mean because once I got back to South Africa from France, I didn't want to jinx it. I had a good 20 minutes against Wales in Bloemfontein, which proved to me I could still play at this level after the doubts I had while playing at Perpignan. Then with each Test appearance, everyone started to talk about how close I was to 100. The media wanted to do interviews and I was very superstitious about talking about it because it takes just one knock to end your season and I knew there wouldn't be a 2009 Test season for me. If I had not come back after 94 Tests then fine, but to come back and aim for 100 and get injured on 98 or 99 would have been heartbreaking.'

In the week of Montgomery's 100th Test, he did very little talking to the media, and he turned down every request for feature article interviews. He knew he still had to get through the Friday captain's run and talking up the moment in the week could only be taunting the gods of superstition.

'In my mind, the 100th cap would be a reality the moment I ran out and took up my place for the anthems, but it was difficult not to think about it all week because wherever I went people were congratulating me and I was saying, "Hey, I haven't got there yet!"'

Unbeknown to Montgomery, HO de Villiers had been asked to present the Springboks with their match jerseys on the Friday morning before the Test, specifically because of the influence HO had on Montgomery's career as a schoolboy.

When I interviewed De Villiers for this book after the 2007 World Cup, he said one of the biggest disappointments for him was not being able to present Montgomery with a Bok jersey. De Villiers had been asked to do the jersey presentation once before, but it was in a week that Montgomery had been dropped from the Springbok team.

'I was honoured to be singled out and asked to make the presentation but at the same time it would have been even more special had I been able to call up the boy who I had spent so many sessions with at SACS,' said De Villiers.

I told the anecdote to SA Rugby's manager of national teams, Andy Marinos, who was doubling up as Bok manager in the 2008 Tri-Nations. I also told the story to Annelee Murray, the Boks' public relations manager, who shared it with Peter de Villiers. All three were unanimous that it was only right to have one legendary fullback, in HO de Villiers, present another with his 100th Test jersey.

The exceptional Murray, having returned to the Boks as team public relations manager after a year working for the International Rugby Board (IRB) as commercial manager, ensured Montgomery would be thanked on every level for his contribution to South Africa. The South African Rugby Union (Saru), as a gift, paid for a two-week holiday to Hawaii for Montgomery, his wife and two children. They also commissioned an oil painting portrait of Montgomery (done by Richie Ryall) to honour his 100th Test and a gold Springbok cap – the opposite of the traditional green Bok cap – was specially made for him. Sasol, the Bok team sponsor, presented Montgomery with a watch of his choice worth R50 000 and he would also get a special match jersey with his full name 'Percival Colin Montgomery' and '100th Test' stitched on the front to sit prominently between the Canterbury logo and the Springbok emblem. Montgomery showed me the jersey on the Friday and seemed embarrassed at how big his name inscription was. 'Do you think it is over the top? Don't you think it should just have said "Monty" and been written a lot smaller?' My response was they couldn't have written it big enough and that for once in his career, he needed to put modesty to one side and enjoy the boldness in the jersey celebration. He described the jersey presentation as the most emotional of his career and said there were two occasions while HO de Villiers was speaking that he nearly burst into tears, and he said he could see it was as emotional for his mentor. The media that week had quoted several icons of the game, who all complimented Montgomery's achievements, longevity and excellence as one of the stars of world rugby. But nothing anyone else could say would compare with hearing his mentor talk with such reverence to him in a room full of Springboks.

The New Zealanders were as flattering in their applause of Montgomery's contribution to the game. All Blacks captain Richie McCaw shook Montgomery's hand immediately after the match and applauded his achievement. The rest of the All Blacks players followed and when Montgomery had returned to the Bok change room, fullback Mils Muliaina, on behalf of all those All Blacks who had played against Montgomery over the past decade, presented him with a signed All Blacks jersey.

'Everything I got afterwards was a surprise. I knew I would have to do a TV interview, but I didn't know a special gold cap had been made for me and it was a big moment when Mils came to our change room and gave me that jersey. To have the opposition recognise you in such a way is one of the biggest compliments a player can get.'

On a Saturday where everything but the result was memorable for Montgomery, the only thing Saru and WP bizarrely couldn't organise was to accommodate Montgomery's parents in a private suite to watch their son play his 100th Test. You would have thought they would be the first couple to be hosted by either the provincial or national president, but they had to be content with sitting in the stands, something they were willing to do as they did not expect – and have never expected – any favours or preferential treatment from anyone.

Highbury Safika Media CEO Kevin Ferguson was appalled that Montgomery's parents would not be treated like royalty, so Montgomery Senior and Lillian were given the treatment they deserved in the company's suite. It proved priceless for me because I got to see the reaction of his parents from 2m away when their son ran out at Newlands for the last time as a Springbok, but for the first time as a Springbok centurion. Montgomery's parents don't show emotion easily and neither of them said anything as their son was introduced to the 50 000 who chanted his name, but the old boy's pumping of his fist as his son waved to the crowd was more powerful than any words.

Two weeks later, Montgomery would play his last Test for South Africa, having started his international career wearing No 13 and ended it wearing No 22. Fittingly, the Boks produced their best performance of the 2008 Tri-Nations to thrash the Wallabies 53-8 (Australia's worst-ever Test defeat), with Montgomery coming off the bench in the 51st minute. He kicked two conversions to take his points tally in Tests to 893.

In his 102 Test-match career, Montgomery played 87 times as a fullback for the Springboks. To illustrate just how big that achievement is you have to know that no other player in the history of the game (at the time of writing in 2008) had played more Tests at fullback, and in the South African context of the 60 men to have played fullback for the Springboks, only André Joubert, with 34 Tests, had exceeded 30. There had been 710 Springboks, of which 384 played in less than five Tests and 157 played in just one Test. But Percy Montgomery is the first to have made it past 100, and that is why he says he can never forget that day at Newlands when he became Springbok rugby's first centurion. For him personally, that day was never about winning or losing.

21

MAKING A POINT, AND A CASE, FOR GOAL KICKERS

It irritates Percy Montgomery that the kicker in professional rugby is so undervalued because big games are so often won by these players. A kicker separated World Cup winners from losers in 1995, 2003 and 2007. A kicker is either maligned or celebrated and rarely is there an in-between. If a kicker kicks well then it is assumed he has played well. Montgomery says there are matches in which he excelled as a player, but kicked poorly. The media analysis was that he had been poor. In other matches he'd kicked flawlessly but not been as good in his general play, but it merited a decent write up.

Kickers, in rugby union, are the surgeons of the game. Which other player in the XV is ever exposed to such dramatic scrutiny as the kicker is when attempting a conversion or penalty? Which other player has his temperament tested in such extreme circumstances, with elements like wind, rain and the ire of the opposition supporters? Perhaps the hooker when throwing a ball in at the lineout, but even that does not compare to the goal kicker because there isn't the tangible pressure of a two- or three-point gain or loss. Which other player for a minute at a time, every time he takes aim, commands the attention of every person at the ground? There isn't another position that asks so much of one player and gives so little reward. If the kicker succeeds, it is accepted he has done his job, for which he is paid millions. If he misses then his salary, his commitment and his pedigree are cursed and questioned.

In a career spanning more than 320 first-class games, Montgomery will tell you people remind him more of the ones he missed. He still hears about his three misses on his Springbok debut against the British & Irish Lions in 1997 and his three against the All Blacks at Newlands in 2001. Those were two matches used as an argument to dismiss his claims to Springbok selection and now to a place among Springbok rugby's greats.

It is ironic because a man who missed more at Test level than Montgomery has never had his pedigree as a kicker questioned. Naas Botha, goal-kicking icon and drop-goal specialist, is regarded as the best Test goal kicker South Africa ever produced, while in the last 30 years, Gerald Bosch, De Wet Ras, Robbie Blair and, more recently, Joel Stransky, Jannie de Beer and Braam van Straaten, were also lauded as lethal kickers. But they all missed on occasion, be it with a penalty, conversion or drop goal. Botha had a 68% conversion success rate in his 28 Tests and a 70% penalty success rate. He kicked more drop goals than any other Springbok but he also missed more than any other Springbok. Some days it was a case of three from three, but there were also days of zero from three or one from four. Statisticians in those days didn't see the necessity of recording accuracy. I know Botha's Test statistics because I did a study of them for a column I wrote many years ago to illustrate the point that as good as he was, he was also vulnerable to failure and that study included footage and reports of every Test he played. It is only in the last five years that goal-kicking statistics have been given the deserving relevance and a kicker's true value can be assessed on his accuracy and not just by way of how many points scored.

Montgomery, before his departure in 2002 for Newport, was regarded as a hit-and-miss specialist when kicking at goal for the Boks. It was an assessment based on two Tests. In Montgomery's first 50 Tests he was used as the first-choice or 'relief' kicker on 17 occasions. The Boks lost only three times when he performed a goal-kicking role, against the Lions in 1997, the All Blacks in 2001 and the defeat against England at Twickenham in 1998 when he kicked one conversion but missed a penalty.

Montgomery, the hit-and-miss specialist, averaged 69% as a goal kicker in the first half of his Test career whereas Naas Botha averaged 69% with his conversions and penalties.

The first time Montgomery started as a Test goal kicker was against Wales at Loftus in Pretoria on 27 June 1998. It was his 17th Test and he scored a then record 31 points. He would better that record with 35 points against Namibia 10 years later, after De Beer had held it since 1999 for his 34 points against England in the World Cup quarter-final in Paris. In 1997, Montgomery would start all four Tri-Nations Tests as the Boks' first-choice goal kicker, slotting vital kicks to beat Australia in Perth and New Zealand in Wellington and finally succeeding with seven from eight in South Africa's win against Australia at Ellis Park. His only miss that day was a penalty from 52m.

In 1999 and 2000, Montgomery was not used as a goal kicker because Honiball, De Beer and Van Straaten all did the goal kicking. Honiball missed the first two penalties against the Lions in the second Test in Durban in 1997 before Montgomery's three failures. André Joubert also missed the conversion of the Boks' third try. But ask the average punter why the Boks lost that series and you'll hear it was because Montgomery missed three kicks and Neil Jenkins kicked all of his. The more accurate response is that Jenkins kicked five penalties, Jeremy Guscott succeeded with the most famous drop goal of his career and the Springboks, using three kickers, missed six attempts at posts and refused to go for a drop goal in the last few minutes (they believed a fourth try was possible and three points would only have given them a draw, which meant they could not win the three-Test series). Montgomery's goal kicking could have won that Test for South Africa, but he alone did not lose it.

Montgomery, before missing three out of four against the All Blacks at Newlands in 2001, kicked 18 points against France and three conversions and four penalties against Italy in Port Elizabeth. But in his first 50 Tests for South Africa, the misses against the British & Irish Lions and the All Blacks were the excess baggage that would not get lighter in selection debates.

Springbok coach Harry Viljoen felt after that defeat against the All Blacks that Montgomery was not kicking or playing well enough to be a selection certainty. Jake White was the team's technical adviser at the time when Conrad Jantjes was selected at fullback against Australia, and Van Straaten was restored as the first-choice kicker. White argued for Montgomery's retention as a flyhalf, centre or wing if Viljoen felt the player was not good enough to start ahead of Jantjes at fullback. White also believed Montgomery's axing slowed the evolution of the Boks' back play because of Van Straaten's limitations as a Test flyhalf or inside centre – the two positions in which the latter was played.

'The axing of Monty from that team put the Springboks back by at least two years,' White told *SA Rugby* magazine in 2005. 'If you consider what he has done for the Springboks, the career that he has enjoyed and the immense value he has brought to his team, it was absolutely criminal that Percy was dropped because of just one bad day at the office. Our rugby took a huge backward step that day, and we are still picking up the pieces.'

Montgomery was the first overseas-based South African player White picked for the Springboks in 2004 and he selected him to kick the points.

'I made it very clear when we met in Cardiff that year that he would be the first-choice goal kicker and that I demanded an initial 75% success rate from him,' recalls White. 'Teams that had won the World Cup always had excellent goal kickers and the task I set Monty was that by the 2007 World Cup, he had to be viewed as one of the best goal kickers in the game with a strike rate close to 80%. [England flyhalf] Jonny Wilkinson had set the yardstick at the 2003 World Cup with 81% and for most of the time in the build-up to that World Cup he was kicking at 90% while his direct opposites were averaging in the 50s when playing against England. That was why England were winning the tight games. As a coach, I wanted that same comfort at the 2007 World Cup. I told Monty that if it came down to a shoot out in the 2007 World Cup, he needed to believe it would go his way because he had the track record. In return, I promised him unconditional support and that his position would never be a discussion point if he was doing his primary role of kicking well.'

Montgomery says the responsibility and the knowledge that he would be the first-choice goal kicker meant his mental approach was different in 2004 compared to his first 50 Tests.

'In most of those matches, I was picked as a player who could kick. When Jake took over, he told me I was a kicker who could play. My role had been defined for the first time in my Test career and it was up to me to succeed. That meant putting in the hours, before and after training, on days off and when not with the Boks. It changed my approach to matches because I knew that so much was expected of me and I never wanted to fail.'

Montgomery played 44 Tests under White and scored 612 points at an average of 13.9 and became the leading Bok point-scorer in Test history. He out-kicked Wilkinson twice in South Africa in 2007 and did not miss a kick in the World Cup semi-final and final to finish the competition with an 80% strike rate. He was also the top point-scorer in France with 105 (two tries, 22 conversions and 17 penalties).

'When the moment came, he was good enough to win games for us and on days we struggled with our general play he was good enough to keep us in the game,' says White. 'Teams feared conceding penalties within 40m of the posts because Monty seldom missed. I felt that by the time we got to France, he had the goal-kicking aura that Wilkinson had at the 2003 World Cup – that gave us a big psychological advantage in every match we played.'

World Cup-winning Springbok captain John Smit agrees that Montgomery was worth a dozen points before each Test and psychologically worth even more when it came to the opposition being afraid to infringe.

'If Monty did not believe he could get it over, he would tell me and it wasn't often that he said no to a chance of adding points. He understood himself so well and knew his capabilities. As a captain, it was a treat to turn to him and jog back knowing that we'd be three points better off. The surprise came if he missed and in the early days, the perception of people and even his team-mates, including me, certainly was more of a surprise when he kicked with consistency.'

Smit first met Montgomery on the Springboks' end-of-year tour in 2000 and says the guy who left for Wales in 2002 and returned in 2004 to play under his leadership was a world apart.

'When I first came into the Bok team, there were plenty of rock stars and in my view he was one of them. They were untouchable within the team set-up and appeared to a young guy like myself to be bigger than the game. When Jake told me he was bringing back Monty to kick the points, I asked him if he was sure about it. I questioned Monty's character in relation to what we wanted to build as a team. I would find out over the next four years just why Jake was that confident and why Monty was so integral to Jake's plan of winning the World Cup.'

Montgomery, having kicked his first rugby ball 30 years ago as a four-year-old, has never been coached to kick. He admits the first book he ever bought and finished reading was Naas Botha's guide to kicking. It is a book he still has.

The most intensive tutoring he got was at a Bok training camp in 2001 when former Aussie Rules kicking specialist Mike Byrne spent a fortnight working with the Bok kickers. Montgomery assumed it finally meant recognition for the player who invariably wins or loses that big game, but Byrne's involvement was brief and the South African Rugby Football Union (Sarfu) determined the services of a kicking specialist were a luxury and not a necessity.

'I could never understand that. I thought he was brilliant and he went on to have a lot of success with Scotland and the All Blacks,' says Montgomery.

Byrne had worked with Aussie Rules, rugby league and union teams, and had been instrumental in developing utility back Stirling Mortlock into a frontline goal kicker for the Wallabies. Ironically, Montgomery's three misses from four kicks against the All Blacks in 2001 would come when Byrne had just completed his introductory course to South African kickers. It is an irony not lost on Montgomery.

'I don't think my goal-kicking performance at Newlands did Mick's chances of being employed by Sarfu any good, but it was so short-sighted of our rugby bosses not to invest in his experience and expertise.'

Byrne, who had impressed Viljoen and White on a trip to Australia in 2001, did not continue with the Boks because Viljoen, under pressure to consider Naas Botha as his kicking coach and not to invest in any more Australian consultants, did not have the energy to continue the fight for another foreigner in his management set-up.

In my capacity then as Bok communications manager and personal adviser to Viljoen, I had been involved with all the communication between SA Rugby, the commercial arm of Sarfu, and Byrne, whose credentials were first class. His attention to detail on various forms of kicking and catching out of hand had been exceptional at the Bok camp in Plettenberg Bay in 2001.

Even former Bok coach and another of Viljoen's assistant coaches in 2001, André Markgraaff, was impressed when he witnessed Byrne's coaching for the first time at the Bok pre-season camp in Plettenberg Bay, 2002. I mention Markgraaff because he was opposed to the idea of foreign involvement on the Springbok management team, believing there were people as qualified in South Africa to do the job.

Byrne was an instant hit with the players. He wanted to be with the Springboks and to be in South Africa, but if he was to relocate his family to South Africa and commit to a five-year national plan to improve all the country's best kickers at senior and junior level, it would come at a cost. He was settled in Australia and highly rated in three different codes. He was also a top bloke who immediately made an impact with everyone, wanted to learn Afrikaans, and was fascinated with the different mix of languages among the players, be it English, Afrikaans or Xhosa. He also immediately showed respect to the players and the tradition of the Springboks. When he was given a Bok tracksuit, he sought the acceptance of the senior players first before wearing it.

But the obsession among the conservative rugby media in 2001 and the equally conservative Sarfu administration when it came to foreigners, and the obsession with Botha, meant common sense would never be applied to decisions pending Byrne's longevity in South Africa.

Viljoen and I had been dismissive of Botha's involvement with the Boks because coaching kickers was not his full-time job. He had other interests and was employed by broadcaster SuperSport as its leading rugby analyst. It was our belief he would not add to the bigger picture, which was to provide a resource on a full-time basis for all the country's kickers, be it the Boks, the Emerging Boks, SA U21, SA U19 or SA Schools. Viljoen had unintentionally alienated the provincial presidents by not embracing Botha and I had fully supported the view that Byrne was the right guy for the kicking specialist position because working with kickers was his job. Viljoen and I underestimated the internal politics among the administration, the xenophobia that existed and we would only learn later how the provincial presidents, who would have to approve any Bok management appointment, were awed by Botha's achievements as a player and his ability to influence public opinion through his TV profile.

Botha was not a favourite with the Springbok players, who respected his credentials as a player but always felt he betrayed the ethos of the Boks with what they felt was sniping criticism in the media. What irked them the most was Botha's contention, said often, that the Boks lacked passion or commitment whenever they struggled or lost. The players would ask how any guy who had played for the Boks could ever question the passion and commitment of a player wearing the green and gold jersey. The players thought Botha, as a TV critic, was in a powerful position to educate the public and the one criticism they could never agree with was that they did not have passion. They may not have played well or been good enough, but they would do anything for the jersey.

This is important as background because it influenced Viljoen's decision not to invest in Botha as a kicking consultant. For all Byrne's brilliance, there was a counter-argument and it was one that was actively aired in the media. Byrne, as an Aussie Rules player, had never kicked a conversion or penalty in his life, so how could he possibly be a better investment than Naas? Our response was that we were not recommending a guy on his playing pedigree but on what he was currently doing, which was working with rugby union and rugby league kickers. I prepared the motivation for Byrne to stay, move his family over and work for SA Rugby and be available to the provinces.

Rian Oberholzer, MD of SA Rugby in 2001, was not opposed to Byrne's involvement, but he wanted to know how much Harry was prepared to fight for him. That would determine how big a fight Oberholzer was prepared to get into against the 14 provincial presidents – they dominated the President's Council, which had to give sign off to national team decisions. Oberholzer, after intense discussion, asked Viljoen if the employment of Byrne was a want or a need. Was it really necessary or was it nice to have? Viljoen, frustrated and irritated, said it was a need but at that stage, not a necessity and that was the end of Michael Byrne as a kicking specialist in South Africa. Byrne left and Botha, in 2001, made the occasional visit to watch the kickers.

Jake White also initially used Botha on occasions when he became Bok coach, against the wishes of the senior players. The likes of Montgomery got on with educating themselves. White and Botha had a good relationship because Botha was the team manager for White's U21 World Championship-winning side in 2002 and White rated Botha's contribution. But the players, and Montgomery in particular, did not want him with the Springboks.

'Naas was never going to be the answer as a team manager for the 2007 World Cup,' says Montgomery. 'The senior players did not want him there. When Jake suggested Naas should become the Bok manager, I was the one who went and told him the senior players did not want Naas with the team. In our view, Naas had done too much damage with his comments on TV in constantly criticising the Boks and there was no trust between him and the senior players. Players had not forgotten the time he said he felt embarrassed to be a Springbok and that he wanted to give back his Bok blazer. Bugger, you don't say that kind of thing. Not when you have played for the Boks and have been in the set-up. There is a

Bok brotherhood and the guys have a code of conduct and part of that code is to always respect your fellow Bok. I know he is a TV critic now, but it doesn't mean he has to forget how it felt when he was there, and it is one thing to criticise the team's performance but players felt he got personal in his criticism.'

Montgomery and Botha have never had an issue and there is no history based on an issue between them. Montgomery's always maintained the respect he has for Botha's ability as a player and Botha was generous in his praise of Montgomery's goal-kicking success at the 2007 World Cup.

'Percy just gets down to business and does his job,' he told *Cape Times* rugby writer Ashfak Mohamed. 'It is as simple as that. And he was brilliant. He took the responsibility on to his shoulders and kicked the goals. And remember, he has been one of the few guys to kick well with this new Gilbert ball. It just shows how good he is that he can adapt. His line kicking has also been excellent. He kicks with a torpedo when he goes for touch, so that has helped him.'

Botha, in discussing Montgomery's refined one-and-a-half step kicking style, also cautioned young players against copying it.

'It works for him, but one of the biggest pieces of advice I can give to kickers is: Don't kick like anybody else. You have to do what you are comfortable with. There are a lot of factors that come into the equation: your height, body weight and athleticism. The problem I find with youngsters is that they don't do the basics right and they forget to keep their balance, or to kick through the ball.'

Botha also said Montgomery's four from four in the final defined his goal kicking at the World Cup because he kicked them when it mattered most. 'If you miss any in the final, nobody cares about the rest of the tournament, so I would say those four were pretty big. That's all that counts.'

Montgomery would come into contact with Botha again in 2008 when Springbok coach Peter de Villiers asked the former flyhalf to present the jerseys to the team and address them before the first Test against Wales in Bloemfontein.

'I thought he spoke very well and with inspiration about being a Bok and the meaning of the jersey, but it didn't change what he had been saying for years on TV,' says Montgomery. 'I think that is what disappointed me the most. When I heard him in our team room talking about being a Springbok it was so different to hearing him talk about the Boks on TV. I can't or won't deny that when I spoke to Jake in 2006 about not wanting Naas as Bok manager that I had lost respect for Naas and did not want to work with him. It is something that will always disappoint me as he was someone I idolised as a schoolboy. I tell my mates that I used to have a poster of Naas on my wall when I was young, but you won't find a poster of him in my house today.'

Montgomery believes the loss of Byrne meant losing a concept that could only have enhanced South African rugby. It was an opportunity lost and it still is.

'I know the Bulls use Vlok Cilliers and WP have used Louis Koen and Eric Herbert in recent times as kicking coaches, but the recognition of a kicking coach and of the role of the kicker is still not what it should be in South African rugby.

'I can't tell you how many times I've practised my goal kicking before a Test and there haven't been enough balls for me. The kickers in the squad also had to mostly use old balls, when match balls travel further and are very different to kick. The cost of ensuring a kicker practises with a couple of new balls before every Test should be seen as part of the team's expense.'

Montgomery also says the training demands of kickers should be factored into any training schedules.

'The Bok coaching staff at the 2007 World Cup is the best I've ever worked with, but even they did not have specialised kicking times worked into schedules. Kicking was something the kickers either did before or after training. That is something that has to change as the demands on goal kickers increase. Kicking is as important to the game as scrumming or lineouts. If you give the kicker the responsibility of winning your matches then give him the time within a training session to fine-tune this skill. What he does after training and before training should be the additional work, where all of my career it has been the only time available to a kicker. I would kick three or four times a week, depending on how I was feeling and how my game went the week before. Kicking, to me, is more a mental thing and I always had to be confident in my fitness. When I have had a niggle and played, it impacted on my performance, but when I knew I was in the best possible shape, there could never be a goal-kicking excuse in my mind.

'You also need a routine and that has to include kicking from the less favourable angles – you only know your range through missing regularly. In practice in Newport, I altered my approach to goal kicking by slowing everything down and being a lot calmer. I had kicked against the best and worked with some of the best in Jannie de Beer and Braam van Straaten. Those guys loved kicking and loved to practise and their strength was they found what worked for them and stayed with it. When I've chatted socially to other kickers – like Andrew Mehrtens, Joel Stransky, Matthew Burke and Dan Carter – they all have one consistent factor and that is settling on what makes them comfortable, and that there is not a right or wrong way. For me it was important to find that comfort, which I probably only did in Newport.

'When I started kicking regularly for teams, I also started keeping all my practice percentages. I would compare that to what I kicked in a game so by the time I came to the World Cup, I knew my range and I certainly knew my angles. For me, it was never about judging my kicking practice sessions by how long they were. I always felt more comfortable kicking from 30 to 45m out and understanding what I wanted to achieve with every kick out of hand or at posts. During the season, I'd have my routine and if the match was on a Saturday I'd start on the Tuesday with 30 place kicks to all parts of the field and then 16 punts, toe punts and torpedo kicks. I wouldn't do a structured kicking session on the Wednesday, but go back-to-back on the Thursday and Friday, with 45 place kicks and 32 punts on a Thursday and 21 place kicks and 16 punts at the captain's run on a Friday. On match day, before our warm-up, I'd be very strategic in where I kicked my eight place kicks from and my eight punts.'

Montgomery says the only 2007 World Cup game that he lacked confidence in his goal kicking was the quarter-final against Fiji in Marseilles.

'I was on a high that season, especially after my two performances against England in Bloemfontein and Pretoria. I kicked 10 from 10 in Bloem and was more accurate than Wilkinson that day. I was also more accurate than him in the second Test in Pretoria. That was a turning point for me mentally as he is rightly regarded as the most accurate goal kicker in the business. To better him in two successive Tests gave me confidence that I could do it again at the World Cup and up until the quarter-final, I kicked as well as I could have. But I struggled against Fiji and it wasn't because of poor preparation. I did everything the same way and knew that I was in form, but when I took my first penalty kick in the match, I felt like my foot was on an accelerator and it just didn't want to stop moving. I rushed everything in my approach. The kick hit the post and it took me a while to find my range. A week later, I was back to striking the ball calmly against Argentina in the semi-final in Paris and it was a calmness I had throughout the final against England. I didn't feel any nervousness when taking my kicks then but against Fiji, it could have been a case of us all being afraid of failure because of Australia and New Zealand losing the previous day. Maybe we felt we had everything to lose and all the pressure was on us as no one gave Fiji a chance to beat us. We certainly felt that pressure and of all the games

I played at the World Cup, I was more relieved than elated when that one was over. I hadn't kicked as well as I could have but we had won and at that stage, winning was all that mattered.'

Montgomery's goal kicking at the 2007 World Cup was the best of his career but when he returned to South Africa in 2008, he was the starting kicker in just two out of eight Tests and finished with six from 12. Why did his success rate suddenly drop to 50%?

'Kickers don't always get it right and it has a lot to do with the mindset of a player,' explains Montgomery. 'Jake was specific about my role, which was to kick goals and that meant a very different type of focus to my game than when I came back to South Africa in 2008. I knew my role in the Bok squad was that of an outgoing squad member, whose responsibility was to work with my successor and to pass on whatever knowledge I had. Butchie [Butch James] was starting most of the Tests and I was among the reserves, and he had the goal-kicking responsibilities from the outset.

'When I did get a start in Dunedin it began very well and I slotted my first three before missing a difficult touchline conversion. With the next two kicks, I hurried them and missed. In Cape Town, in my 100th Test, I overcompensated for a tricky wind and missed both. In the warm-up, there was little wind and I was slotting all my kicks. There is no excuse for the misses in the match. The ball was good, the conditions were good and the crowd was fantastic. I factored the wind to be stronger in the kick than it actually was and that is why I pulled both kicks.

'It happens and it is unfortunate, but it reminded me why I always tell the other players it doesn't matter whether you have played one Test or 100, you can take nothing for granted. You can never assume because you kicked 10 from 10 one week, you won't miss any the next. I would have loved a better goal-kicking ending to my international career, but when I look back over 102 Tests and more than

320 first-class matches, the good days certainly dominated the bad.'

Montgomery would retire from international rugby as the holder of nearly every Springbok goal-kicking record. But with a wry smile, he said he knew there would be those who would remember two misses against the All Blacks in 2008 more than they would the 18 consecutive successes at the Stade de France in the World Cup.

'I guess it is a bit like golf. You never master that damn ball, and to do well you just have to keep working hard and never underestimate the value of doing the basics well. There is no secret to goal kicking. You have to want to do it and because of that you have to want to practise.'

Montgomery, in 102 Tests, scored 893 points – a total that would place him seventh in the all-time list of point-scorers at the time of his retirement. It was a feat only made more incredible because he was the goal kicker in only 63 of those Tests.

22

JONAH, JAKE AND PLENTY OF GREEN AND GOLD JEWELS

In completing the rugby story of Percy Montgomery, I asked him to name his best Springbok XV of his career. I also asked him to pick the best overseas players, the best captain and the best coach. It was easier said than done, and as we started sifting through 11 years, 102 Tests, more than 320 first-class games and several coaches, there were few names that stood out, but many that he admired equally.

Montgomery says Jonah Lomu, in his prime, was like no other player he experienced. The All Blacks wing was the only one Montgomery would separate from the hundreds he had teamed up with or opposed.

'Jonah was exceptional from 1995 to 2000 and I've yet to see another player cause defences that much trouble and occupy that much of a team's attention in the build-up to games. He was incredible at his best. There are some very good players out there, but in my view there was only one Jonah and I haven't seen anyone as spectacular since. No other player could consistently break the first tackle or two, and then take a pack of forwards with him, on occasions piggybacking them. And that was only one aspect of his game. He also had pace and balance when he ran and was more than a finisher. Those who played on his inside and off him certainly gained a lot because of how much attention he demanded from a defence. I don't believe there is such a thing as the complete player, so there are areas of Jonah's game that weren't without fault. But in terms of his presence, his menace and his influence on games, he was colossal. I played against him at Super Rugby and Test level, but it was also good to play alongside him for the Barbarians [the famous invitation side comprising players from all around the world] and to experience first hand his humility and the respect players had for him.

'My Barbarians matches were always enjoyable because they were so different to any I played as a professional. The atmosphere was relaxed and the main reason for being there was to provide entertainment to the crowd. It was the only time in my career that I knew I had total freedom to go out and express myself without consequence in team selection or fear of making a mistake. I was fortunate to have benefited from playing in some very strong Barbarians teams and we won seven of our nine games. They were good times because there was never any pressure on me and every match was a rugby celebration. It also allowed me to get to know a few [non-South African] players socially. The demands of the modern game often limit interaction between teams away from the field. It is very different, for example, to be playing against [All Blacks fullback] Christian Cullen or [Wallabies fullback] Chris Latham every year, than to play in the same team and spend a week hanging out with them, socialising, laughing and seeing another side to their on-field character. [French utility back] Thomas Castaignède was someone I always got on well with at the Barbarians and [Wallabies centre] Tim Horan was probably the naughtiest of the overseas players. He was always pulling a prank on someone and always seemed to be up to something, but when he got on the field, he always produced a quality performance. In many of the games I played, there was a strong contingent of South African players so I never felt isolated or alienated, although I don't think anyone plays for the Barbarians and leaves the squad feeling that way. One of the unwritten rules is how everyone makes each other feel comfortable and, regardless of nationality, you just get on with having a good time and involving everyone.'

Test rugby was a different animal and the must-win nature of the professional game meant friendships were harder to form because it was more of a work environment.

'You are playing to stay there most of the time and to earn the respect of those around you. If you make friendships, it is a bonus and when I reflect on my career, I see more good working relationships than friendships. I always got on well with my team-mates in South Africa, Wales and France, but I have few friendships – in the true sense of a friendship – from playing the game.'

Montgomery had many player influences on his career, including the mentorship from James Small and Christian Stewart in 1997, but he does not believe there was one player who significantly influenced his career more than others.

'There are so many good players in South Africa and I don't believe you can compare different eras. The Springbok team that won 17 successive Tests and the 2007 World Cup-winning side were the two best Bok teams I played in, but I find it impossible to pick one XV from both, or to say with any conviction which was the better of the two teams. Who do you choose on the flank between André Venter and Juan Smith, for example? Is Gary Teichmann or John Smit the better Bok captain? When I played under Gary, I was a youngster, who had no relationship with him away from the game. With Smitty at the World Cup, it was completely different because I was a senior player and we were mates off the field. They both have strengths as leaders, but you see things so differently when you are playing your first Test compared to when you play your 100th. I wouldn't be able to give you a definitive answer as to why I would choose one over the other.

'I was lucky to have played fullback in both of those teams, almost a decade apart, and to win rugby's two biggest trophies [for a southern-hemisphere player] in the Tri-Nations and World Cup. There is also the matter of where I was in the evolution of my career when assessing team-mates. If I had played alongside James as a 33-year-old, my impressions would have been very different from the 23-year-old. I would also have viewed the winning of the World Cup as a 23-year-old in another light to when we did win it in 2007. People like hearing "a best of this and a best of that", but I've never taken those kinds of things seriously or paid too much attention to those lists because I think they are impossible to compile. I know there are some players who I would prefer to be in my team ahead of others if it was wet weather and we were playing in the northern hemisphere, but the same guys may not be the best option for a fast-paced game in sunshine in Australia. For me, there are too many variables to say, with certainty, that one of the many quality players I teamed up with was better than the other one.'

Of the coaches Montgomery played under, he speaks fondly of his experience with Jake White and Newport's Mike Ruddock and Alan Griffith.

'They were very good to me, but again at a very different time of my career to guys who coached me in my early days. Jake and Mike managed me as much as they coached me and showed me a trust that probably only came because of the stage I was at in my career when our paths crossed. I have also played under very good coaches in Nick Mallett and Gert Smal, who were technically outstanding. Nick was the most dominant coach I have known. He was larger than life, and as a young player I was shit scared of him, but I did not like how he managed senior players. He would treat all players equally, complimenting or shitting someone out with the same enthusiasm, regardless of how many Tests he had played. I didn't like that, even as a youngster, because I have always believed in a pecking order in a team environment and in senior players being afforded respect. You don't humiliate a senior player in front of a youngster and in an ideal environment, you don't humiliate any player in front of another. Technically, and judged purely on rugby, there aren't many coaches who are better than Nick, but when I look at what I responded to the best in a coach, then it would have been Jake and Mike's approach. Both of them seemed to appreciate the value and the voice of senior players, and that always made me more comfortable and more secure that I could speak or make a contribution.'

Montgomery says he will always have a soft spot for Carel du Plessis, because he was the man who first picked him to play Test rugby. He adds that all of his coaches – from his schoolboy mentor HO de Villiers, to Tubby Tubes, who was instrumental in his move from Tech Gardens to Villager, to his Villager club coach Anton Chait, to White – helped with his all-round development as a player.

'Take someone like Harry Viljoen. I learned a lot from him, although not necessarily about improving technical aspects of my game. In 1997, Harry was a revolutionary in terms of his ideas about the game and players being professional in a professional environment. That certainly made an impression on me. We eventually fell out when he dropped me from the Test side, but the way it ended between us doesn't change the impact he made on me when he coached Western Province in 1997.

'I worked under Alan Solomons after Harry left and he was completely the opposite. Solly's a traditionalist and a pragmatist and he gave balance to a lot of things, but he was passionate about the game. I've had good guys around me most of my career, who have backed me, and as a player, you can't ask for more than that from a coach. I've also taken it on the chin when I was dropped because I was not performing, but I have never forgotten how a guy like Nick refused to buckle to media and public pressure to drop me in 1999 and kept on putting his faith in me. I like to think I vindicated that with my performances at the 1999 World Cup.

'What set Jake apart was that he knew exactly what he had in me and he had a clear vision for how he wanted to use me. I just had to ensure I delivered on that expectation. The exception among professional rugby coaches for me was Chris Anderson, who coached us for a year at Newport. He may have been a rugby league legend, but as far as I was concerned he was out of his depth in rugby union and didn't have the knowledge to have the attitude he had. He was my worst experience, but over 11 years, he was very much in the minority when it came to me and coaches – and I have played under quite a few.'

Montgomery played under five Bok coaches in Du Plessis, Mallett, Viljoen, White and Peter de Villiers – and you won't find him having a go at the last man on that list.

'Why would I? He gave me one last crack at Test rugby and an opportunity to be part of a winning Springbok team in New Zealand, to experience the feeling of playing my 100th Test and to finish my international career on my terms. He was up front with me when we first met in Perpignan in early 2008, telling me I was not his first-choice fullback, but that he felt I had a role to play in helping bring through my successor. He never veered from that view that season.

'I backed him as I did every Springbok coach I played for because you don't play for the individual, you play for the jersey. In doing that, you play for the guy who is coaching the Springboks. It's about the jersey. That's the advice I always gave the younger players when they made the Boks. The reason they played this game was to become a Springbok and that is where their loyalty must always be – not to a team-mate or the coach, but to the Springbok jersey.'

MONTGOMERY'S SPRINGBOK RECORDS (at 30/08/2008)	
AGAINST AUSTRALIA	5
Most capped	20
Most career points	140
Most career conversions	13
Most career penalty goals	31
Most career drop goals (shared)	2
AGAINST ENGLAND	5
Most capped	12
Most career points	99
Most career conversions	20
Most career penalty goals	18
Most conversions in a Test	7
AGAINST FIJI	1
Most conversions in a Test	3
AGAINST FRANCE	4
Most career points	78
Most career penalty goals	18
Most drop goals (shared)	1
Most penalty goals in a Test	7
AGAINST IRELAND	6
Most capped	6
Most career points	56
Most career conversions	10
Most career penalty goals	12
Most conversions in a Test	4
Most penalty goals in a Test (shared)	4
AGAINST ITALY	2
Most career penalty goals (shared)	4
Most penalty goals in a Test (shared)	4

MONTGOMERY'S SPRINGBOK RECORDS *(continued)*	
AGAINST NAMIBIA	5
Most career conversions	12
Most career penalty goals	2
Most points in a Test	35
Most conversions in a Test	12
Most penalty goals in a Test	2
AGAINST NEW ZEALAND	6
Most capped (shared)	19
Most career points	106
Most career conversions	16
Most career penalty goals	20
Most career drop goals	3
Most drop goals in a Test (shared)	2
AGAINST PACIFIC ISLANDS	6
Most career points	18
Most career conversions	3
Most career penalty goals	4
Most points in a Test	18
Most conversions in a Test	3
Most penalty goals in a Test	4
AGAINST SAMOA	3
Most career penalty goals (shared)	3
Most points in a Test	29
Most penalty goals in a Test	3
AGAINST SCOTLAND	8
Most capped (shared)	7
Most career conversions	19
Most career points	101
Most career penalty goals	16

MONTGOMERY'S SPRINGBOK RECORDS *(continued)*

AGAINST SCOTLAND *(continued)*	8
Most points in a Test	26
Most conversions in a Test	8
Most penalty goals in a Test	7
Most tries in a Test (shared)	2

AGAINST TONGA	1
Most penalty goals in a Test (shared)	1

AGAINST USA	4
Most career penalty goals (shared)	1
Most points in a Test	15
Most conversions in a Test	6
Most penalty goals in a Test (shared)	1

AGAINST WALES	7
Most capped	9
Most career points	91
Most career conversions	18
Most career penalty goals	10
Most points in a Test	31
Most conversions in a Test	9
Most penalty goals in a Test	4

TRI-NATIONS RECORDS	5
Most capped	34
Most career conversions	26
Most career penalty goals	43
Most career points	210
Most drop goals in one tournament (shared)	2

MONTGOMERY'S SPRINGBOK RECORDS *(continued)*

WORLD CUP RECORDS	7
Most career points	111
Most career conversions	22
Most career penalty goals	17
Most points in a tournament	105
Most conversions in a tournament	22
Most penalty goals in a tournament	17
Most points at the 2007 World Cup	105

FIRSTS		11
First to score 400 career points in Tests	vs England, London	20/11/2004
First to score 500 career points in Tests	vs Australia, Pretoria	30/07/2005
First to score 600 career points in Tests	vs Scotland, Port Elizabeth	17/06/2006
First to score 700 career points in Tests	vs Samoa, Johannesburg	09/06/2007
First to score 800 career points in Tests	vs England, Paris	14/09/2007
First to score 100 career conversions in Tests	vs England, Bloemfontein	26/05/2007
First to score 150 career conversions in Tests	vs Argentina, Paris	14/10/2007
First to score 100 career penalty goals in Tests	vs Scotland, Port Elizabeth	17/06/2006
First to score 200 career points in Tri-Nations tournament	vs New Zealand, Dunedin	12/07/2008
First to score 900 career points in all matches	vs New Zealand, Dunedin	12/07/2008
First to play in 100 Tests	vs New Zealand, Cape Town	16/08/2008

MONTGOMERY'S SPRINGBOK RECORDS *(continued)*	
OVERALL CAREER RECORDS	9
Most capped	102
Most career points in Tests	893
Most career conversions in Tests	153
Most career penalty goals in Tests	148
Most capped in all matches	104
Most career points in all matches	906
Most career conversions in all matches	157
Most career penalty goals in all matches	148
Most Test opponents in a career (shared)	18
MATCH RECORDS	3
Most points in a Test	35
Most conversions in a Test	12
Most penalty goals in a Test	7
SEASON RECORDS	2
Most points in a season	219
Most conversions in a season	52
POSITION RECORDS	5
Most Tests as a fullback	87
Most consecutive Tests as a fullback	24
Most tries in Tests as a fullback	18
Most tries in all matches as a fullback	19
Most Tests as a back-three combination with Stefan Terblanche and Pieter Rossouw	13
TOTAL NUMBER OF BOK RECORDS	94

SPRINGBOK TESTS								
DATE	OPPONENTS*	POSITION	T	C	P	D	PTS	RESULT
28/06/1997	British & Irish Lions (2)	Centre	1	0	0	0	5	L 15-18
05/07/1997	British & Irish Lions (3)	Centre	1	0	0	0	5	W 35-16
19/07/2007	New Zealand (1) (TN)	Centre	0	0	0	0	0	L 32-35
02/08/1997	Australia (1) (TN)	Centre	0	0	0	0	0	L 20-32
09/08/1997	New Zealand (2) (TN)	Centre	1	0	0	0	5	L 35-55
23/08/1997	Australia (2) (TN)	Centre	2	0	0	0	10	W 61-22
15/11/1997	France (1)	Fullback	1	0	0	0	5	W 36-32
22/11/1997	France (2)	Fullback	0	0	0	0	0	W 52-10
29/11/1997	England	Fullback	0	1	0	0	2	W 29-11
06/12/1997	Scotland	Fullback	2	8	0	0	26	W 68-10
13/06/1998	Ireland (1)	Fullback	0	0	0	0	0	W 37-13
20/06/1998	Ireland (2)	Fullback	0	4	0	0	8	W 33-0
27/06/1998	Wales (1)	Fullback	2	9	1	0	31	W 96-13
04/07/1998	England (1)	Fullback	0	1	2	0	8	W 18-0
18/07/1998	Australia (1) (TN)	Fullback	0	0	3	0	9	W 14-13
25/07/1998	New Zealand (1) (TN)	Fullback	0	1	2	0	8	W 13-3
15/08/1998	New Zealand (2) (TN)	Fullback	0	2	0	0	4	W 24-23
22/08/1998	Australia (2) (TN)	Fullback	0	2	5	0	19	W 29-15
14/11/1998	Wales (2)	Fullback	0	0	0	0	0	W 28-20
21/11/1998	Scotland	Fullback	0	2	2	0	10	W 35-10
28/11/1998	Ireland (3)	Fullback	0	3	2	0	12	W 27-13
05/12/1998	England (2)	Fullback	0	1	0	0	2	L 7-13
12/06/1999	Italy (1)	Fullback	1	0	0	0	5	W 74-3
19/06/1999	Italy (2)	Fullback	1	0	0	0	5	W 101-0
26/06/1999	Wales	Fullback	1	0	0	0	5	L 19-29
10/07/1999	New Zealand (1) (TN)	Fullback	0	0	0	0	0	L 0-28
17/07/1999	Australia (1) (TN)	Fullback	0	0	0	0	0	L 6-32
07/08/1999	New Zealand (2) (TN)	Fullback	0	0	0	0	0	L 18-34
14/08/1999	Australia (2) (TN)	Fullback	0	0	0	0	0	W 10-9
03/10/1999	Scotland (RWC)	Fullback	0	0	0	0	0	W 46-29
15/10/1999	Uruguay (RWC)	Fullback	0	0	0	0	0	W 39-3
24/10/1999	England (RWC quarter-final)	Fullback	0	0	0	0	0	W 44-21
30/10/1999	Australia (3) (RWC semi-final)	Fullback	0	0	0	0	0	L 21-27
04/11/1999	New Zealand (3) (RWC 3rd/4th)	Fullback	0	0	0	2	6	W 22-18
10/06/2000	Canada	Fullback	1	0	0	0	5	W 51-18

SPRINGBOK TESTS *(continued)*								
DATE	OPPONENTS*	POSITION	T	C	P	D	PTS	RESULT
17/06/2000	England (1)	Fullback	0	0	0	0	0	W 18-13
24/06/2000	England (2)	Fullback	0	1	1	0	5	L 22-27
08/07/2000	Australia (1)	Fullback	0	0	0	0	0	L 23-44
22/07/2000	New Zealand (1) (TN)	Fullback	0	0	0	1	3	L 12-25
29/07/2000	Australia (2) (TN)	Flyhalf (R)	0	0	0	0	0	L 6-26
12/11/2000	Argentina	Flyhalf	0	3	0	0	6	W 37-33
19/11/2000	Ireland	Flyhalf	0	1	2	0	8	W 28-18
26/11/2000	Wales	Flyhalf	0	0	0	0	0	W 23-13
02/12/2000	England (3)	Fullback	0	0	0	0	0	L 17-25
16/06/2001	France (1)	Fullback	0	0	6	0	18	L 23-32
23/06/2001	France (2)	Centre (R)	0	0	0	0	0	W 20-15
30/06/2001	Italy (1)	Flyhalf	1	3	4	0	23	W 60-14
21/07/2001	New Zealand (1)	Fullback	0	0	1	0	3	L 3-12
10/11/2001	France (3)	Centre (R)	0	0	0	0	0	L 10-20
17/11/2001	Italy (2)	Wing (R)	0	0	0	0	0	W 54-26
19/06/2004	Ireland (2)	Fullback	0	2	4	0	16	W 26-17
26/06/2004	Wales (1)	Fullback	0	6	2	0	18	W 53-18
17/07/2004	Pacific Islands	Fullback	0	3	4	0	18	W 38-24
24/07/2004	New Zealand (1) (TN)	Fullback	0	3	0	0	6	L 21-23
31/07/2004	Australia (1) (TN)	Fullback	0	1	3	0	11	L 26-30
14/08/2004	New Zealand (2) (TN)	Fullback	0	3	3	0	15	W 40-26
21/08/2004	Australia (2) (TN)	Fullback	0	2	3	0	13	W 23-19
06/11/2004	Wales (2)	Fullback	1	3	4	0	23	W 38-36
13/11/2004	Ireland (3)	Fullback	0	0	4	0	12	L 12-17
20/11/2004	England	Fullback	0	1	3	0	11	L 16-32
27/11/2004	Scotland	Fullback	0	4	1	0	11	W 45-10
11/06/2005	Uruguay	Fullback	0	6	1	0	15	W 134-3
18/06/2005	France (1)	Fullback	0	3	2	1	15	D 30-30
25/06/2005	France (2)	Fullback	0	3	2	0	12	W 27-13
09/07/2005	Australia (1)	Fullback	0	0	4	0	12	L 12-30
23/07/2005	Australia (2)	Fullback	0	3	4	0	18	W 33-20
30/07/2005	Australia (3) (TN)	Fullback	0	1	3	1	14	W 22-16
06/08/2005	New Zealand (1) (TN)	Fullback	0	1	4	0	14	W 22-16
20/08/2005	Australia (4) (TN)	Fullback	0	0	3	1	12	W 22-19
27/08/2005	New Zealand (2) (TN)	Fullback	0	3	2	0	12	L 27-31

SPRINGBOK TESTS *(continued)*								
DATE	OPPONENTS*	POSITION	T	C	P	D	PTS	RESULT
05/11/2005	Argentina	Fullback	1	2	3	0	18	W 34-23
19/11/2005	Wales	Fullback	0	0	3	0	9	W 33-16
26/11/2005	France (3)	Fullback	0	2	1	0	7	L 20-26
10/06/2006	Scotland (1)	Fullback	1	2	4	0	21	W 36-16
17/06/2006	Scotland (2)	Fullback	0	0	7	0	21	W 29-15
24/06/2006	France	Fullback	0	0	7	0	21	L 26-36
15/07/2006	Australia (1) (TN)	Fullback	0	0	0	0	0	L 0-49
22/07/2006	New Zealand (1) (TN)	Fullback	0	2	1	0	7	L 17-35
05/08/2006	Australia (2) (TN)	Fullback	1	0	0	0	5	L 18-20
26/08/2006	New Zealand (2) (TN)	Fullback	0	0	2	0	6	L 26-45
26/05/2007	England (1)	Fullback	0	7	3	0	23	W 58-10
02/06/2007	England (2)	Fullback	1	5	1	0	18	W 55-22
09/06/2007	Samoa (1)	Fullback (R)	1	1	0	0	7	W 35-8
16/06/2007	Australia (1) (TN)	Fullback	0	1	3	0	11	W 22-19
23/06/2007	New Zealand (1) (TN)	Fullback	0	1	2	0	8	L 21-26
15/08/2007	Namibia	Fullback	1	12	2	0	35	W 105-13
25/08/2007	Scotland	Fullback	0	3	2	0	12	W 27-3
09/09/2007	Samoa (2) (RWC)	Fullback (R)	1	1	0	0	7	W 59-7
14/09/2007	England (3) (RWC)	Fullback	0	3	4	0	18	W 36-0
22/09/2007	Tonga (RWC)	Fullback (R)	0	1	1	0	5	W 30-25
30/09/2007	USA (RWC)	Fullback	0	6	1	0	15	W 64-15
07/10/2007	Fiji (RWC quarter-final)	Fullback	0	3	1	0	9	W 37-20
14/10/2007	Argentina (RWC semi-final)	Fullback	0	4	3	0	17	W 37-13
20/10/2007	England (4) (RWC final)	Fullback	0	0	4	0	12	W 15-6
07/06/2008	Wales (1)	Centre (R)	1	0	0	0	5	W 43-17
14/06/2008	Wales (2)	Fullback (R)	0	0	0	0	0	W 37-21
05/07/2008	New Zealand (1) (TN)	Fullback (R)	0	0	0	0	0	L 8-19
12/07/2008	New Zealand (2) (TN)	Fullback	0	0	3	0	9	W 30-28
09/08/2008	Argentina	Fullback (R)	0	0	0	0	0	W 63-9
16/08/2008	New Zealand (3) (TN)	Fullback	0	0	0	0	0	L 0-19
23/08/2008	Australia (2) (TN)	Fullback (R)	0	1	0	0	2	L 15-27
30/08/2008	Australia (3) (TN)	Fullback (R)	0	2	0	0	4	W 53-8
102 TEST MATCHES			**25**	**153**	**148**	**6**	**893**	
RECORD			**P: 102 W: 67 L: 34 D: 1 Win %: 66**					

** The number in brackets next to the opponent indicates which match of a sequence against that opponent that year. TN = Tri-Nations; RWC = Rugby World Cup*

SPRINGBOKS (NON-TEST MATCHES)								
DATE	OPPONENTS	POSITION	T	C	P	D	PTS	RESULTS
11/11/1997	French Barbarians	Fullback	1	0	0	0	5	Lost
09/12/2000	Barbarians	Flyhalf	0	4	0	0	8	Won
2 MATCHES			**1**	**4**	**0**	**0**	**13**	
RECORD			**P: 2 W: 1 L: 1 D: 0 Win %: 50%**					

SPRINGBOKS XV (NON-CAP)								
DATE	OPPONENTS	POSITION	T	C	P	D	PTS	RESULT
12/09/1999	Eastern Province XV	Fullback	0	1	0	0	2	Won
03/06/2006	World XV	Fullback	0	0	9	0	27	Won
2 MATCHES			**0**	**1**	**9**	**0**	**29**	
RECORD			**P: 2 W: 2 L: 0 D: 0 Win %: 100**					

EMERGING SPRINGBOKS								
DATE	OPPONENTS	POSITION	T	C	P	D	PTS	RESULT
17/06/1997	British & Irish Lions	Centre	0	1	0	0	2	Lost
1 MATCH			**0**	**1**	**0**	**0**	**2**	
RECORD			**P: 1 L: 1 Win %: 0**					

WESTERN PROVINCE (NITE SERIES)								
DATE	OPPONENTS	POSITION	T	C	P	D	PTS	RESULT
26/03/1997	Eastern Province	Centre	1	0	0	0	5	Won
04/04/1997	SE Transvaal	Centre	0	0	0	0	0	Won
11/04/1997	SWD Eagles	Centre	0	2	4	0	16	Won
18/04/1997	Boland	Centre	0	0	0	0	0	Won
25/04/1997	Border	Centre	0	0	0	0	0	Won
02/05/1997	Northern Free State	Centre	0	0	0	0	0	Won
07/05/1997	Griquas	Centre	1	1	0	0	7	Won
14/05/1997	Boland	Flyhalf	0	0	1	0	3	Won
8 MATCHES			**2**	**3**	**5**	**0**	**31**	
WIN RECORD			**P: 8 W: 8 Win %: 100**					

WESTERN PROVINCE (FRIENDLIES)								
DATE	OPPONENTS	POSITION	T	C	P	D	PTS	RESULT
21/10/1995	Northern Transvaal	Position (R)	0	0	0	0	0	Won
11/03/1997	Mendoza	Centre	1	7	0	0	19	Won
15/03/1997	North East Region	Flyhalf	0	5	3	0	19	Won
18/03/1997	Buenos Aires	Centre	0	1	5	0	17	Won
22/03/1997	Rosario	Centre	1	5	0	0	15	Won
31/05/1997	British & Irish Lions	Flyhalf	0	3	0	0	6	Lost
6 MATCHES			**2**	**21**	**8**	**0**	**76**	
RECORD			**P: 6 W: 5 L:1 Win %: 100**					

WP/STORMERS (SUPER 12 & SUPER 14)								
DATE	OPPONENTS	POSITION	T	C	P	D	PTS	RESULT
16/03/1996	Highlanders	Fullback	0	0	0	0	0	Lost
22/03/1996	Crusaders	Fullback	0	0	0	0	0	Drew
23/04/1996	Hurricanes	Centre (R)	0	0	0	0	0	Won
27/02/1998	Hurricanes	Centre	2	4	1	0	21	Lost
07/03/1998	Sharks	Centre	0	0	0	0	0	Lost
14/03/1998	Bulls	Fullback	1	0	0	0	5	Won
28/03/1998	Waratahs	Fullback	0	1	1	0	5	Won
03/04/1998	Brumbies	Fullback	1	0	0	0	5	Won
11/04/1998	Reds	Fullback	0	0	0	0	0	Lost
18/04/1998	Crusaders	Centre	0	0	0	0	0	Lost
26/04/1998	Blues	Fullback	0	0	0	0	0	Lost
02/05/1998	Chiefs	Fullback	0	0	0	0	0	Lost
09/05/1998	Highlanders	Fullback	0	0	0	0	0	Lost
16/05/1998	Cats	Centre	1	0	0	0	5	Lost
27/02/1999	Bulls	Fullback	0	0	0	0	0	Won
07/03/1999	Hurricanes	Fullback	0	0	0	0	0	Won
19/03/1999	Brumbies	Fullback	0	1	0	0	2	Lost
26/03/1999	Waratahs	Fullback	0	0	0	0	0	Won
03/04/1999	Reds	Fullback	1	0	0	0	5	Won
10/04/1999	Sharks	Fullback	0	0	0	0	0	Won
18/04/1999	Crusaders	Fullback	0	0	0	0	0	Won
01/05/1999	Blues	Fullback	0	0	0	0	0	Won
08/05/1999	Chiefs	Fullback	0	0	0	0	0	Won
15/05/1999	Cats	Fullback	0	0	0	0	0	Lost

WP/STORMERS (SUPER 12 & SUPER 14) *(continued)*								
DATE	OPPONENTS	POSITION	T	C	P	D	PTS	RESULT
22/05/1999	Highlanders	Fullback	0	0	0	0	0	Lost
26/02/2000	Waratahs	Fullback	0	0	0	0	0	Won
04/03/2000	Cats	Fullback	0	0	0	2	6	Lost
11/03/2000	Bulls	Fullback	0	0	2	0	6	Drawn
18/03/2000	Brumbies	Fullback	0	0	5	0	15	Lost
26/03/2000	Crusaders	Fullback	0	1	0	0	2	Lost
29/04/2000	Highlanders	Fullback	0	0	0	0	0	Won
07/05/2000	Hurricanes	Fullback	0	0	0	0	0	Won
13/05/2000	Sharks	Fullback	2	0	0	0	10	Won
24/02/2001	Cats	Fullback	1	0	0	0	5	Lost
04/03/2001	Waratahs	Fullback	0	0	0	0	0	Lost
09/03/2001	Hurricanes	Fullback	0	0	0	0	0	Won
18/03/2001	Highlanders	Fullback	0	0	0	0	0	Lost
24/03/2001	Brumbies	Flyhalf	1	0	0	0	5	Lost
07/04/2001	Reds	Flyhalf	0	0	0	0	0	Won
14/04/2001	Crusaders	Fullback	0	0	0	0	0	Won
21/04/2001	Blues	Fullback	0	0	0	0	0	Lost
27/04/2001	Chiefs	Fullback	0	0	0	0	0	Won
05/05/2001	Bulls	Fullback	0	0	0	0	0	Won
12/05/2001	Sharks	Fullback	0	0	0	0	0	Lost
22/02/2002	Sharks	Wing	1	0	0	0	5	Won
02/03/2002	Waratahs	Fullback	0	0	0	0	0	Lost
08/03/2002	Hurricanes	Fullback	0	4	4	0	20	Won
16/03/2002	Highlanders	Fullback	0	0	5	0	15	Lost
23/03/2002	Brumbies	Fullback	0	1	1	0	5	Lost
06/04/2002	Reds	Fullback	0	3	5	0	21	Lost
12/04/2002	Crusaders	Fullback	0	3	0	0	6	Lost
20/04/2002	Chiefs	Fullback	0	3	3	0	15	Won
26/04/2002	Blues	Fullback	0	0	2	0	6	Lost
04/05/2002	Cats	Fullback	0	4	1	0	11	Won
11/05/2002	Bulls	Fullback	0	2	4	0	16	Won
55 MATCHES			**11**	**27**	**34**	**2**	**217**	
RECORD			**P: 55 W: 26 L: 27 D: 2 Win %: 47%**					

* *Western Province played in the 1996 Super 12 and did not qualify in 1997*

STORMERS (FRIENDLIES)								
DATE	OPPONENTS	POSITION	T	C	P	D	PTS	RESULT
17/02/1998	Namibia President's XV	Centre	1	6	0	0	17	Won
1 MATCH			**1**	**6**	**0**	**0**	**17**	
RECORD			**P: 1 W: 1 Win %: 100**					

WESTERN PROVINCE (CURRIE CUP)								
DATE	OPPONENTS	POSITION	T	C	P	D	PTS	RESULT
06/07/1996	SWD Eagles	Wing	1	0	0	0	5	Won
13/07/1996	Griquas	Wing	0	0	0	0	0	Won
20/07/1996	NFS Griffons	Wing	0	0	0	0	0	Won
14/06/1997	Gauteng Falcons	Centre	2	0	0	0	10	Won
30/08/1997	Mpumalanga Pumas	Centre	1	0	0	0	5	Won
07/09/1997	Eastern Province	Centre	1	0	0	0	5	Won
14/09/1997	North West Leopards	Centre	1	0	0	0	5	Won
20/09/1997	Griquas	Centre	0	0	0	0	0	Won
04/10/1997	Northern Transvaal	Centre (R)	0	0	0	0	0	Won
18/10/1997	Golden Lions (semi-final)	Centre	0	0	0	0	0	Won
25/10/1997	Free State Cheetahs (final)	Centre	0	0	0	0	0	Won
05/09/1998	Boland Kavaliers	Fullback	0	0	0	0	0	Lost
13/09/1998	Mpumalanga Pumas	Fullback	0	0	0	1	3	Won
19/09/1998	Golden Lions	Fullback	0	4	3	0	17	Won
27/09/1998	Free State Cheetahs	Fullback	1	2	1	0	12	Lost
03/10/1998	Blue Bulls	Fullback	0	4	0	0	8	Won
10/10/1998	SWD Eagles	Fullback	1	1	1	0	10	Won
17/10/1998	Natal Sharks	Fullback	0	1	4	0	14	Won
24/10/1998	Griquas (semi-final)	Fullback	0	1	4	1	17	Won
31/10/1998	Blue Bulls (final)	Fullback	0	0	1	0	3	Lost
05/08/2000	Blue Bulls	Fullback	1	1	1	0	10	Won
17/09/2000	Mpumalanga Pumas	Fullback	2	0	0	0	10	Won
23/09/2000	Golden Lions	Fullback	0	0	2	0	6	Won
30/09/2000	Natal Sharks	Fullback	0	1	0	0	2	Lost
07/10/2000	Free State Cheetahs	Fullback	1	0	0	1	8	Won
14/10/2000	Boland Kavaliers	Fullback	2	0	0	0	10	Won
21/10/2000	Golden Lions (semi-final)	Fullback	0	0	0	0	0	Won
28/10/2000	Natal Sharks (final)	Fullback	0	0	0	0	0	Won
04/08/2001	SWD Eagles	Fullback	1	5	1	0	18	Won

WESTERN PROVINCE (CURRIE CUP) *(continued)*								
DATE	OPPONENTS	POSITION	T	C	P	D	PTS	RESULT
01/09/2001	Mpumalanga Pumas	Fullback	0	0	0	0	0	Won
07/09/2001	Border Bulldogs	Fullback	0	0	0	0	0	Won
15/09/2001	Blue Bulls	Fullback	0	0	0	0	0	Won
22/09/2001	Golden Lions	Fullback	0	0	0	0	0	Won
29/09/2001	Falcons	Fullback	0	0	0	0	0	Won
06/10/2001	Free State Cheetahs	Fullback	1	0	0	0	5	Won
13/10/2001	Natal Sharks	Fullback	0	0	0	0	0	Lost
20/10/2001	Free State Cheetahs (semi-final)	Fullback	0	0	0	0	0	Won
27/10/2001	Natal Sharks (final)	Fullback	0	0	0	0	0	Won
27/07/2002	NFS Griffons	Fullback	1	0	0	0	5	Won
02/08/2002	Border Bulldogs	Fullback	0	0	0	0	0	Won
23/08/2002	Border Kavaliers	Fullback	1	1	0	0	7	Won
31/08/2002	Griquas	Fullback	1	0	0	0	5	Won
06/09/2002	Falcons	Fullback	1	0	0	0	5	Won
14/09/2002	Free State Cheetahs	Fullback	1	0	0	0	5	Lost
21/09/2002	Natal Sharks	Fullback	1	0	0	1	8	Lost
28/09/2002	Blue Bulls	Fullback	0	0	0	0	0	Lost
12/10/2002	Golden Lions	Fullback	0	1	1	0	5	Lost
47 MATCHES			22	22	19	4	223	
RECORD			P: 47 W: 38 L: 9 D: 0 Win %: 81					

NEWPORT (CLUB SIDE)								
DATE	OPPONENTS	POSITION	T	C	P	D	PTS	RESULT
20/12/2002	Bridgend	Fullback	0	0	0	0	0	Lost
26/12/2002	Llanelli	Fullback	0	0	0	0	0	Lost
01/01/2003	Cardiff	Fullback	0	0	0	0	0	Won
25/01/2003	Pontypridd	Fullback	0	1	4	1	17	Won
02/01/2003	Ebbw Vale	Fullback	1	2	5	1	27	Won
02/05/2003	Neath	Fullback	1	2	2	0	15	Lost
20/08/2003	Bedwas	Fullback	0	0	0	0	0	Won
15/03/2003	Swansea	Fullback	2	0	0	0	10	Won
20/03/2003	Caerphilly	Fullback	0	4	1	0	11	Won
05/04/2003	Ebbw Vale	Fullback	0	4	1	0	11	Won
12/04/2003	Bridgend	Fullback	1	3	3	0	20	Lost

NEWPORT (CLUB SIDE) *(continued)*								
DATE	OPPONENTS	POSITION	T	C	P	D	PTS	RESULT
19/04/2003	Bridgend	Fullback	0	0	9	0	27	Won
22/04/2003	Llanelli	Fullback	0	2	3	0	13	Won
03/05/2003	Llanelli	Fullback	0	0	2	1	9	Lost
07/05/2003	Pontypridd	Fullback	0	3	2	0	12	Won
13/05/2003	Swansea	Fullback	0	3	0	0	6	Lost
17/05/2003	Ebbw Vale	Fullback	2	5	3	0	29	Won
17 MATCHES			**7**	**29**	**35**	**3**	**207**	
RECORD			**P: 17 W: 11 L: 6 D: 0 Win % 65**					

NEWPORT GWENT DRAGONS (REGIONAL SIDE)								
DATE	OPPONENTS	POSITION	T	C	P	D	PTS	RESULT
07/12/2003	Ulster	Fullback	1	0	0	0	5	Won
14/12/2003	Leicester Tigers	Flyhalf	0	0	1	0	3	Lost
02/01/2004	Border Reivers	Fullback	1	3	4	0	23	Won
10/01/2004	Stade Français	Fullback	0	2	1	0	7	Won
18/01/2004	Stade Français	Fullback	0	0	0	0	0	Lost
24/01/2004	Leicester Tigers	Fullback	1	0	3	0	14	Lost
30/01/2004	Ulster	Fullback	0	0	0	0	0	Lost
06/02/2004	Leinster	Centre	1	5	0	0	15	Won
13/02/2004	Llanelli Scarlets	Centre	0	0	5	0	15	Won
20/02/2004	Ospreys	Centre	0	0	3	0	9	Lost
28/02/2004	Ulster	Centre	0	1	5	0	17	Won
05/03/2004	Glasgow Warriors	Centre	1	0	5	0	20	Lost
12/03/2004	Munster	Centre	0	1	3	0	11	Won
26/03/2004	Celtic Warriors	Centre	0	2	2	0	10	Won
02/04/2004	Edinburgh	Centre	0	1	2	0	8	Won
17/04/2004	Cardiff Blues	Centre	1	6	2	0	23	Won
01/05/2004	Connacht	Centre	1	3	2	0	17	Won
07/05/2004	Border Reivers	Centre	0	7	0	0	14	Won
14/05/2004	Leinster	Centre	0	3	1	0	9	Lost
01/10/2004	Leinster	Centre	0	0	0	0	0	Won
08/10/2004	Ulster	Centre	0	0	0	0	0	Won
15/10/2004	Border Reivers	Centre	0	0	0	0	0	Won
23/10/2004	Newcastle Falcons	Centre	0	0	0	0	0	Lost
31/10/2004	Edinburgh	Centre	0	0	0	0	0	Won

NEWPORT GWENT DRAGONS (REGIONAL SIDE) *(continued)*								
DATE	OPPONENTS	POSITION	T	C	P	D	PTS	RESULT
04/12/2004	USA Perpignan	Fullback	0	0	0	0	0	Won
11/12/2004	USA Perpignan	Fullback	0	0	0	0	0	Lost
27/12/2004	Cardiff Blues	Fullback	0	0	0	0	0	Won
01/01/2005	Llanelli Scarlets	Fullback	0	0	0	0	0	Lost
08/01/2005	Edinburgh	Fullback	0	0	0	0	0	Won
16/01/2005	Newcastle Falcons	Fullback	0	0	0	0	0	Lost
22/01/2005	Glasgow Warriors	Fullback	1	0	0	0	5	Won
30/01/2005	Leinster	Centre	0	0	1	0	3	Lost
18/02/2005	Ulster	Fullback	0	0	2	0	6	Won
04/03/2005	Border Reivers	Fullback	0	4	3	0	17	Won
25/03/2005	Munster	Centre	0	0	0	0	0	Lost
09/04/2005	Edinburgh	Centre	0	0	0	0	0	Lost
16/04/2005	Connacht	Centre	0	0	0	0	0	Won
29/04/2005	Llanelli Scarlets	Centre	0	0	0	0	0	Lost
38 MATCHES			**8**	**38**	**45**	**0**	**251**	
RECORD			**P: 38 W: 23 L: 15 D: 0 Win %: 61**					

BARBARIANS								
DATE	OPPONENTS	POSITION	T	C	P	D	PTS	RESULT
20/05/2001	Wales	Fullback	1	0	0	0	5	Won
24/05/2001	Scotland	Flyhalf	0	6	0	0	12	Won
28/11/2001	Australia	Fullback	0	0	0	0	0	Lost
26/05/2002	England	Centre (R)	1	0	0	0	5	Lost
29/05/2002	Wales	Fullback	0	0	0	0	0	Won
01/06/2002	Scotland	Fullback	0	0	0	0	0	Won
06/03/2003	London Irish	Fullback	1	0	0	0	5	Won
25/05/2003	England	Fullback	0	0	0	0	0	Won
31/05/2003	Wales	Fullback	0	0	0	0	0	Won
9 MATCHES			**3**	**6**	**0**	**0**	**27**	
WIN RECORD			**P: 9 W: 7 L: 2 D: 0 Win %: 78**					

NATAL SHARKS (CURRIE CUP)								
DATE	OPPONENTS	POSITION	T	C	P	D	PTS	RESULT
10/09/2005	WP	Fullback	0	1	4	0	14	Lost
17/09/2005	Griquas	Fullback	0	3	1	0	9	Won
24/09/2005	Leopards	Fullback	0	4	0	0	8	Won
01/10/2005	WP	Fullback	0	1	3	0	11	Lost
4 MATCHES			**0**	**9**	**8**	**0**	**42**	
RECORD			**P: 4 W: 2 L: 2 D: 0 WIN %: 50**					

SHARKS (SUPER 14)								
DATE	OPPONENTS	POSITION	T	C	P	D	PTS	
11/02/2006	Chiefs	Flyhalf	2	3	3	0	25	Won
18/02/2006	Cheetahs	Fullback	1	1	3	0	16	Lost
25/02/2006	Crusaders	Fullback	1	2	2	0	15	Lost
04/03/2006	Waratahs	Fullback	1	0	1	0	8	Lost
11/03/2006	Brumbies	Fullback	0	0	0	0	0	Lost
01/04/2006	Reds	Fullback	0	0	0	0	0	Won
15/04/2006	Cats	Fullback	0	0	0	0	0	Won
22/04/2006	Blues	Fullback	0	1	0	0	2	Won
29/04/2006	Bulls	Flyhalf	1	2	0	0	9	Lost
06/05/2006	Stormers	Fullback	1	3	1	0	14	Won
12/05/2006	Force	Fullback	0	5	2	0	16	Won
03/02/2007	Bulls	Fullback	0	2	1	0	7	Won
09/02/2007	Waratahs	Fullback	0	1	3	0	11	Won
17/02/2007	Highlanders	Fullback	2	2	3	0	23	Won
03/03/2007	Crusaders	Fullback	0	2	2	0	10	Won
14/04/2007	Blues	Fullback	0	0	2	0	6	Won
21/04/2007	Chiefs	Fullback	0	0	0	0	0	Lost
28/04/2007	Lions	Fullback	0	2	2	0	10	Won
05/05/2007	Stormers	Fullback	1	4	1	0	16	Won
12/05/2007	Blues (semi-final)	Fullback	0	2	4	0	16	Won
19/05/2007	Bulls (final)	Fullback	0	0	3	0	9	Lost
21 MATCHES			**10**	**32**	**33**	**0**	**213**	
RECORD			**P: 21 W: 14 L: 7 Win %: 66**					

PERPIGNAN								
DATE	OPPONENTS*	POSITION	T	C	P	D	PTS	
15/12/2007	London Irish (EC)	Fullback	0	0	0	0	0	Won
05/01/2008	Brive (T14)	Fullback	0	0	0	0	0	Won
12/01/2008	Treviso (EC)	Fullback	0	2	0	0	4	Won
19/01/2008	Dragons (EC)	Fullback	0	2	2	0	10	Won
26/01/2008	Biarritz (T14)	Fullback	0	0	1	0	3	Lost
01/02/2008	Montauban (T14)	Fullback	0	2	3	0	13	Won
09/02/2008	Clermont (T14)	Fullback	0	1	0	0	2	Won
01/03/2008	Dax (T14)	Fullback	0	0	0	0	0	Drew
08/03/2008	Stade Francais (T14)	Fullback	0	2	3	0	13	Won
22/03/2008	Albi (T14)	Fullback	0	3	4	0	18	Won
29/03/2008	Bourgoin (T14)	Flyhalf (R)	0	0	0	0	0	Won
05/04/2008	London Irish (EC, quarter-final)	Fullback	0	0	3	0	9	Lost
19/04/2008	Bayonne (T14)	Fullback	0	4	0	0	8	Won
26/04/2008	Brive (T14)	Fullback	0	1	2	0	8	Won
03/05/2008	Biarritz (T14)	Fullback	0	1	3	0	11	Won
10/05/2008	Montauban (T14)	Fullback	0	1	2	0	8	Lost
17/05/2008	Clermont (T14)	Fullback	0	0	3	0	9	Lost
21/06/2008	Clermont (T14, semi-final)	Fullback	0	1	0	0	2	Lost
18 MATCHES			**0**	**20**	**26**	**0**	118	
RECORD			**P: 18 W: 12 L: 5 D: 1 Win %: 67**					

* *EC = European Cup; T14 = Top 14*

SA HONOURS	
Player of the Year nominee	1997
President's Special Award	2004
Player of the Year nominee	2007

INDEX